In the Name of Italy

AUSTRIA

SWITZERLAND

Sondrio   Trieste

ISTRIA   DALMATIA   YUGOSLAVIA

Zara

Brazza

ITALY   Adriatic Sea

• Rome

Luigia Barbarovich Paulovich's Italy
1930–1932

In the Name of Italy

NATION, FAMILY, AND PATRIOTISM
IN A FASCIST COURT

Maura E. Hametz

FORDHAM UNIVERSITY PRESS
New York 2012

Frontispiece: Map of Luigia Paulovich's Italy, 1930–32

Library of Congress Cataloging-in-Publication Data

Hametz, Maura Elise.
   In the name of Italy : nation, family, and patriotism in a fascist court / Maura E. Hametz.
         p. cm.
   Includes bibliographical references and index.
   ISBN 978-0-8232-4339-6 (cloth : alk. paper)
  1. Barbarovich Paulovich, Luigia.   2. Trials—Italy—Trieste.
3.   Italianization.   4. Administrative courts—Italy.   5. Law—
Political aspects—Italy.   6. Fascism—Italy.   7. Italy—Politics and
government—1922–1945.   8. National characteristics, Italian.
9. Trieste (Italy)—History—1918–   I. Title.
   KKH46.B37H36 2012
   342.4508'5—dc23

                                                2012002895

Printed in the United States of America

14 13 12   5 4 3 2 1

First edition

Contents

For Todd,
Jonathan, and Zachary
and
For my parents—
My mother, who taught me what a strong woman can do and
My father, who inspired my fascination with the law

Abbreviations and Name Correspondences

Rome, ACS, CdS - Sez. IV	Rome, Archivio Centrale dello Stato, Consiglio di stato - Sezione quarta: Giurisdizionale
Rome, ACS, PCM, UCNP	Rome, Archivio Centrale dello Stato, Presidenza consiglio dei ministri, Ufficio centrale per le nuove provincie
Rome, ACS, SPDCR	Rome, Archivio Centrale dello Stato, Segreteria particolare del Duce: Carteggio riservato
TS, AdS, CGCVG	Trieste, Archivio di Stato, Commissariato Generale Civile per la Venezia Giulia
TS, AdS-PPT/DI	Trieste, Archivio di Stato, Prefettura della Provincia di Trieste, Divisione I: Riduzione Cognomi
TS, AdS, Pref. Gab.	Trieste, Archivio di Stato, Prefettura di Trieste, Gabinetto (1923–52)
TS, BC, Racc. Pat.	Trieste, Biblioteca Civica, Raccolta patria

Basovizza	Bazovica (Sl.)
Brazza	Brač (Cr.)
Carso	Karst (Ge.), Kras (Sl.)
Cattaro	Kotor (Mo.)
Fiume	Rijeka (Cr.)
Grado	Gradež (Sl.)
Istria	Istra (Cr. and Sl.)
Pirano	Piran (Sl.)
Pola	Pula (Cr.)
Postumia	Postojna (Sl.), Adelsberg (Ge.)
Ragusa	Dubrovnik (Cr.)
San Pietro della Brazza	Supetar, Brač (Cr.)
Sebenico	Šibenik, (Cr.)
Spalato	Split (Cr.)
Trieste	Trst (Sl.), Triest (Ge.)

Venezia Giulia	Julijska krajina (Sl. and Cr.), Julian March (En.)
Zara	Zadar (Cr.)

Languages indicated in parentheses are: Croatian (Cr.), English (En.), German (Ge.), Montenegrin (Mo.), and Slovene (Sl.).

Acknowledgments

Over the course of more than a decade since my discovery of Luigia Paulo-vich's brush with the fascist court, I have incurred innumerable debts in bringing her story and this book to light. A summer research fellowship in 2006 and sabbatical semester in the spring of 2010 from the College of Arts and Letters and Old Dominion University provided assistance that enabled me to complete the project.

The staff at the archives and libraries has been exceedingly patient and kind. At the Archivio di stato Trieste, where the entire staff has made me feel welcome, Grazia Tatò, Pierpaolo Dorsi, and Carla Triadan offered invaluable assistance. At the Archivio centrale dello stato, Mariapina Di Simone helped me to navigate labyrinthine files to uncover evidence re-lating to the Paulovich case and naming practices in Trieste. My work would have been impossible without the help of Beverly Barco, Stuart Frazer, and the Perry Library Interlibrary Loan staff at Old Dominion University.

Colleagues and friends have offered assistance, suggestions, and timely advice and criticism along the way. Alexander De Grand and Nancy M. Wingfield have been exceedingly generous in reading the manuscript and offering unflinching support for this project and my work. Ivan W. Hametz and Sanja Juric read early drafts and offered keen legal eyes. Alice Kelikian inspired me to take a closer look at women in fascist Italy. John Davis, Judith Szapor, Marina Calloni, Tullia Catalan, Marta Petrusewicz, Marla Stone, and Mia Fuller helped to shape my thinking on gender issues in interwar Italy and assisted with the project along the way. The book has benefited from the observations, questions, and criti-cisms raised by audiences with whom I have shared the Pauloviches' story from the Conference on Women, Gender, and the Extreme Right orga-nized by Kevin Passmore at Cardiff University in 2001 to the Conference on the Culture of Judicial Independence organized by Shimon Shetreet at the University of Vienna in 2011. Among others, I wish to thank Jože Pirjevec, Marion Kaplan, Ruth Ben-Ghiat, Andrea Pëto, Larry Wolff, Mark Mazower, Cora Granata, Roland Sarti, and Agatha Schwartz for their invitations to present my work. Colleagues at Old Dominion University including Austin Jersild, Heidi Schlipphacke, Jane Merritt, Michael Carhart, Kathy Pearson, Erin Jordan, Annette Finley-Croswhite, and Chandra de Silva provided invaluable support.

Research in Italy would have been impossible without the assistance, friendship, and hospitality of Michela Bassanese and the Bassanese family, Silvia Cotroneo, Maurizio Borelli, Riccardo Kriscjak, Barbara Giordano, Marina Petronio, Silvio Delbello, Roberto Ambrosi, and Rita Braico.

No book can be published without editorial support and technical assistance. At Fordham University Press, Fredric Nachbaur offered enthusiastic support for the project, William Cerbone and Katie Sweeney offered gracious assistance, and Michael Koch edited the manuscript with a keen eye. I am grateful to Donald K. Emminger at Old Dominion University who designed the map.

I have received assistance and encouragement from all of these individuals and from unnamed others, to whom I offer heartfelt thanks. In spite of their best efforts, no project ever appears quite finished to the author, and obviously responsibility for the contents of the book and any shortcomings rest with the author.

Introduction

"By decree of the Prefect of Trieste, issued this 26th day of June 1930, the widow Paulovich's name is restored to the Italian form Paoli."[1] Asserting her right to maintain her husband's family name, Luigia Barbarovich Paulovich rejected the Italian form Paoli and launched a legal appeal that challenged fascist authorities working to nationalize the populations in Italy's eastern borderlands. By the end of 1931, the appeal reached the Administrative Court of the Council of State (Section Four of the Consiglio di Stato) in Rome. Justices at the highest echelons of the fascist judiciary considered the widow's complaint against the prefect of Trieste and the directive that "restored" her married surname. The appeal was truly extraordinary. Of the tens of thousands of people in Italy's Adriatic border provinces whose surnames the fascists altered between 1927 and 1943, Paulovich was the second of only a dozen who sought legal redress in Rome.

Luigia Barbarovich Paulovich's case, at the core of this study, offers a window on fascist government officials' and legal professionals' response to dynamic conceptions of law, morality, and patriotism. Paulovich's dispute with local administrative authorities exposes the philosophical dilemmas legal professionals and government representatives faced in the wake of authoritarian takeover and shows how they reconciled liberal training and beliefs with fascist exigencies. It illustrates how, in the climate of shifting perceptions of individual rights and community responsibilities, the Italian legal system and fascist governing system continued to evolve after the "seizure of power," the crystallization of the dictatorship, and into the "years of consensus."[2] It demonstrates that some individuals saw Mussolini's government as a change in Italian leadership but refused to accept fascism as a transformation of the Italian system.

Maneuvering in the interstices of law, morality, and social expectations, Luigia Paulovich set local officials and national jurists at odds. Her objection to the fascist directive forced legal professionals at the prefectural and national levels to articulate the bounds of the government's authority in efforts to impose a nationalist agenda. Despite the fascist commitment to Italian nationalism, the court rewarded the elderly widow willing to stand against the prefect and eager to assert her faith in Italian justice. Amidst the violence that stands as a mark of the fascist government's efforts to Italianize the border population, Paulovich's experience appears uncharacteristic as an indication of administrative tolerance and reliance on legal processes.

The clash of nationalist perspectives—from Rome (the site of fascist central administration and the Administrative Court), Trieste (Paulovich's home and part of the new Italian territories), and Dalmatia (the Paulovich family's land of origin and "unredeemed" territory over which Italian irredentists sought control)—demonstrates how standards for patriotism, loyalty, and national belonging could vary over time and space even under the eyes of the dictatorship. The superior power and will of the center were clear in the court's straightforward directive to the prefect of Trieste to void the name restoration decree but, the implications of the ruling were far from clear.

While fascist anti-Slavism and political persecution continued, contradictory impulses of the fascist state allowed Paulovich to escape the effects of Italianizing policy. Officials eager to maintain stability promoted the fascist state; judges committed to maintaining legal traditions and precedents cooperated in government and legislative reform; civil servants and authorities at all government levels turned a blind eye to the periodic violence and fascist repression. Yet, those responsible for educating modern fascist citizens and for integration of the borderland remained wedded to social conventions and traditions inherited from the liberal era that idolized loyal Italians and women committed to family, motherhood, and country.

The legal ambiguities and contradictions brought to light in Paulovich's case were not simply an aberration of fascism. Although *legality* is portrayed often in black and white terms—something is either legal or illegal, within the bounds of law or outside them—understandings of the legality of particular actions or the scope of the law regarding them is subject to interpretation, dependent on individual or collective interpretations of right and wrong under the law. Malleable and even fickle social trends affect interpretations of what constitutes law. Dynamic conceptions of social justice render the law *living* rather than static, and Western jurisprudence relies on the law's subjectivity to interpretation and its evolution.

Fascism intended to undermine the spirit of liberalism inherited from the French Revolution that served as the foundation for traditions of individual freedom and ideas of the individual's social contract with the modern state. Those serving fascism, however, remained bound to their liberal legal, social, and cultural inheritance. That embedded political and cultural understandings shaped the administration of fascist justice seems self-evident. That notions of *legality* were malleable appears equally understandable given the nature of the seizure of fascist power and the necessity for fascists to compromise with traditional power bases in the extension and exercise of fascist rule. That legal expectations and understandings guiding fascist justices and legal professionals were grounded in the same principles that guided Western democracies offers food for further thought and study.

Expectations and understandings of the liberal period persisted into the interwar period, limiting the success of efforts to remold the state and reeducate Italian citizens to fit fascist designs. Appearing to walk in lockstep with the fascist government, magistrates in Italy's highest Administrative Court at the same time proudly acknowledged their adherence to liberal precepts and traced their understandings of the law and their responsibilities to liberal traditions. Fascism presented an authoritarian face and the fascists asserted their power by force, but within the scope of fascist society the law was subject to interpretation based on lawmakers' aims, legal professionals' understandings, and public perceptions. Conservative ideas regarding national identity, women's status, and traditional politics intertwined with fascist revolutionary aims. Debate over ideological and practical matters of governance continued in the interwar period as a by-product of competition among national officials, local authorities, and party representatives. These conflicts impeded revolutionary political and administrative reforms that aimed to transform the state, the society, and the individual. Not only in Italy but in other interwar successor states as well, where ultra-conservative nationalist agendas clashed with liberal interests, contradictory impulses encumbered officials responsible for the enforcement and oversight of national policies.

The decree that restored the name *Paulovich* to *Paoli* was emblematic of fascist officials' heavy-handed attempts to Italianize the population and to justify Italian possession of newly acquired eastern borderlands. Such nationalizing policies characterized the approach of governments throughout the successor states in the wake of World War I. Ethnic conflicts took center stage as political leaders struggled to consolidate national states. The ideological foundations and conceptions that guided the formation of nation-states and the nature of nations and nationalism are highly contentious, as are the definition of terms such as *nation, nationalism*, and even *nation-state*. The analysis of Paulovich's case relies on conceptual models inspired by Benedict Anderson's ideas of "imagined communities" and by Anthony Giddens's assumptions of the relationship of the nation as "collectivity" to the reach of unitary authority. Both identify the processes of the extension of modern state bureaucracies and the modern delineation of borders as central to national articulation and state-building.[3] The surname legislation, intended as a nationalizing tool, was a means to define membership in the Italian nation (Anderson's socially constructed "imagined community") within the newly drawn borders of the state (Giddens's "power container"). Its effect was to persecute those who did not fit the state's expectations. Toying with citizens' names abrogated their rights under the Italian civil code, which held names to be sacrosanct.

Yet, the politics and processes of surname alteration were linked to the peculiarities of the settlements of World War I. With respect to guarantees of minority and ethnic rights, the Italian case was uncharacteristic of the successor states. Italy had leverage and privileges as a victor state. While Vittorio Orlando's presence at the peace table did not secure all hoped-for territorial gains and his failures fed Italian perceptions of the "mutilated victory," attention to Italy's disappointments distracted attention from questions relating to non-Italian ethnic populations included within the expanded state's borders. The *Risorgimento* (or Italian unification era) myth of an ethnically homogenous, albeit regionally diverse, Italian state formed by natural boundaries and "encircled by the Alps and the sea" continued into the fascist period.[4] As internationally renowned jurist Julius Stone remarked in 1937, "Italy is a homogeneous state from the national point of view. It is not afflicted save in the Tyrol and Istria, and there not seriously, with the problem of minorities."[5]

Such assumptions of homogeneity echo in the scholarly literature to the present day. Studies of Italian nationalism concentrate on the amalgamation of various ideological perspectives and effacement of regional (or geographical) particularities rather than on ethnic politics. Scholars trace fascism's appeal in interwar Italy to its ability to link "intimate local place" to the "abstract national world."[6] They emphasize the persistence of regional identities and the legacy of historical political fragmentation. Extensive local literatures examine the northern and eastern borderlands inhabited by ethnic minority populations, but much that has been written focuses on persecution and reflects a tendency to justify specific claims or to assess blame for persecutory policies or failures at integration. Several studies examine clashes in the Brenner provinces or the evolution of the South Tyrol Question, but few discuss the impact of minority politics in the Adriatic regions on the history of the modern Italian state.[7]

This examination of Italian governance and of the interaction of local and national administrators in the Adriatic territories complements studies of the Southern Question and South Tyrol Question that address the role of the state in dealing with clientalism, autonomy, violence, and regional particularities. Center versus periphery issues and regional allegiance and loyalty questions that predominate in studies of the Italian South and the northern German-speaking provinces were no less salient in the eastern borderlands. Yet, due to the politics of irredentism and the eastern borderland, Triestines have presented an ultra-conservative and nationalist face to the central government since annexation. As a result, Rome has been able to ignore regional discontents, offer palliatives, or dismiss tensions as by-products of Italian-Yugoslav conflict. This account reveals Triestines' underlying disappointments with Rome that are often hidden by the mask of official conservative nationalist support. Oft-mentioned binational confrontations between Italians and Slavs (generically defined) relate only to a specific projection of Adriatic identities, a vision tied to the history of Western prejudices, the politics of pan-Slavism, the formulation of Italy and multiethnic Yugoslavia in the wake of World War I, and the bipolar political alignments that emerged with World War II.

In the newly acquired borderlands, the nationalization process involved Italianization to integrate the new territories and to assimilate new populations into the Italian Fatherland.[8] Paulovich's case reveals the dilemmas that confronted officials attempting to extend Italian legal and administrative systems and to uphold standards of Italian justice while at the same time introducing fascist reforms in territories unaccustomed to Italian national administration. It also exposes the difficulties fascist officials faced in their attempts to impose ethnic uniformity in communities that did not share the Italian state's ethnic or national assumptions or expectations.

The fascist government came to power with the support of nationalists of a variety of stripes, many of whom pass through these pages. Monarchists, irredentists, interventionists, moderates, and conservatives mixed with hard-line fascists to support the formation of the government and assist in the development of fascist institutions.[9] Triestine officials' perspectives on nationalism, loyalty, and nationalist affiliation diverged from that of their counterparts in other regions and their superiors in Rome.

The Paulovich family's name, heritage, and political leanings related intimately to the politics of the Italian borderland, and the proceedings of the Paulovich case testify to the continuing effects of misapprehensions concerning the cultural, social, and political identities of borderland populations. The widow and her husband both hailed from Dalmatia, the contested Adriatic coastland boasting a patchwork history of control by Romans, Slavs (primarily Croats), Venetians, French (in Napoleon's Illyrian Provinces), and Habsburgs. From the nineteenth-century Italian Unification, Italian nationalists called for redemption of Italians stranded outside Italy's borders. Italy's failure to gain coveted Dalmatian lands in the wake of World War I played an important role in the construction of the Italian nationalist myth. Italian eyes were riveted to poet-patriot Gabriele D'Annunzio's escapades in Fiume (Rijeka) and the national struggles to rein in the eastern borderland. Even after the March on Rome in 1922, Mussolini and fascist politicians harped on the importance of "border fascism" to beat back Italy's enemies and further Italian ambitions and claims.

Fascist propaganda touted the importance of the "redemption" of Italian populations and emphasized borderland populations' "sacrifice" for Italy, but the government paid little attention to the challenges integration posed in the Adriatic provinces. Preoccupation with territorial possession did not translate to careful oversight or national intervention, except where borderland unrest or instability seemed to threaten the security of the state. National authorities designed and enacted policies with the vague intention of promoting integration but left their enactment to the discretion of local officials. Paulovich won her case because local officials overestimated Rome's commitment to enforcing legislation that painted a veneer of *italianità* over the polyglot and multiethnic autochthonous populations in the Adriatic borderlands.[10] The prefect and members of the local naming commission proved unable to "legitimate their choices" regarding the application of the surname measure within the fascist legal framework.[11]

Paulovich's refusal to accept fascist intervention in her personal affairs and the legal proceedings emanating from her challenge to the prefect's decree form the foundation for the narrative, a microhistorical study that examines various aspects of the Paulovich case. The study's approach resembles that of such works as Helmut Walser Smith's *Butcher's Tale: Murder and Anti-Semitism in a German Town* and Edward Berenson's *Trial of Madame Caillaux*.[12] In the Italian context, the work draws inspiration from Carlo Ginzburg's *The Cheese and the Worms* and David Kertzer's works *The Kidnapping of Edgardo Mortara* and *Amalia's Tale*.[13] Yet, the cases Kertzer explored challenged the authority of institutions like the Catholic Church or the Italian medical establishment. The Paulovich case did not. It did not bear the imprint of emotion, drama, courtroom theatrics or press interference. The matter remained within the halls of Italian justice, and officials and legal representatives remained in the shadows of the fascist bureaucracy. Members of the legal profession and government authorities in service to the government and intent on carving out their powers and upholding their responsibilities within Italy's legal system debated the merits of Paulovich's appeal at an administrative hearing.[14] Officials', magistrates', and lawyers' positions offer a window on the workings of the internal legal culture and reflect on the environment "created by jurists for jurists" in which fascist administrators debated precedents, policy, and aims.[15] The records of Paulovich's hearing produced by the court and lawyers offer a top-down legal institutional perspective. But, unlike transcripts of arguments in criminal or civil trials, they are not biased by attempts to establish guilt or innocence or to assign blame. Rather, they include open and frank debates over legal issues and the state's intents to correct or fine-tune administrative functions.[16]

The nuances important to understanding the case lie in the legalistic jargon, the minutiae of legal arguments, the contested definitions of particular terms, and the differing interpretations of individuals' rights. The study retains the specific legal terminology as far as possible to capture the plurivocality of legal language, to articulate legal professionals' aims and explain their legal interpretations in the climate of official censorship and oppression.[17] Since name *changes* were subject to different laws and procedures, the contention that the decree transforming Paulovich to Paoli constituted a *change* not a *restoration* served as an important basis for the legal challenge. Name alterations appear as restorations, restitutions, or corrections to conform to the language of the legislation, the court papers, and transcripts. Similar attention is given to assertions regarding rights, laws, duties and responsibilities. A handbook on surname restoration and correction published in 1929 reproduces in full the relevant Italian laws and outlines the process of the surname campaign in Trieste.[18] Documents and published materials held in the Central State Archive (Archivio centrale dello stato), particularly the Council of State (Consiglio di Stato) collection, in Rome and in the State Archive (Archivio di stato) in Trieste provide the specifics of the case.[19] Čermelj's *Life-and-Death Struggle* discusses the Administrative Court's decision.[20]

While Paulovich's complaint was exceptional, the progress of her case was not. The legal case proceeded on a strictly bureaucratic course, following a path outlined in the legislation. Administrative protocol and precedent shielded the court proceedings from the public view, but the Administrative Court's verdict was published openly as part of its public interface. Records of the hearing became part of the court record, and the prefect of Trieste published notice of the voiding of Luigia Paulovich's name restoration decree. The Administrative Court's decision and its reception therefore offer a window on the internal legal culture's relationship to the external legal culture, the relationship between the individual and the government that court officers sought to convey to "users" or "potential users of legal services."[21]

Paulovich's case demonstrates Mussolini's failure to impose "organizational totalitarianism," and the fascist government's inability, even after November 1926, to impose uniformly the will of the fascist "police state" described by Adrian Lyttelton and others.[22] Those serving the government recognized that the participation of the masses was necessary for "organizational" success in implementing reforms and enforcing new laws. Widespread public support could more easily be achieved through creative regulation and enforcement than through repression and violence.[23]

At the historical moment of the Paulovich case, the regime was engaged in a dynamic process of reforming state institutions and molding public opinion to fit the exigencies of fascist rule. Officials involved in the Paulo-vich proceedings sought to define the boundaries of dictatorship, the reach of fascist influence, and the extent of fascist control. They employed tactics of persuasion and used new laws to impose the fascists' will, but they were not ignorant of, blind to, or contemptuous of the needs and desires of individuals. Liberal political liberties eroded slowly under fas-cism. At least in the first ten years of fascist rule, juridical officers and public officials maintained a belief in the rule of law and adhered to the essential principles of Italian justice established in the nineteenth-century Risorgimento. The fascist government pushed through new legislation and oppressive policies, but also remained content to co-opt, adapt, and even simply accept prefascist legislative, political, and cultural precedents where convenient.

Little attention has focused on civil servants' and public administrators' interpretations of fascist policies.[24] Scholars of Nazi Germany pay consid-erable attention to the Nazi bureaucracy and the relationship between the traditional and conservative powers of the legal state and the extraordinary powers invested in the Nazi Party and leadership.[25] Civil servants' role in shaping the public's experience of fascism and in making fascism palatable for many Italians has been largely overlooked.

Civil servants and legal authorities reacted with pragmatism to the development of the fascist administrative and legal state. Loss of liberties was not "a relatively unimportant feature of political life, which when all was said and done, went on much the same despite this loss."[26] Nor was there necessarily a gap between "legal Italy" and "real Italy," a contest between fascist administrators and the Italian people, in which the "real Italy" ultimately triumphed.[27] Rather, a fitful, piecemeal, and multifac-eted attack on domestic civil liberties produced incremental changes that were all but imperceptible to those living under the regime. Through the distorting lens of fascism, few saw the power of "legal Italy." Civil servants and legal professionals accustomed to mediation and compromise rarely recognized the steps they followed leaving the legal culture of the liberal state to enter into the service of the fascist regime. Most Italians had little confidence in the power or willingness of professionals in the legal and administrative system (of liberal, fascist, or even later in republican Italy) to influence the climate of "real Italy" to their benefit. Here, Paulovich was an exception.

This account does not examine the widow as an individual with particular rights ensconced in her own local social network. No surviving accounts describe Luigia Barbarovich Paulovich's character or physical appearance. The apartment building in which she lived in Trieste bears no trace of the Paulovich (or Barbarovich) families, its former occupants. The name Paulovich appears only eleven times in the national Italian white pages, and none of the contemporary Italian Pauloviches can provide any information about Luigia Barbarovich Paulovich or her family.[28] She appears here as the "*donna in oggetto*" or "the woman in question" in a legal proceeding.[29] Evidence of her life survives only in thin files relevant to her case buried in masses of prefectural and national administrative records in the archives in Trieste and Rome. Paulovich did not enjoy exalted social status or fame. As a woman, an elderly person, and a citizen of the borderland, Luigia Barbarovich Paulovich would likely have been invisible to the fascist government, merely a widow among the masses.

Neither local nor national officials had any reason to draw attention to the Paulovich case. Only cases that the fascist government wished to publicize came to the public's eye, and these cases were molded, sensationalized and even staged by fascist officials to fit the government's aims. Authorities could hope to gain little (and may perhaps have lost credibility) by publicizing the complaint of an elderly widow with unimpeachable nationalist credentials.

Paulovich did not pose a threat to the regime, nor was her protest an overt attack on fascism. Government officials could not condemn her as a malcontent, subversive, or criminal, nor was she associated with the political resistance or opposition. Through the force of circumstance, by shrewd use of institutional frameworks, and by skillful manipulation of cultural and social expectations, Paulovich forced officials to address her complaint. Her appeal revealed cracks in the façade of widespread popular support and exposed the bounds of individuals' quiescence. Her protest questioned assumptions with regard to individuals' understandings of nationalism and the regime's expectations for loyalty. The analysis borrows methods of the *Alltagsgeschichte* (everyday history) approach pioneered by Alf Lüdtke to explore the quotidian experience of fascist governance in the early 1930s through the lens of the experience of an individual who defied fascist expectations. It sets the experiences of those in the Adriatic borderland against the backdrop of fascist institutional expectations and assumptions regarding acceptable modes of cultural life. Paulovich's anonymity and ordinariness, her traditional lifestyle, and her faith in Italian justice were the keys to her success in challenging the fascist decree. Yet, her opposition to fascist legislation demonstrated an "historical form of individuality" that, ironically, set her up as an exemplar of the loyal fascist citizen.[30]

The unraveling of intricate and complex meanings of the law through the lens of the Paulovich case demonstrates how legal professionals crafted creative and multifaceted responses to legal challenges even under the oppressive regime. Paulovich and her lawyer took advantage of embedded systems of law, legal institutions, and legal practices and assumptions developed over the course of the nineteenth century. Judges employed by the fascist state took seriously their duties to uphold laws related to the fair treatment of Italian citizens, for whom the state was meant to be responsible and to whom the state had been responsible in the years prior to fascism.

For decades, scholars have debated whether or not the Nazi judiciary was complicit in the Nazi takeover and repression in Germany.[31] The impact of fascism on the Italian judiciary remains relatively unexplored except for scattered studies that examine the Special Tribunal for the Defense of the State (particularly its role in the repression of the political Left), the Italian judiciary in the post–World War II fascist purge trials, or in later trials dealing with organized crime and sensational public scandals.[32] This study examines the judicial climate of the Administrative Court in the early 1930s and opens the door for more focused and systematic studies of the development and functioning of the fascist judicial system—including the administrative, criminal, and extraordinary courts—and the liberal legacy, fascist innovations, and ultimately, the role of public institutions in fascism's demise.

Resistance to Italian fascism has often been studied in terms of *visible* and *organized* action against the regime.[33] While the study of civilian resistance has been effectively separated from analyses of military resistance, individuals' activities have been pegged generally on a spectrum from passive to active resistance to government initiatives.[34] The bulk of literature on antifascism has emphasized the development of resistance and antifascism in the years after the Italian fascist alliance with Nazi Germany. Antifascist resistance in the first decade of fascist rule and up to

1935 appears as scattered, armed resistance and political opposition. Stories of personal heroism and regional resistance predominate.[35] Paulovich's case hints at underlying discontents in the first decade of fascist rule. While fascist dictatorship appeared in many guises, dissent could adopt many masks. Opposition and resistance to the imposition of the "fascist way of life" were multilayered and multifaceted.

Scholarly literature has turned away from questions framed in terms of broad consensus for dictatorship sparked by Renzo DeFelice's *Mussolini il duce: Gli anni del consenso, 1929–1936*, but questions regarding the nature of popular support for fascism continue to intrigue scholars.[36] Targeted repression may have quashed "any possibility of articulating alternatives to the fascist way."[37] But violence, physical threat, and intimidation were tools used to facilitate the rise to power or in response to perceived threats to the state order. Blatant and aggressive attacks on traditional liberties provoked political and public outcry. Protest against the 1924 assassination of Italian socialist deputy Giacomo Matteotti and questioning of the 1938 racial laws frame the core period of fascist rule prior to Italy's entry into the Axis Alliance and World War II. The study of the Paulovich case provides a vision of the "years of consensus" marked by "stability and relative calm" and characterized by "lack of protest," not as a time of blind acceptance or acquiescence, but as a period in which no event or action crystallized national opinion or sparked public protest against the regime. Fascists and their supporters intimidated critics, and piecemeal resistance was easily suppressed. In some cases, as in the highly publicized trial in 1930 in Trieste where the Special Tribunal sentenced four to death for the firebombing of *Il Popolo di Trieste* (purportedly an act of Slavic conspiracy), fascism's penchant for violence and the seeming success of the fascist government demoralized dissenters. Antifascists were isolated and unable to launch or lead national opposition. But, the seeds planted in the late 1920s and early 1930s would sprout in successful antifascist and partisan movements during World War II.

The Paulovich case reveals that while resistance was met by violence, dissent was not always met with force. In less sensational or public circumstances, quiet compromise or accommodation could prevail. The Council of State's willingness to hear Paulovich's case suggests the need for further study of the institutional role in shaping the contours of popular quiescence in fascist Italy. Such institutional and systemic approaches have been for decades at the fringes of scholarly assessments relating to interpretations of cultural hegemony, political power, and the role of the political and professional elite inspired by Antonio Gramsci and his philosophies. However, much work remains to be done. Examination of the function of the Administrative Court in the fascist legal system offers an alterative avenue for exploration of public response to fascist directives that has been documented in the well-known campaigns for grain, demography, and autarky and in participation in initiatives sponsored by the fascist youth and *dopolavoro* (afterwork leisure) organizations that aimed to win public support.

Studies of the surname and nationalizing measures tend to concentrate on the legislation's oppressive and discriminatory nature and intents as part of the broader aggressive fascist campaign to assert Italy's power. Assessments focus on denationalization as cultural and political persecution and at the extreme, as evidence of intents to commit "cultural genocide."[38] Studies of the surname campaign uncritically follow in this current of thought.[39] Recent emphasis on the "hybrid" Adriatic identity, rooted in the historical rhetoric of Italians of the Adriatic borderland, speaks to recognition of the history of overlapping and competing identities that transcended state definitions.[40] Yet, the term *hybridity* assumes that identities derive from dissimilar elements or stocks to form a combination or mixture. Ultimately the term relies on a combination of essential differences that reify the very categories it purports to transcend. Study of the public's reception of the surname campaign suggests that individuals operated in a variety of contexts and situations that required flexibility. Rather than accepting hybrid identities, they nurtured multiple and fluid associations and affiliations. Individuals recognized and accepted that identities were socially constructed and politically engineered. For those in the borderland, names, like ethnic identities, were not sacrosanct but subject to circumstantial, official, or unofficial interpretation and modification. Some abhorred the state's intervention in formulating names. Others saw it as an inconvenience or an inevitable consequence of daily governance, a process that, like the requirement to pay taxes or qualify for professional licenses and permits, was annoying or even painful, but was a normal consequence of life. Still others accepted alteration of their surnames through spelling and phonetic alterations or translations as a means to simplify their relationship with ruling authorities. Finally, there were those who welcomed the restorations or sought corrections as an opportunity for social advancement to speed assimilation into the Italian state.[41]

Italianization was not only a means to assert Italian control. It formed part of the process of fascist bureaucratization—the expansion of record-keeping, registration, and numbering controls and checks—pursued as a facet of modernization. Extension of the bureaucracy conveniently increased the fascists' capabilities for surveillance and repression, but its intents also included the facilitation of access to social benefits. State-making required state-naming.[42] In its approach to the development and centralization of the state, this study builds on such works as David Horn's *Social Bodies*, Ruth Ben-Ghiat's *Fascist Modernities,* Carl Ipsen's *Dictating Demography*, and more recently Roger Griffin's *Fascism and Modernity* that examine tensions between the traditional and modern that were a hallmark of fascist ideology and practice.[43]

Fascist bureaucratization also affected women's treatment under Italian law. This study complements others that concentrate on women's struggle for suffrage and legal rights by highlighting the efficacy of individual action and the ability of individuals, particularly women, to take advantage of legal and social contradictions embedded in institutional and legal frameworks. Gender is a central category of analysis, and the work shares some aims of feminist scholarship in its quest to "penetrate more deeply into an understanding of social relations and strategies . . . to see the radical cutting edge of the antagonism between the choices of individuals and groups, rather than classes or categories."[44] However, the approach is neither overtly feminist nor activist, and sexuality is not explicitly explored. The study travels a path pioneered in the early nineteenth century examining women neither "as passive victims of historical injustice nor as constant heroines struggling to change society," but rather as individuals wielding influence in a society in which they had little political power or legal standing.[45]

The contradictory impulses in the fascist approach to and treatment of women have fascinated scholars for decades. Alexander De Grand's seminal article "Women under Italian Fascism," written in 1976, suggested avenues for further inquiry into the multiple associations that defined women's positions in fascist Italy and interwar European society.[46] Victoria De Grazia's *How Fascism Ruled Women* and Michela De Giorgio's *Le Italiane dall'Unità* offer visions of Italian women and explore the ways in which they were *seen* in public and private, in art and literature, and by the government and individuals.[47] De Grazia's work and Robin Pickering-Iazzi's *Mothers of Invention* identify coincident trends of progressive and regressive redefining of femininity, women's roles, and women's contributions in the interwar period. Pickering-Iazzi points to "internal contradictions" in fascist ideology and practice that empowered women to become incorporated in national life, which are particularly relevant to discussing Paulovich's experience.[48] This study builds on these works to focus on the relationship between the women's self-conceptions and the state's conceptions articulated in the legal system.[49] While Paulovich was clearly a "bourgeois," fascist attitudes toward women workers and women's public roles, articulated by such scholars as Luisa Passerini and Perry Willson, affected the court's vision of women and its deliberations in the widow's case.[50] This account also contributes to the scholarship that explores women's antifascism or explores comparative perspectives on resistance to the regime.[51]

Despite the appearance of important studies of women in interwar Italy, analyses of Italian women under fascism remain scant beside those of women under Nazism.[52] Paulovich's experience is common to that of women of her generation in fascist Italy and to that of women throughout Central Europe dealing simultaneously with the quickening pace of emancipation after World War I and the rise of conservative regimes in the successor states. The widow's birth in the Adriatic provinces of the Habsburg monarchy and acquisition of Italian citizenship in the aftermath of World War I as well as her residence in a contested frontier zone of overlapping nationalist and ethnic identities in provinces which would be claimed as part of the German Reich in 1943 (as opposed to attached to the Italian Republic of Salò), make her case particularly interesting in comparative analysis of women's positions, ethnic nationalism, and loyalty in the Adriatic and Central Europe in the interwar period. The book contributes as well to a growing literature on women's citizenship, sovereignty, and national legal status in interwar Europe. After World War I, most native inhabitants of Italy's newly acquired territories gained Italian citizenship, but new citizens, particularly women with fewer legal rights, had to learn to navigate within the Italian legal and juridical contexts. Paulovich's case points to the deficiencies of relying on political affiliation and citizenship to define national association and assimilation.

As protectors of hearth and home, women like Paulovich bore responsibility for the proper conduct, moral development, and health of the family. Family politics, particularly those linked to the promotion of border fascism, form an important part of this study. Conservative family values derived from traditional perspectives. In the wake of the 1929 Concordat and the reconciliation between the Italian state and the Church in the early 1930s, as the Paulovich case passed through the justice system, issues relating to Italian family life, moral conduct, and religion garnered public attention. While Paulovich did not refer specifically to Catholic values, she did appeal to conservative attitudes rooted in patrilineal society and Church beliefs.

Emphasis on the legislation affecting surnames places the study in the genre of onomastics or name studies—or more specifically of surname studies, a subfield of linguistic onomastics that has emerged over the past two decades as a fruitful field for inquiry across a wide disciplinary spectrum.[53] Recognizing surnames' importance as cultural markers, this study examines the fascist state's attempts to render names more "legible" for bureaucratic and state-making purposes and its efforts to use surnames to promote cultural nationalism.[54] Meron Benvenisti's *Sacred Landscape* and other studies of nationalist naming have explored the impact of "administrative toponymy" and the assignment of place names.[55] The rapid state-making projects of the interwar period made names and renaming a matter of importance throughout the successor states.[56] The Paulovich case demonstrates how the fascists attempted to use surname restoration and correction legislation to subvert and erase Habsburg traditions, affiliations, and loyalties and how individuals asserted fluid and malleable identities that challenged the state's nationalist assumptions. Although matronyms are often used, patronyms (or names inherited from male ancestors) serve as the basis for social organization in Italian culture. The case's reliance on questions related to the transmission of the surname Paulovich provides a means to view intersections of nationalist, cultural, and political policies with gendered social legislation and practices related to marriage, inheritance, and legal rights.

The study of names in Central Europe and the Adriatic lands is a minefield studded with explosive ethnic, racial, and nationalist passions and agendas. Italy's eastern borderlands remained contested throughout the fascist period, and the borders have shifted and sovereignty (and with it names) has changed several times since World War II. Dalmatia is now an integral part of Croatia. Istria is shared between Slovenia and Croatia. Italian names in the eastern Adriatic that were common in Paulovich's time now seem outmoded or archaic. However, in the text Zara appears rather than Zadar, Brazza rather than Brač, and Fiume rather than Rijeka to reflect the documents and usage of the widow and her family, fascist officials, and the court. A table offers name correspondences in the variety of languages used in the various Adriatic regions. "Adriatic Littoral" refers to the upper Adriatic provinces as they were under Austrian domination after 1866, an area of uncertain borders and unclear associations not analogous to but encompassing largely the same territory as the "Julian March" (or Julijska Krajina) some of which was incorporated into Italian Venezia Giulia after 1918. Italy's northern provinces, too, are referred to by the Italian names used at the time or by the common English names, for example Alto Adige or South Tyrol in place of Südtirol, Hochetsch, or Oberetsch, despite the German ethnic majority in some areas.[57] Risorgimento Italy refers to the lands included in the modern Italian state at the end of the Unification period in 1870. This term, which does not appear in the sources, simplifies the delineation between old (pre–World War I) citizens and new (post–World War I) citizens, old territories and new territories, and avoids the use of core nation and periphery, designations that imply hierarchies.

The text follows, as far as possible, the personal names used in the court record. Technically, the woman in question was Luigia Barbarovich Paoli. Legally, according to arguments put forth in her case, she should have been Luigia Barbarovich the widow Paulovich. For simplicity and clarity and following her obvious preference, the text refers to her as Paulovich, except where the use of another name better conveys the meaning.

Legal proceedings related to Paulovich's appeal of the prefect's decree frame each chapter. Chapter 1 explores conceptions of Italian national consciousness in the Adriatic territories and focuses on the impact of nationalist ideas and philosophies of education to promote national belonging in Italy's eastern border territories. Chapter 2 examines the evolution of the Italian political and justice systems under fascism with emphasis on Alfredo Rocco's reforms. Both chapters set the stage for Paulovich's protest introduced in chapter 3 that traces the development of the local policy in the surname campaign. Two decrees relating to the Paulovich family's surname *restoration*, frame the analysis in chapter 4 that explores the complex and ambiguous role of the family in interwar Italy. Chapter 5 examines the legal hearing and questions related to Paulovich's rights as an Italian citizen. Chapter 6 concentrates on the arguments designed to appeal to the judges' sense of social justice and embedded gendered beliefs. Chapter 7 explores the impact of the Paulovich decision and discusses the debate that continued until 1943 over the fascist implementation of nationalizing legislation. The conclusion points to the broader applicability of the analysis in terms of women's citizenship, national sovereignty and definitions of nationalism and patriotism. It also examines the legacy of fascist surname Italianization after World War II and its impact on contemporary reform efforts in the Adriatic that began in the aftermath of the political realignments of Europe after 1989.

1   Inculcating *Italianità*

Luigia Barbarovich Paulovich's road to Rome began with the passage of Royal Legislative Decree (RDL) no. 17 on January 10, 1926. Article 1 of the fascist surname measure designed to redeem ethnic Italians called on authorities in Trent to restore names "deformed from Latin or Italian roots." It also required surnames "of toponomastic origin, derived from place names that had been translated into other languages or deformed by foreign spelling" to be corrected or restored to their original (Latin or Italian) forms. Article 2 allowed individuals to request "correction" of surnames to an Italian form. Article 3 outlined the administrative processes to secure the measure's passage through Parliament and to set up guidelines for execution of the decree. [1]

The measure, extended in April 1927 to include all those living in territories annexed to Italy in the wake of World War I, called for an ethnic adjustment of surnames to enable those in the borderland to demonstrate their commitment to Italy not only through their deeds but through elevation or recovery of their Italian identity as well. Acting under the terms outlined in article 1, on June 26, 1930, the prefect of Trieste ordered the widow Luigia Barbarovich Paulovich to assume the name Luigia Barbarovich Paoli.

Late June 1930 was not the first time the widow's family had encountered the surname legislation. In 1928 Paulovich's elder son Enrico italianized his surname under the provisions of article 2 of the measure, which allowed petitioners with "foreign surnames or surnames of foreign origin" to request "reduction" or "correction" to an Italian form. Enrico adopted the surname form Paolucci. Although undoubtedly familiar with the nationalist impulses that motivated her son, Luigia Barbarovich Paulovich did not share his enthusiasm for italianization. Neither she, nor her daughter Ines, nor her younger son Ernesto followed Enrico's lead.

Italian nationalists who pushed for the surname law claimed that italianization remedied injustices perpetrated by oppressive and illegitimate former rulers and recovered names suppressed by those trying to eliminate evidence of the region's innate *italianità* (or Italianness). The measure affirmed Italy's commitment to assimilate individuals the borderland as equal citizens, indistinguishable from those in Risorgimento Italy. Surname restoration and correction intended to capture the collective Italian consciousness of borderland populations to assert the primacy of Italy and Italian civilization in territories newly annexed, recently redeemed, or liberated (depending on the point of view). Triestine officials' heavy-handed application of the surname restoration legislation transformed the measure to a tool of oppressive denationalization. The disjuncture between local understandings of nationalism in the former provinces of the Habsburg Adriatic Littoral and fascist visions of the Italian nation set the stage for the Paulovich family's clash with the prefect. Paulovich's willingness to question the validity of the nationalizing decree was rooted in her understanding of *italianità*. It reflected her perceptions of national allegiance, patriotism, and loyalty, and her national consciousness as an Italian, in an Italy that, from her perspective, just happened to be under fascist rule at the time.

National Consciousness in the Adriatic Coastlands

In 1918 Italian nationalist historian and native Triestine Attilio Tamaro described the "principle of nationality" as "that according to which each nation organically creates its existence and its personality." Noted for his irredentism and his expertise on Italy's eastern and Adriatic provinces, Tamaro saw "collective conscience" grounded in the experience of "history" as the basis for nationality.[2] His perspective reflected French philosopher and philologist Ernest Renan's conceptualization of the nation as a "spiritual principle" or a "spiritual family." Renan saw the nation in the liberal tradition, resting on the consent of individuals to live a common life and in its existence representing a "daily plebiscite." His characterization of modern Italy as a nation "unified through its defeats" would have been unpalatable to the fascists who emphasized Italian glory and Roman prestige, but his contention that a "large aggregate of men, healthy in mind and warm of heart" formed the nation through a "kind of moral conscience" resonated with fascist nationalist expectations. Moreover, Renan's assertion that proof of moral conscience lay in "sacrifices which demand the abdication of the individual to the advantage of the community" echoed fascist calls for individual sacrifice for the national community.[3] Officials fashioning the surname legislation sought to strengthen the Italian "collective consciousness," to reconcile "discrepancies," and to promote the Italian moral consciousness of the peoples recently welcomed as citizens of the modern state.

Decades before the fascists extended the surname legislation to cover the eastern borderlands, officials, clerics, and nationalist sympathizers initiated nationalization efforts aimed at populations in the upper Adriatic provinces. The widow Paulovich's origins in Dalmatia made her cognizant of the impact of historical efforts to nationalize Adriatic populations. Her response to the surname measure was grounded in her experiences of the particularities of the Dalmatian politics of her childhood and young womanhood and her life in Habsburg Trieste. The widow was born Luigia Barbarovich in the village of Milna, a sandy port founded in the late sixteenth century on the western side of the island of Brazza. The largest island in Dalmatia and the third largest in the Adriatic archipelago, Brazza lay opposite the port of Spalato, a city that lived in the shadow of Roman Emperor Diocletian's magnificent Roman palace built of local stone. Barbarovich's birth date is uncertain, recorded as May 14, 1854, in the parish records of San Pietro della Brazza but claimed by the family as June 26, 1856.

Whichever the exact date of her birth, Luigia Barbarovich was born in Habsburg Dalmatia, buffeted over the centuries by winds of Illyrian, Roman, Byzantine, Croat, Venetian, and Ottoman control, where the Austrian administration had replaced the collapsed Venetian Republic in the wake of the Napoleonic Wars and with the Restoration at the turn of the nineteenth century. In 1822 the Habsburgs transformed the southern Illyrian provinces, including eastern coastlands of the Adriatic Sea and islands of the Adriatic archipelago into Königreich Dalmatien or the Kingdom of Dalmatia, an administrative unit that survived until the monarchy's collapse in 1918.

Dalmatia developed as a multilingual Habsburg territory enjoying varying levels of autonomy. The political climate spurred the development of Dalmatian linguist and writer Niccolò Tommaseo's philosophies that relied on multinationalism and pluralism as building blocks for federal states throughout Europe. Born in Sebenico in the Illyrian Provinces in 1802, Tommaseo conceived an Italian nationalism based in heterogeneity rather than homogeneity and insisted on a decentralized governmental structure without a single capital. His ideas rooted in diversity as a building block for Italy contrasted with Giuseppe Mazzini's unitary republican model, which provided the ideological foundations of the modern Italian state.[4]

The issues raised by the clash between Tommaseo's federalist and Mazzini's unitary models of state and nation formed the ideological background for the divergence between Luigia Paulovich's vision of Italian nationalism born of experience in Dalmatia and Trieste and fascist ideas of nationalism rooted in Roman history and the development of the modern state. Fascism relied on conceptions of Rome as the center of the nation-state and as the historic center of the nation. The fascist state propagated visions of Italian nationalism based on the Roman perspective and carefully orchestrated their dissemination.[5] Raised in Dalmatia, Paulovich understood Italianness in terms of Romantic notions of spirit, community, home, and language emphasized by Tommaseo rather than in terms of territorial subjugation, the history of domination, or symbolic images of Rome. These ideas contrasted with Mazzini's Romantic notions that emphasized duty and sacrifice in the name of the unitary core Rome. These notions of responsibility and sacrifice drove the prefect of Trieste's vision of nationalism in the fascist state.

From the era of the Risorgimento, Dalmatians' notions of heterogeneity conflicted with peninsular Italians' ideas of unity. Dalmatia's Autonomous Party had its roots in the 1860s in the Habsburg promotion of Dalmatian regionalism against Croat nationalism. In 1867 the Dalmatian Autonomous Party welcomed the Compromise that divided the Habsburg lands into Hungarian Transleithania and Austrian Cisleithania. By including Dalmatia in Austrian lands, the Compromise effectively thwarted Croat aspirations to join the coastland to the Croatian interior and to Fiume included in the Hungarian lands. It appeared to support and reinforce Dalmatian autonomy. At the same time, creation of the dual monarchy stoked ethnic passions, encouraging other subject nationalities including Italians to seek privileges similar to those accorded to the Hungarians. The progress of the Italian Risorgimento on the peninsula inspired Italian nationalists who staked claims to territory on the eastern Adriatic shores. Moderates placed the Italian border at the Isonzo River, leaving Trieste, Istria, and Dalmatia ensconced in the multinational monarchy. Ultra-nationalists caught the attention of the Italian right and conservative nationalist public opinion with cries to include all Italians in modern Italy.[6]

Over the course of the second half of the nineteenth century, shifting currents in Habsburg domestic politics and the developing relationship between the Habsburg monarchy, Italy, and emerging states in the eastern and southern Balkans affected the political development of Dalmatia. Habsburg attempts to woo Croats in the Adriatic coastlands with promises of greater attention to Slavs' aspirations raised the suspicions of those in the Autonomous Party. Dalmatian Autonomists bristled at calls to unify the Dalmatian lands with Zagreb, the Croatian capital in Transleithania. They responded with calls for the defense of the multilingual, multiethnic population of the territory that translated to protecting the rights of ethnic Italians. This produced the impression that Autonomists favored the Italians. While the party fought for Italian rights and to maintain Italian language privileges, its aims were not primarily territorially irredentist. Italian protectors on the peninsula misinterpreted the situation, and under the impression that German Habsburgs and Croat Slavs persecuted Adriatic Italians, sent aid and support from the new Italian state.[7]

Local support for Dalmatian autonomy under the Habsburg umbrella remained strong despite increasing political polarization along ethnic lines in the lands of the monarchy. In 1910 the founder of the Croat Democratic Party in Dalmatia, Josip Smodlaka, a representative from Spalato, argued before the Austrian parliament in support of Dalmatian autonomy, but he did not advocate a break with the Habsburgs. He complained that the Viennese government had failed to continue to develop Dalmatia as Napoleon had in the Illyrian provinces and called for separate administration and better consideration of the needs of the region that was "too far off" and too dissimilar in its "climate, people and needs" to be tied directly to Vienna.[8]

The combination of Dalmatian poverty and rise of support for Croat nationalism devastated the Italian community on Luigia Barbarovich's native island of Brazza. Like many other ethnic Italians, she must have left Brazza in search of a larger Italian community.[9] The details of her path are sketchy, but she appears to have moved north along the Adriatic coast from Brazza to Zara. Historically the capital of Dalmatia, Zara boasted a strong, although by no means preponderant, Italian community and a Venetian commercial tradition. Life in the city shaped her political perspective and also sealed her fate. Zara was the native city of her husband Antonio Paulovich.[10]

The Habsburg Zara of Antonio Paulovich's youth was a city of approximately 12,000 inhabitants. At the time of Luigia and Antonio's marriage in 1883, Zara appeared to an Italian observer as an "eminently Italian city."[11] Dotted by ruins of Venetian defensive walls built to keep the Ottomans at bay, Zara boasted a Venetian shipyard built in the 1770s.[12] The famed Venetian winged lion topped the city's towers and gates, including the landward Porta Terra Firma (built and designed by the famed Veronese architect Michele Sanmicheli) and the seaward Porta Marina.[13] Italian propagandists cast Zara as an Italian space and emphasized the "care" taken to preserve "her old Roman Tower, her Roman aqueduct, and her ancient Loggia del Comune, with its 34,000 volumes and invaluable Latin and other manuscripts."[14] But, keen observers noted that behind the pointed Venetian doorways lived a mixed population in which "the blood of many races mingle[d]."[15] Croats, Hungarians, and Ottomans influenced the culture of the city. Pan-Slavic voices provided a counter-narrative to the Italian perspective. Citing the city's importance to the Illyrian and Slav movements, some touted Zara as the site of "Slavic intellectual awakening" in 1848, emphasizing that the city had a Slav mayor and had responded to calls from the Slav Congress in Prague.[16]

By the 1880s, Zara was the last stronghold of the Autonomist Party in Dalmatia. At the turn of the twentieth century, Zara was an important center for the Lega Nazionale (Italian National Association), the seat of several pro-Italian political groups including the Società politica dalmata (Dalmatian Political Society), and the Società degli studenti italiani della dalmazia (Italian Student's Society of Dalmatia). It hosted Italian political and cultural periodicals including *Il Dalmata*, *Il Risorgimento*, and *La Rivista Dalmatica*. Luigia and Antonio Paulovich and their three children Ines, Enrico, and Ernesto, born between 1885 and 1891, were involved in the Italian life of the city.

According to evidence presented in the name restoration case, Antonio Paulovich, an ardent supporter of the Autonomist Party, fought aggressively for the cause of ethnic Italians.[17] But, at the turn of the century, the Italians were clearly losing ground. Dalmatian deputies representing Croat parties sought expanded rights for Croats in the Habsburg realms.

The Rijeka and Zadar Resolutions of October 1905 called for reunification of Dalmatia with the Croat nation and the recognition of Croat solidarity.[18] The resolutions announced by various Serbian and Croatian Dalmatian factions as well as other Croat representatives reacting against Vienna, were the product of a temporary rapprochement between local Slavic groups. But the Rijeka Resolution's suggestion that the Croats would seek "a favorable influence upon the consideration of those of our race who live in other lands, particularly at the most exposed point, namely in the sister land of Istria" irked ethnic Italians.[19] The Serb representatives' promise that they would support Croat aspirations for "reincorporation of Dalmatia, with Croatia and Slavonia" in return for assurances of equal treatment for Serbs and Croats provoked considerable concern as well.[20] The Autonomists' tenuous political position and the Serb and Croat representatives' affirmation that "*the Croats and Serbs are one nation*" combined with the pledge "to work shoulder to shoulder" on Dalmatian political questions convinced many that the climate was ripe to seek opportunities elsewhere.[21]

The Pauloviches migrated up the Habsburg Adriatic coast to Trieste in 1905. Travelers, traders, and migrants frequently passed along this route from Zara to Trieste, a nine-hour trip by express steamer. The Pauloviches left behind the world of languid, picturesque Adriatic islands "dominated by Venetian style towers and piazzas" trading it for the Habsburg commercial hub laid out in the "imposing grid style" of Empress Maria Theresa.[22]

At the turn of the twentieth century, Trieste was "brisk, wealthy, and bursting with vitality . . . curious and arresting." Yet, it was not considered a grand city. Rather, it retained "an air of wishing to become eventually imposing."[23] The Habsburgs announced policies intended to transform it from a port of transit to a financial and economic node of the monarchy. By 1904 work began to enlarge and modernize the port facilities. By 1909, the new Monti Tauri rail line linked the port directly to markets in the Austrian interior and southern Germany.[24] Trieste was a city "born bourgeois" in "an era of the affirmation of the European bourgeoisie."[25]

Since the mid-nineteenth century, common educational background and commitment to education in Austro-German universities and opportunities for advancement in the Habsburg government and *porto franco* had forged an affinity of intellectuals and professionals in Trieste, a city known for its role in eastern Mediterranean commerce, its cosmopolitan

population, and its progressiveness with respect to technological innovation.[26] Most Triestines shared in the liberal commercial fortunes of the
city. However, by the end of the nineteenth century, increasingly vocal
Italian, Slovene, and Croat movements propounding ethnic-based agendas began to transform the political climate, subverting the voices of the
commercial classes.

In the half-century prior to the Pauloviches' arrival in the Adriatic
port, Trieste's population had more than doubled as a result of immigration linked to commercial modernization, industrialization, and Habsburg patronage.[27] Italian-speaking immigrants from the eastern Adriatic
coastal lands, increasingly affected by ethnic tensions in the monarchy,
found a refuge and a home in the commercial port. Ethnic antagonisms
and migration decimated small Italian communities along the Dalmatian
coast, like that in Luigia Barbarovich's birthplace Brazza. By 1910 only a
few hundred in Brazza's population of approximately 23,000 considered
themselves Italians.[28] Of those who had recently migrated from San Pietro
della Brazza, only 82 had remained in Dalmatia, 388 had left for other
Habsburg lands. The pattern was similar for Zara, where 1,610 internal
migrants stayed in Dalmatia while 3,447 moved elsewhere in the Habsburg
monarchy.[29]

Urban Ethnicity in Trieste

Turn-of-the-century Trieste may have boasted "nothing to detain the tourists," but the bustling, rapidly growing port "devoted to Mercury," or to
commerce related to the affairs of the Austrian monarchy was a haven for
migrants.[30] Trieste teemed with immigrants, many from less urbanized
Adriatic coastlands. Between 1890 and 1900 the city's population rose by
12.4 percent to 176,200 inhabitants. In the following decade, at the mid-
point of which the Pauloviches arrived, the population increased by an
astonishing 33.5 percent to 235,000.[31] More than 5,000 of Trieste's residents in 1910 were born in Dalmatia.[32]

Although Habsburg supporters, commercial agents, and international
shippers and traders touted Trieste as a crossroads of the Italian, Germanic, and Slavic worlds, various movements and parties fought for recognition of nationalist Italian, Slovene, and Croat, as well as united South
Slav (or Yugoslav) interests in a climate inflamed by propagandists on all

sides who criticized the Austro-German Habsburg rule.[33] Liberal commercial interests controlled the Habsburg port city through a pro-Italian city council. But, as the pace of immigration quickened and the electorate expanded, traditional leading elements felt themselves under siege. Local commercial leaders called for assimilation of the new immigrants, but Italian nationalists saw their arrival as a reflection of Slavic desire for conquest, orchestrated by Czech banks and based on principles of pan-Slavism.[34]

Italian nationalists jealously guarding political power became increasingly aggressive in defense of Trieste's *italianità*. Tamaro called the Adriatic "an Italian gulf" and emphasized Trieste's history of independent "municipalism" dating back to the fourteenth century as a brand of perennial resistance to Habsburg authority.[35] Nationalists in the Adriatic city, like those in Dalmatia, solidified ties with irredentists on the Italian peninsula. Slovene intellectuals in the city, caught between the rising currents of conservative ethnic nationalism and increasingly shrill demands for Italian assimilation, became disenchanted with liberal democratic agendas. The expansion of suffrage weakened their position and introduced nationalistic and reactionary mass elements into the voting force. Tensions increased and conflict escalated as nationalist parties gained popularity in areas where political life had not previously been construed in racial or ethnic terms.[36]

Despite some critiques of irredentism, most famously from socialist writer Angelo Vivante in *Irredentismo Adriatico* published in 1912, Italian nationalists continued to insist that Slavic nationalists (referring to all groups associated with pan-Slavism) were radical, revolutionary elements that sought to destabilize the city. Vivante, a member of an Italian bourgeois family, caused considerable consternation with his insistence that Trieste's prosperity lay in its ties to eastern Adriatic hinterlands and in its acceptance of the "equilibrating force" of Austria.[37] Italian journalist Virginio Gayda's scathing condemnation of Austrian treatment of Italian populations in the Adriatic coastlands in his book *L'Italia d'oltre confine* (1914) and in a pamphlet entitled *Gli Slavi della Venezia Giulia* (1915) was more typical of the nationalist attitude in the city and in Italy. Gayda charged the Habsburg government with pan-Germanism.[38] He identified the Austrians as Italy's main enemy, arguing that the city of Trieste was actually under assault by "a powerful combination of the governing powers in Vienna and the heads of the Slovenes in Carniola" for whom the Slovenes in the coastal regions were a "blind instrument."[39] His particular vehemence against Slavs and contempt for Germans stemmed, at least in part, from his travels in central and eastern Europe as a journalist for *La Stampa* in the years prior to World War I and his wartime work as an attaché to the Italian ambassador in St. Petersburg where he was instrumental in arranging for the exchange and transport of ethnic Italian Austrian prisoners to Italy.[40] In the same camp as Gayda, Tamaro went even farther with the idea of Slavs' disenfranchisement over time. "The contrast between Italians and Slavs in the Julian Region has always been an opposition of autochthonous, indigenous Italians against migratory foreigners," he charged.[41] Aggressive Germans sought to dominate through control of the weak and malleable Slavs. In the Italian imagination, autochthonous non-Italian populations in the borderlands were not dangerous in and of themselves, but as pawns of international intriguers.[42]

Italian nationalists routinely exaggerated the superiority of Italy, the strength of Italian influence over the Adriatic, and the oppression Italians suffered at the hands of "foreign" powers in the Adriatic. In the first decades of the twentieth century, their zeal and bias provoked the ire of Habsburg officials and even annoyed Italian government agents on the peninsula. Amedeo Nasalli Rocca, the prefect of Venice from 1908 to 1913, complained to Rome about irredentists who denounced him as an Austrophile and charged that he was "paid by Austria to repress the *italianità* of the unredeemed territories." He asked for the Italian government's assistance to deal with the disruptive influence of irredentists who "under the pretext of patriotism too often claimed the right to violate the law."

Italian leadership in Rome made light of the situation. Prime Minister Giovanni Giolitti placated Nasalli Rocca with assurances of the government's faith in his abilities and counseled him to ignore such remarks that "offended only those who published them." Yet, he recognized the dangers of extreme irredentism and acted to thwart irredentist designs. In one case, Giolitti ordered Nasalli Rocca to prevent the election of an irredentist that might cause "complications and bring great embarrassment to the Country."[43] Italian politicians' ambivalence left the Venetian prefect in a frustrating position. Charged with responsibility for controlling nationalist extremism and inflammatory irredentism, Nasalli Rocca faced Giolitti and other government ministers unwilling to support overtly his antiextremist stance. Giolitti's attitude reflected the politics of Rome and the position of moderate nationalist intellectuals who sympathized with ethnic Italians in the Adriatic but did not wish to provoke Austria.

In *Irredentismo Adriatico*, Vivante criticized irredentists who charged the Habsburg government with promoting Slavs at the expense of Italians. He saw the growth of the urban population and the increasing entrance of Slavs into the Habsburg civil service as a natural consequence of liberal development.[44] His observations that members of the working classes of Trieste had varied political involvements and interests that did not correspond to ethnic associations fell on deaf ears. Italian nationalists concentrated on the threat of socialist politics and programs that appealed to workers, many of whom came from the surrounding countryside. Although considerable numbers of migrants came from the Italian peninsula and many workers were ethnic Italians, Slavs became the main targets of anti–working class agitation. The Slovene and Croat national movements promoted distinctive cultural traditions, language, and political identities that were anathema to ruling Italian interests and appeared to undermine liberal commerce.[45]

Arriving in Trieste in 1905, the Pauloviches made their home in the neighborhood of Cologna, a recently developed urban district whose name reputedly referred to the land's attachment to the Roman colony ("agro colonico") at Tergeste (Trieste).[46] Cologna, originally a village separated from the city, had 59 houses and 236 inhabitants in Napoleon's time. As Trieste expanded in the nineteenth century, the city encroached on the village, and in 1880, the parcel of green land separating Trieste and Cologna that had belonged to the Benedictines until 1844 became the site for Trieste's public garden, making the village contiguous with the city. By 1884 the new city neighborhood of Cologna had nearly 2000 inhabitants living in 213 houses.[47]

In 1905 Cologna was abuzz with activity. The Pauloviches appear to have acquired an apartment on Piazza Leonardo da Vinci, a square developed between 1899 and 1902 as part of an urban expansion project that encompassed part of the former Spinger estate.[48] The planners' tribute to the renowned Italian painter, sculptor, and inventor Leonardo da Vinci in naming the *piazza* or square was no accident. Working in tandem with the city council, they sought to evoke visions of Italy, Italian invention, and Italian innovation to make clear to arriving immigrants Triestines' affinities for Italy and the benefits of Italian ingenuity. They dubbed the street at the base of the piazza Via Luigi Galvani, in memory of the eighteenth-century Bolognese surgeon and physicist famed for his discovery of principles of bioelectricity.[49] Via Alessandro Volta, celebrating the Italian physicist and inventor from Como renowned for his discovery of the electric cell and work in electricity at the turn of the eighteenth century, ran along the edge of the public garden, dedicated to Muzio de Tommasini, a local botanist and Habsburg civil servant who served as Trieste's chief magistrate and then mayor.[50]

The new development reflected Italian tastes, but Cologna was already well-established as an industrial zone with a polyglot population. Home since 1858 to the award-winning Pullitzer Soap and Chemical Products factory that employed Central European immigrants, it was also the site of Angelo Valerio's factory that employed French workers in the production of *cioccolata a vapore*, or steamed chocolate.[51] Industrial development had also brought political organizations and, by the turn of the century, socialist politics to the district. The Fabbrica Caldaie, a socialist cooperative factory, was located on Via Cologna in 1897.[52]

A few blocks from the Pauloviches' apartment building on Piazza Leonardo da Vinci ran the new tram line to Villa Opicina, a Slovene village more than three hundred meters above the city in the Carsic hills. The tramway was a technical marvel worthy of the new century. Built in 1902, it incorporated a funicular and rack railway system and made use of cable tractors to connect Trieste to Villa Opicina and the Sudbahn railway running along the mountain crest, eliminating the circuitous trip of more than thirty kilometers using the standard rail track.[53] The tram departed from Piazza della Caserma (renamed Piazza Oberdan in 1922) and wound its way through Cologna and up the mountainside to stop at the Obelisk, a monument constructed by the Triestine Merchant Board in 1830 in honor of the birth of future Habsburg emperor Franz Joseph and to commemorate the opening of the new road between Vienna and Trieste. The Obelisk stop provided access to the Napoleonica, the road purportedly used by Napoleon's troops as they made their way down the Adriatic coast through the Illyrian provinces.

The tram facilitated the movement of labor from the Carso countryside to the city. It also brought the city to the countryside. Urban residents eager to escape Trieste took the tram up the hill to stroll along the mountain ridge, promenading and picnicking along the Napoleonica trail that afforded vistas of the sea and the city below. From some vantage points, they could glimpse the Habsburg's Miramare Castle, where the ailing Empress Charlotte, the former princess of Belgium and the consort of Maximilian I of Mexico, lived at the turn of the century.[54]

If Cologna's industry and technical marvels made it a microcosm of the new city at the turn of the century, its inhabitants reflected the new urban denizens and political arrangements of the late Habsburg monarchy. The café at the nearby public garden was the site of a pro-Austrian demonstration in 1898, a reaction to the assassination of the Habsburg Empress Elizabeth at the hands of Louis Lucheni (or Luigi Luccheni), a Parisian-born Italian anarchist. Reportedly intending to mock the Italian city of Trieste, demonstrators drove patrons from the café, venting their anger and eating the leftover ice cream straight from the dishes without using spoons. Thus, according to legend, it was in the Cologna district that supporters of the Austrian monarchy earned the epithet *leccapiattini* or plate lickers.[55]

By the turn of the twentieth century, the pro-Italian city council and strong irredentist sentiment in Trieste created a welcoming environment for ethnic Italians like the Pauloviches. On September 20, 1903, the thirty-third anniversary of the breach of the Porta Pia and the joining of Rome to the modern Italian state, pranksters raised a large Italian flag over Trieste's city hall using an "ingenious contrivance" rigged from the clock tower and accessible only by climbing a turret staircase. By "strange coincidence" the turret was locked, and the key proved difficult to find. The Italian flag flew over the city for several hours. Italian nationalists pointed with glee to nationalist pranks, but such actions inflamed ethnic and political passions that corroded cosmopolitan interests. They also irritated Habsburg officials trying to counter nationalist extremism, who found their inability to marshal forces to track down the culprits in the wake of the incident particularly vexing.[56]

Irredentism and Nationalist Visions

Italian nationalists affirmed the superiority of Italians and Italian culture and were vocal in their support for Italy and Italian causes, but prior to the World War I many saw irredentism primarily as a means to assert Italian culture and protect the rights and privileges of ethnic Italians outside of

Italy's borders. Tamaro defined irredentism as "the political action by which the Italian populations under Austrian domination manifested their desire to be independent and at the same time the action by which Italy affirmed its responsibility and its right to liberate them from the foreign yoke."[57] He justified the call for the Adriatic territories' "return from Austria to Italy" on the basis of the history of political domination in the region. "The justice or injustice of a domination," he claimed, was based in "the ways in which it is accepted or submitted to or combated by the dominated populations." *Who* dominated a land was less important than *how* powers dominated a land, "what they have done for the benefit of a country and even more for the benefit of civilization."[58] Despite the emphasis on the justice of irredentism, in a subtle way, his definition adhered to local notions of autonomy characteristic of Trieste and the Adriatic provinces. It made more of Italy's responsibility to aid subjugated Italians than of Italy's right to annex the Habsburg territory.

In the first decade of the twentieth century, many individuals were susceptible to increasingly shrill calls for expansionism, international assertiveness, and imperialism that characterized the European international diplomatic scene.[59] The Paulovich family's involvement with Italian nationalist politics followed a common path from support for Italian minority autonomy in the Habsburg monarchy to calls for inclusion in Italy. Antonio Paulovich's support for ethnic Italians and Dalmatian autonomy in Zara translated in Trieste to irredentism in favor of Italian control. According to documents presented in the Paulovich case, Antonio and Luigia's sons Enrico and Ernesto served "at the vanguard of best actions of the irredentist party" between 1905 and 1915, actively seeking to join the Adriatic lands to Italy.[60]

In intellectual circles, irredentists in the Adriatic found common cause with those in the northern Brenner provinces. Geographer and historian Ettore Tolomei, a native of Trent who worked obsessively to promote the *italianità* of South Tyrol, was in contact with irredentist Triestines and sympathized with the plight of Adriatic Italians.[61] In Florence, he was acquainted with the prominent Triestine born intellectual and scholar Salomone Morpurgo, the director of the National Library in Florence from 1905 to 1923.[62] Like Tolomei, Morpurgo was born in the Habsburg monarchy. An immigrant to Italy, he was active in irredentist and republican circles and served as an important link between Triestine and Florentine intellectuals.[63] In the final years of Habsburg rule, meetings between committed irredentists like Morpurgo and Tolomei forged a unity of Adriatic and Brenner interests that kept irredentism in the public eye. Italian psychologist and criminologist Scipio Sighele's "Letter to the Students of the Trieste," published in 1913 by the National Association, typified irredentist exhortations emanating from Florence. It encouraged collective action in favor of the Italian nation and justified aid to populations in the borderlands on the premise that "the pulse of the *patria* beats more strongly on the periphery than at the heart."[64]

After World War I, arguments raged over the positioning of borders between Italy and the new Kingdom of South Slavs and between Italy and the new Austrian state. Ambiguities in the 1915 Treaty of London (on the basis of which Italy had denounced the Triple Alliance and entered World War I on the side of the Entente powers) heightened tensions. Article 5 of the treaty had promised Italy "the province of Dalmatia within its present administrative boundaries," but had called for the neutralization of areas further south on the coast that were considered Dalmatian lands. An additional note promised Adriatic territories to Croatia, Serbia and Montenegro.[65] The Italian Memorandum of Claims filed in February 1919 after the end of hostilities included claims to the Dalmatian coast based on Roman heritage and Venetian patterns of settlement and to meet Italy's defensive needs in the Adriatic. Italy also sought Fiume, on the northeastern tip of the Istrian peninsula as part of Venezia Giulia, ostensibly to protect its Italian population and to ensure better coordination of the ports in the northeastern Adriatic.[66]

In the treaties of St. Germain and Rapallo, ratified in September and December 1920 respectively, liberal Italy obtained New Provinces dubbed Venezia Tridentina in the north at the Brenner Pass and Venezia Giulia in the east in the Habsburg Adriatic Littoral. However, these new territories fell short of irredentists' hopes. While Italians rejoiced at the annexation of Trento and Trieste, tempers flared over the failure to win parts of Istria and Dalmatia. Occupied by Italian troops in November 1918, Zara became Italian with the Treaty of St. Germain, but its hinterlands remained contested. The Treaty of Rapallo assigned to Italy "the commune of Zara and portions of some neighboring communes, amounting roughly to a radius of seven kilometers around the city." It incorporated the remainder of the surrounding territory and the bulk of Dalmatia into the South Slav

Kingdom. Special conventions regulated relations between Zara and its hinterlands.[67] The partition of Zara and the failure to redeem lands on the Dalmatian coast, including Luigia Paulovich's home island of Brazza, remained at issue for Italian nationalists throughout the interwar period, forming part of the Italian myth of "mutilated victory" that spurred fascist nationalism and expansionism.[68]

Immediately following the war, continuing conflict over territory and questions relating to the placement of the border between Italy and Yugoslavia complicated the situation in the Adriatic territories. The terms of the Paris Peace called for an autonomous Fiume, declaring the intention to establish the Hungarian port and a small surrounding area as an autonomous city under international control. In September 1919, in violation of the agreements, Italian nationalist writer and poet Gabriele D'Annunzio seized the port in the name of Italy but without the Italian government's sanction. The Italian government's refusal to recognize what many saw as his heroic act, patriotic act led D'Annunzio to proclaim the Italian Regency of Quarnaro, under which he and his *legionnaires* occupied Fiume for the next fifteen months. In the meantime, the 1920 Treaty of Rapallo created the Free State of Fiume / Rijeka. Placed in an embarrassing situation, Italian Prime Minister Giovanni Giolitti ordered regular Italian forces to the city and in January 1921, they succeeded in ousting D'Annunzio and his followers.[69]

From 1920 to 1924, Italy and the South Slav Kingdom bickered over the fate of the weak autonomist-led free state until, under pressure from Mussolini's fascist government, the South Slav Kingdom ceded control of the port city and some surrounding Istrian lands to Italy in the Treaty of Rome. In return, Italy agreed to the South Slav Kingdom's annexation of a small portion of the free state including the port of Sušak. With the annexation of Fiume, Mussolini scored a nationalist triumph, partially repudiating the disappointments of St. Germain and Rapallo. The highly publicized and propagandized extension of Italy's eastern borderland intensified the fascists' desire to fully integrate border populations to ensure Italian control in recently acquired provinces.

In the years immediately following the World War I armistice, the fate of the Habsburg Adriatic Littoral was a sticking point in international negotiations but, as with many border territories considered at the Paris Peace Conference, few really understood the local ethnic alignments.

Triestines and others in Venezia Giulia heard nationalist demands for Dalmatia, but they remained more interested in the cities of Fiume and Zara, with their relatively strong ethnic Italian communities, than in much of Dalmatia where the majority was of Croat sympathies. Most in the new Italian territories, eager to get on with annexation and reconstruction, were not keen to squabble over the fate of scattered individuals in small Italian enclaves in traditionally multilingual, multiethnic areas along the Adriatic coast.[70]

"Civilizing" the Borderland

Under the conventions of the World War I treaties, as a new state, the South Slav Kingdom agreed to recognize and respect the rights of minority groups and to allow them to maintain associations, schools, and access to legal redress in their native tongues.[71] Such guarantees were not required of Italy, a successor state to the Habsburg monarchy but not a newly established one. In the Upper Adriatic provinces, this produced an awkward imbalance ensuring the protection of the rights of Italian speakers in Yugoslavia but leaving Slavic speakers to Italy's good graces.[72]

Ethnic Slovenes and Croats entered an Italy unaccustomed to dealing with issues related to the absorption and assimilation of linguistic minority groups. Risorgimento Italy was not devoid of linguistic minorities, but census figures of 1911 indicated that only 74 of every 10,000 inhabitants of Italy were "foreign speakers." Annexation of the New Provinces considerably altered this situation. In 1922 the number of "foreign speakers" rose to 350 per 10,000 inhabitants including the populations in Venezia Giulia, Venezia Tridentina, and Istria.[73] While as a percentage of the population this number was relatively small (particularly as compared to the percentages in other successor states), it represented a nearly fivefold increase, giving the impression of a threat to the integrity of the Italian nation. Prior to 1918, many Italian nationalists shared Gayda's perception that Slovenes in Venezia Giulia would be easily assimilated into the Italian environment because smaller nations of Europe (such as Slovene or Croat) were less rooted in their histories. After the war, *foreign speakers* appeared instead as members of populations of *foreign extraction*, people of organic foreign origin and sensibilities incompatible with those of the Italian nation.[74] Italian nationalists increasingly associated Slavs with national threat, defining them generically in ethnic terms (eliding Slovenes, Croats, etc.) and associating them with the South Slav state. Defense of *italianità* became associated with defense of Italy against a foreign element tied to a foreign power, the Kingdom of the Serbs, Croats, and Slovenes.

Nonetheless, Western European bias made Italianization of "new Slavic brothers" (more than 400,000 Slovenes, Croats, and Serbs in the eastern provinces of Italy) seem far easier than Italianization of the 250,000 "Germans" (in the new Brenner territories and Gorizia-Gradisca). Despite the defense "by Pan-Slavs in Lubljana, Zagreb, and Belgrade" and the support of elements in "Washington, London, or Paris . . . [engaged in giving] paladins' speeches against the rights of Italy," the Slavs "unfortunately had an inferior civilization." Italian nationalists noted confidently that Slovene identity in Friuli had faded considerably since the Risorgimento, particularly in Udine and in Cividale "once a Slovene hamlet, [but] where no one speaks [Slovene] any longer."[75]

Italian leaders trying to accelerate assimilation overlooked the borderland populations' primary concerns, which were related to economic and social reconstruction. The collapse of the Habsburg trade networks and commercial markets coupled with physical devastation related to the war crippled Trieste. Sunken vessels clogged the port, and merchant ships of the Austro-Hungarian fleet lay at anchor for nearly two years after the armistice, pending international agreement on their fate. Trieste's natural or traditional, geographic commercial hinterlands lay across the border in the new South Slav Kingdom. Established trading networks based on rail lines that ran up both the eastern and western sides of the Italian peninsula competed with Trieste's networks to serve Italy's needs in the Adriatic city's traditional markets in Central Europe.

Local authorities recognized the volatility of the eastern borderland. Political disappointments linked to dissatisfaction with the territorial settlements, economic decline, and the Italian governments' inability to normalize local life appeared to magnify ethnic discontents. Administrative duties linked to the Italian takeover distracted local officials. For the commercial classes, economic concerns outweighed ethnic considerations. The leadership of the Slovene national movement in Trieste resumed its prewar political program and activities designed to further the interests of Slovenes in the city.[76]

In the countryside near Trieste and in Istria, politically motivated violence escalated. Attacks by bands of criminals assumed to be crude, uncivilized non-Italian elements terrorized locals and annoyed police. In 1919 police in Parenzo claimed that Istrian police agents' work was "particularly difficult among the segment of the population with natural proclivities toward violence." The police report acknowledged that problems in the region were not new, "the rude nature of the inhabitants, the majority Slavs (Morlachs, Serbs, and Hercegovinans, etc.)." contributed to "delinquency" in the region that had been "somewhat accentuated also under the previous regime."[77]

By July 1920, tensions attributed to the "rude nature" of rural populations in the new territories spilled over into urban violence. An attack on the Slovene culture center in Trieste Narodni Dom, sparked by an incident in Spalato that left two Italian sailors dead, testified to escalating anger at "foreign elements" in lands assigned to Italy. Violence also erupted in the former Austrian naval port at Pola. Outbreaks heightened nationalist Italians' fears and justified government intervention to protect and defend "vulnerable" ethnic Italian populations throughout the New Provinces. In Trieste, police stationed near Narodni Dom did not act decisively to stop looting and burning of Slovene and other Slavic assets. The national government did not condone their inaction, and the troops' failure to respond was not linked to official policy. It was symptomatic of official indifference and indicative of individuals' sympathies for the Italian cause.[78] The Slovene press and other Slavic outlets interpreted the weak response to Italian government support for attacks on Slavic minorities and the desire to force assimilation and eliminate ethnic minorities' presence.

Educating Borderland Populations

Between the armistice and official annexation, the Italian government initiated education efforts to assimilate the new borderland population. Professor of Philosophy Giovanni Gentile, a supporter of Italian intervention in World War I, who would be the leading ideologue of fascist education in the 1920s, emerged as one of the key figures in Italian efforts to convince those of "foreign extraction" of the benefits of Italy and the privileges of being an Italian citizen. Gentile rejected definitions of national community based on geographic boundaries, residence, and legal citizenship in favor of Romantic notions that relied on ideas of Italian spirit, the history of the nation, and its greatness. He saw the nation as a "creation of the mind," and argued that the state was merely the nation's "concrete, political manifestation."[79] The assumption that the nation was defined "spiritually" rather than "legally" according to modern state boundaries, based in the nineteenth century philosophies of Renan and his followers, justified the assimilation of populations of contested borderlands and legitimated programs for the nationalist education of "sympathetic" peoples abroad.

Ideological architect of the Italian Risorgimento Giuseppe Mazzini had recognized education as one of three main pillars (along with labor and the franchise) of nation-building. Mazzini saw education as a means to promote liberty and encourage self-sacrifice, while making national citizens dependent neither "on the *idea* of a single man or the *force* of the majority."[80] Gentile, an idealist philosopher, believed that individuals united in "spiritual communion," could only reach their potential within the community of the state. He rejected the liberal notion of the individual's social contract, instead promoting the state as the "supreme ethical entity" into which the individual should "merge his or her will."[81] The state's desire and responsibility was to "educate citizens to their responsibilities—to awaken the individual to his communal essence."[82]

Gentile published his observations for Trieste and the Adriatic borderland in 1920, in *La riforma dell'educazione* (*The Reform of Education* [English edition 1922]), a collection of his lectures intended to prepare teachers in Trieste to be educators in the new Italy. His proposals and policies promoted classical influences in Latin and Italian patriotic history to instill an understanding of the greatness of the nation and allow the Italian spirit to permeate the people.[83] While idealistically appealing in the climate of nationalist rejoicing at the realization of Italian aspirations for Trent and Trieste, the proposals were impractical and Gentile's advice and guidance were poorly suited to improving or fostering education in the Adriatic environment. The Habsburgs had adopted a centralized educational model that proved far more successful in combating illiteracy and extending education to the masses than the regional French classical model adopted in Italy. Schools in the Adriatic provinces were well adapted to studies of German that were the bread and butter of the commercial city. If Italy hoped to take advantage of Trieste's Central European connections, those educational traditions needed to be continued, not discarded in favor of national education and the inculcation of Italian spirit that Gentile proposed.[84]

Almost immediately upon assuming power in 1922, the fascists initiated a campaign to nationalize the New Provinces. While not officially a member of the Fascist Party until June 1923, Gentile served as Mussolini's Minister for Public Instruction from October 1922 to July 1924. He also served as a member of the fascist Grand Council from 1923 to 1929, presiding over the first fascist educational reforms.[85] Gentile's primary duty as the president of the National Fascist Institute of Culture, an organization he helped to establish and a position he held until 1937, was to "bring fascism to Italian culture."[86] He saw politics as "pedagogy on a grand scale." As fascism encompassed "the whole will and thought and feeling of the nation," education was a means to convey the priorities of the collective and to convince the public of its supremacy over individual interests.[87]

The new fascist society would create proper Italians, or at least promote a vision of dynamic, virile, and loyal Italians that instilled a respect for Italy and its people. Trieste's local cultural periodical *La porta orientale* articulated Gentile's ideal path for national spirit to permeate the borderland explaining, "where naturally stabilized or politically imposed borders are lacking, the flame of the idea [of the nation] is constrained to feed on the penetration of the heart."[88] Emphasis on national education translated to specific aims and policies for the borderland outlined in Triestine Superintendent of Education Giuseppe Reina's bulletin *Scuola al Confine (Border School)*, published from 1924 to 1927. Reina, a fascist of the first hour and a native of Palermo, came to Trieste after World War I. He served as the principal proponent and administrator of local educational reform until his death in 1945.[89] Laws mandating instruction in Italian, among the first fascist educational measures adopted, changed the face of primary education in the Adriatic territory. A natural extension of Gentile's insistence on disciplining the masses, they mimicked the policy initiated in South Tyrol where, in 1921, Italian families were compelled to withdraw children from German schools and to enroll them in Italian facilities. While *italianità* could be determined on the basis of individuals' declarations of ethnic preference, officials included families with Italian surnames or surnames deemed "of Italian origin" in those belonging to "the

Italian population." This made ethnic determinations a matter of state policy rather than individual choice.[90]

In theory, reforms to promote Italian political education and the formation of Italy's new citizens did not target specific groups. Reformers believed that proper methods for inculcation of national principles would lead to development of Italian identity based on the discovery of affiliation with the modern Italian state, and in public discourse, they promoted the measures to increase literacy and participation in the state. The liberal government introduced standards for language instruction in Italian grammar schools, and the fascist regime expanded and significantly strengthened the emphasis on Italian language in legislation of 1923, highlighting Latinness and classical education and sanctioning Italian as the only official language of the state.[91] Emphasis on teaching and learning Italian to combat illiteracy provoked linguistic minorities in Venezia Giulia, Venezia Tridentina, and Piedmont, where literacy rates (for persons over the age of six) were already comparatively high. In 1921, of the eighteen regions in Italy, Venezia Tridentina ranked first, Piedmont (including the Val D'Aosta) was second, and Venezia Giulia and Zara ranked sixth in terms of overall literacy, with literacy estimated at 97.5, 93.2, and 84.9 percent, respectively. This was in stark contrast to illiteracy rates of over 50 percent in southern regions like Calabria and Basilicata. Reforms of the first fascist decade did little to raise the level of literacy. By 1931 the regions' respective rankings in Italy remained the same and literacy had risen only marginally to 98.2 percent in Venezia Tridentina, 95.8 percent in Piedmont, and 87.6 percent in Venezia Giulia. In Calabria and Basilicata, illiteracy continued to hover around 50 percent.[92]

Ostensibly intended to promote Italian national culture, language education had long been recognized as a tool to build a national community and to "solidify permeable community boundaries."[93] As the venerable Milan daily *Corriere della Sera* tried to explain in an article justifying the educational reform of 1928, fascism did not desire "trembling obedience" from the new citizen in the borderland. Rather, it sought "the true and conscious consent of one who understands that he must be disciplined before he can share in the formation of the new Italian spirit."[94] This observation assumed the inferiority of competing cultures and ethnic associations, the ability of populations to assimilate, and their desire to learn what were assumed to be superior Italian ways. Triestine commentator Mario Todeschini writing in 1933 targeted young children for reform. Citing, the "importance of nursery school in multi-lingual and foreign speaking zones," he emphasized the importance of teaching youngsters Italian so that they learned "to speak Italian and to love Italy, not with the cold calculation of reason, but in the simplicity of heart and ardor of faith."[95]

Yet, the fascist reforms did require "trembling obedience." The words "border school policies" became code for forcible Italianization.[96] Slovene activists charged that the fascist educational acts were merely a continuation and amplification of Italianization strategies employed in the Julian March since 1918. Nationalists supported the programs to repudiate what had appeared to them to be the liberal government's lax administration of the New Provinces.[97]

From a practical perspective, the fascist government had little difficulty in enforcing the curricular reforms and linguistic regulations. The fascists' penchant for pressure tactics meant that Gentile's ideal of "transformation of the spirit" through "national education" slipped easily into suspension of non-Italian instruction. The 1923 measures introduced primary instruction in Italian to the exclusion of other languages. Supplemental instruction in other languages remained available at parents' request, but autochthonous German, Slovenian, and Croatian speakers were increasingly ostracized and no longer enjoyed the right to education in their native tongues. Competency tests in Italian intimidated teachers in the eastern borderland and weeded out Slovene and Croat teachers from Italy's civil servant ranks. Individuals who wished to retain their positions adhered to fascist policies, but their compliance was pragmatic not enthusiastic.[98]

With the onset of the dictatorship, the pace of the educational reforms accelerated. In 1926 the fascists ramped up Italian language teaching on the upper levels and banned second language teaching on the lower levels.[99] In Trieste the reforms eliminated vestiges of Habsburg education such as the German School at Servola. Founded in 1904 and supported by Habsburg subsidies since 1906, it ceased to function by the end of World War I. In 1926 no ethnic Germans came forward to defend the school.[100] The situation differed considerably with respect to the schools in districts with strong Slovene and Croat presences, where the fascists faced considerable resistance to Italianization.[101]

The government encouraged initiatives that supported Italianization policies. Ostensibly a private apolitical organization, the Action Group for Schools of the Eastern Borderland sprang up in 1925 to raise the moral and material standards of teachers and to assist impoverished pupils. Its approximately 140 members exhibited "the most Italian sentiments." Its mission included supporting Italian schools and combating the influence of Solsko Drustvo, the Slovene teachers' cultural association.[102]

In 1930, the private school on Via Giuliani in Trieste that taught in Italian but offered supplemental instruction in Slovenian was closed.[103] By 1934 the fascist clamp down on non-Italian speakers, schools, and instruction had reached a fever pitch. Purportedly, government officials went so far as to sequester religious textbooks and notebooks at the Tomadio convent school. Critics charged that, although the catechism texts were in Slovene, 24 sisters were engaged in teaching in Italian to 150 pupils, all girls dressed in the uniforms of the *piccole italiane*. The official that seized the books claimed that the presence of such "indoctrinating materials" testified to "dangerous irredentist activity, meant to disturb the future of Italy."[104]

The fascists paired educational reforms with linguistic reforms that excluded the use of languages other than Italian in all official capacities. Authorities tended to overstate the threat posed by non-Italian speakers. On the national level, the fear of non-Italian speakers reflected, at least in part, deep uncertainties relating to notions of the superiority of Italian identity that Mussolini sought to promote. Fascist nationalist rhetoric held up ancient Rome and the Romans as models of *italianità*, but implied that modern Italians had to be remade to approach this ideal and meet fascist expectations.[105]

In light of traditions of Habsburg public instruction that had favored voluntary assimilation over imposed linguistic requirements, the reforms of the 1920s appeared repressive and characteristic of Italian and fascist oppression of minorities, and they played a role in polarizing and radicalizing local populations. While Gentile claimed that educational reforms fostered Italian spirit and insisted that the use of Italian-sped assimilation, the heavy-handed enactment of the measures alienated autochthonous non-Italian speakers. Increasingly isolated Slovenian and Croatian speakers turned to armed and violent resistance against the cultural oppression. In 1928, in reaction to authorities' closure of Slovene and Croat schools, ostensibly in reaction to Yugoslav provocation by local Slavic elements, protesters set ablaze several Italian kindergartens and elementary schools in Slovene-dominated areas.[106] Firebombing of state-sponsored schools in rural areas had been a common form of ethnic protest when Habsburg authorities had interfered in local education.[107]

Fascist Education and the Surname Measure

The fascist government conceived the surname measure on the basis of which Luigia Barbarovich Paulovich became embroiled in nationalist controversy as part of Gentile's cultural reform. The government's reliance on surnames to determine Italianness for the purposes of the educational reforms in the northern provinces in 1921 sowed the seeds for enactment of the surname policy in Trent in 1926 that was designed to "recover" ethnic Italians in the name of the fascist Italian nation.

As Aldo Pizzagalli, the fascist linguist, writer, and civil servant charged with overseeing the surname campaign in Trieste noted, the royal decree took aim at the "situation Italy found in the newly redeemed provinces," which was, according to fascist officialdom, that "a population nationally and culturally Italian bore, in great measure, surnames of foreign character."[108] Certainly irredentists emboldened by the fascist centralization of power and avid nationalists promoted the surname measure, an act initially intended to underline *italianità*.

The January 1926 surname decree applied solely to those in Trent, a largely Italian-speaking province that was part of the contested Brenner region of the Trentino-Alto Adige, ceded to Italy in 1919 in the Treaty of St. Germain. Assistance for Italian elements kept with the historic prewar traditions of Italian irredentism and the fascist policies for political education. Passage of the surname measure coincided with the broad legislative restructuring and reform intended to usher in policies to mold the "new fascist society" and to assert fascist authority in the social and cultural realms. The measure did not originally apply to the largely German-speaking South Tyrol. In 1926 the fascist government was not yet ready to assume the Herculean task of inculcating the Italian spirit in German-speakers of South Tyrol, who might seek assistance from ethnic brethren in Austria and Germany. But, by April 1927, the fascist government had consolidated its authoritarian hold on the population, and by means of a provision in the legislation that allowed for its application "in entirety or in part to other provinces of the Kingdom," the measure was extended to include "all territories annexed to the Kingdom by the laws of September 26 and December 19, 1920."[109]

The surname measure, as a product of Gentilian fascist cultural ideology, assumed that national spirit was malleable. It relied on the recovery of Latin or Italian roots and, as article 2 allowing for surname corrections made clear, Latinness or Italianness could rely on choice and sentiment and was not tied to blood or organic notions of race. In 1929, three years after the surname measure was introduced, Gentile's withdrawal from active fascist political life signaled a change in the fascist attitude and policy. Gentile's understanding of inclusive national belonging shaped by appropriate education yielded, by the mid-1930s, to a competing vision of organicism, shaped by notions of intrinsic civilized traits and biological association. These ideas were incompatible with assumptions of national association by choice and ideas of malleability underlying the surname legislation.

Cultural ideologies linked to biological theories of race and assimilation that competed with Gentile's views dated to the nineteenth century. Those relying on theories of racial science attributed the Slavic influence (and by extension the prevalence of the Slavic names) to the expansionary tendencies of the Slavs who had "invaded" Roman coastal settlements. In 1930 demographer Haskel Sonnabend, vice-secretary of the Italian Committee for the Study of Population Problems—working under Italian sociologist and nationalist Corrado Gini, head of Mussolini's Central Institute for Statistics (ISTAT)—published a study in which he traced the Slavs' presence to sixth-century migration from the Danube regions. He claimed that by 600 AD, Slavs had "invaded Istria," and by the beginning of the seventh century, they had "attacked Dalmatia" extending their reach down the eastern Adriatic coast.[110] The "expansion of Southern Slavs" did not result from migration of "innumerable masses," he maintained, but rather "invaders" imposed it on the autochthonous inhabitants.[111]

Sonnabend's study testified to the beginnings of fascist demographic science's crystallization around essentialist racial attitudes. Nonetheless, cultural transformation through education or election continued to remain a possibility. Trieste continued to be recognized as a historic gathering point for Central European immigrants, and even nationalists insistent on Triestines' *italianità* had to admit the polyglot origins of the population of the merchant city that had welcomed Italians from the peninsula, Central Europeans, and eastern Mediterraneans who had built and serviced maritime commercial networks.

Austria-Hungary continued to cast its shadow on the borderland. An incident in February 1924 at Trieste's Verdi Theater revealed the tensions hanging in the city's air. At the premier performance of Raimondo Rodriguez's "Antony," a member of the audience ("already badly predisposed toward the opera seemingly of little musical value and not of the level to be presented in the best theater of the city") made hissing sounds in response to tenor Franco Tafura's "off-key singing and ironic hand movements." Tafura responded, calling the anonymous member of the audience a "cretin." The individual hissed. Tafura yelled, "Long live Italy, down with Austria, . . . Austrophiles, Austrophiles" and, according to the reporting officer, "immediately fell to the ground the [victim of] a strong nervous attack." The curtain man came to the performer's rescue, while a respected community member in the audience, retired captain Salvo Mariano, an employee of RAS Insurance, chastised the unknown individual and pointed out that Tafura "as a former combatant soldier recognized that Trieste was always Italian and never Austrian." The insult "Austrians" had been meant for those disturbing the performance not the audience in general. The performance resumed and during a break in the third act, baritone Salvatore Persichetti assured the public that no offense was meant.[112] No further official intervention or response was warranted as the crowd at the theater (a building constructed in Habsburg Trieste but modeled, ironically, on Milan's La Scala and renamed in honor of Italian composer Giuseppe Verdi on his death in 1901) was pacified. Nonetheless, the altercation demonstrated the frailty of the public peace and the depth of national suspicions regarding the local population's loyalties.[113]

The general mood in the city of Trieste might have been sympathetic to loyal *italianità*, but pockets of Austrian or Germanic loyalties survived. In 1925 the Italian authorities charged Rodolfo Dittrich, officially a Czech citizen, of trying to make the small seaside village of Sistiana in Duino-Aurisina northwest of Trieste into "a German colony . . . like an island in the waters of the sea."[114] They suggested he was "one of the type" who saw Italy as a land of conquest for foreigners and who believed that "Italian authorities did not have the prestige or the will to make their power felt." They ordered his expulsion from Italy.[115] The observation that Dittrich was "one of a type" underlined his individual perfidy, and at the same time testified to the lack of esteem for Italian officialdom in some circles.

In the new Italian territories, authorities were particularly concerned about the loyalty of the nobility, suspecting Czech-German affinities.[116] In 1925 a border official complained that a white and red flag flying over the castle of Prince Windisgraetz, just inside the new Italian border near the village of Planina (now Slovenia), "gave the impression of being Czechoslovak." The flag turned out to be the Windisgraetz family's crest, but the official insisted that the prince be required to fly the Italian colors above the family banner due to the impression the flag created on the well-frequented road between Trieste and Ljubljana.[117]

Most famous, perhaps, with respect to charges of Austrophilism was the case of Gofreddo Banfield, an Austrian aviator and officer, bestowed with the title baron for his efforts in support of Habsburg Austria in World War I and the last man to be awarded the Military Order of Maria Theresa. A native of Cattaro, Banfield elected Italian citizenship under the terms of the Treaty of St. Germain but moved to England in the wake of the war, so his naturalization was not finalized. Public outcry erupted in 1925 when he sought to claim Italian citizenship and affirm official residence in Pola. The citizenship commission in Pola refused his request calling him a "bitter enemy of Italy" and citing his notorious success in "bombing missions [directed] against our cities." An article in *La Frontiera*, a magazine published by the Wounded and Combatants of Venezia Giulia and Friuli, blamed Banfield for the bombardment of Venice. Rome overruled the local commission, no doubt owing to the intervention of the baron's influential friends, business associates, and relatives of his wife, Countess Maria Tripcovich, daughter of Triestine shipping magnate Diodato Tripcovich. The Austrian hero's welcome into the Italian national fold incited the anger of the local leader of the Fascist Party Captain Carlo Lupetina, who charged that Banfield was not an Austrian officer who had simply followed orders, but an "audacious" bombardier responsible for air raids that "caused damage and killed innocent victims in Italy."[118]

The Banfield case testified to the delicacy of questions arising with regard to the status of the thousands of individuals affected by new political and territorial arrangements. Inconsistencies, gaps, or discrepancies in international obligations and Italian laws and practices produced hun-

dreds of cases of unclear or contested citizenship. The citizenship commission in Pola that considered the Banfield case was the cognate of
commissions set up in Trieste and other border prefectures in 1922 to deal
with legal issues related to individuals' statehood claims. As the commissioner in Pola explained, the citizenship committees were bound to "work
particularly scrupulously" and their decisions almost always had to be
unanimous, "constituting a precise *but synthetic* judgment on the conduct
of the petitioner with regard to our national interests."

Legal criteria as well as social and cultural assessments affected the
judgment in each case. Questions relating to individuals' status plagued
local officials for at least a decade after the end of World War I. Not until
1927 did *Il Piccolo* announce the Triestine commission's work complete,
having processed more than 20,000 requests and issuing 9,767 decrees
of which 8,532 were favorable toward the granting of Italian citizenship.[119]
In Pola, the commissioner warned, "clemency could constitute a permanent danger to the security of the state" as the committee dealt not only
with those from "Croatia, Serbia, Hungary, Austria and promoters of Austrian authority" but also with workers linked to Bolshevism.[120] Rome's
willingness to overrule the commission in Pola and to provoke the ire of
the Fascist Party in Trieste in Banfield's case testified to the gap between
central understandings and local beliefs with respect to nationalist loyalty
and patriotism.

Issues relating to assimilation and stabilization preoccupied local
administrators. Pizzagalli noted with some satisfaction that while some
groups (stubbornly and unwisely, he implied) maintained their own traditions, "others became Triestines, that is to say Italians." Slavs, and in particular Slovenes, were "country folk of an almost barbarous cultural level"
who were "exclusively agricultural . . . attached to clods of earth in a land
of little fertility with a harsh climate." Descendants of "foreign" and primitive peoples could elevate themselves to become "excellent Italian citizens"
in a process that favored a kind of natural selection into an organically
superior Italian environment. Exposed to the "superior" Italian culture of
the cities and coast, Slavs or Slovenes, even where they constituted a majority in areas like the industrial burg of Monfalcone north of Trieste, would
choose assimilation. "Very few resident intellectuals conserved their own
nationality," Pizzagalli observed. Even wealthy "sons and nephews" of

"German commercial agents and high-ranking Austrian functionaries" had chosen to fight for Italy in World War I, locally referred to as the War of Liberation.[121]

Despite the prejudice characteristic of socially conservative sectors of the Italian population and some nationalists' insistence on a European racial hierarchy, officially the Italian government accepted those of Slavic origin as legal and equal citizens of Trieste. The anti-Slavic prejudices characteristic of sectors of Italian society resonated with fascist nationalist ultra-conservatism, a core component of fascist ideology throughout the *ventennio*.[122] Yet, while propaganda touted Slavs as members of an inferior, primitive, and sometimes menacing race, fascism never segregated ethnic minority populations. In the language of the fascist regime all citizens who were not ethnically native Italians became *allogeni*, a generic term for those of foreign extraction. The term *allogeni* stripped resident minority groups of unique characteristics or territorial associations, neutralizing the language of association with far-reaching implications.[123] The surname legislation accepted without reservation Europeans of all ethnic persuasions, even Slavs who occupied an ambiguous position in racial theories and hierarchies. Premised on ideas of the inherent superiority of *italianità*, it assumed the ineluctable expansion of the Italian state and culture.

The year 1930, in which the Paulovich controversy began, marked a turning point in official inclusiveness and welcome. The shift from Gentile's educative assimilation to racial and ethnic organicism became most evident in changing attitudes towards religious minorities, particularly Jews, but affected attitudes towards Slavs as well. Perhaps as a result of the intensifying international economic crisis or as a result of the increasing vehemence of anti-Semitism and the beginnings of the rise of Nazism in Central Europe, the Italian government began to be suspicious of Jews entering Trieste. A circular from the minister of the interior sent to the prefect in May 1930 expressed concern over recent grants of citizenship to "foreign Jews" and prohibited extending citizenship to "semitic elements coming from eastern and central European states." The minister cited specifically the increasing number of requests for naturalization from Hungarian, Polish, and Romanian Jews (*ebrei*) who, he argued, held "ideas and sentiments predominating among the mass of their co-religionists in their countries of origin." Their foreign loyalties could give rise to "serious inconveniences" or imperil the state, he warned. In the same memo, he was careful to exclude from the ban Jews (*israeliti*) "born or resident from childhood or youth in the New Provinces, those who have been educated in an Italian manner, and who are already assimilated in the Italian environment." They remained free to be naturalized.[124] While politically targeted and suspect, ethnic Slavs were not officially quarantined like Jews. Those of ethnicities associated with foreign states (including Germans and Yugoslav Slovenes and Croats) could still be educated to become loyal Italian citizens. The surname restoration and correction campaign demonstrated that Italy welcomed them to the nation with full privileges, rights, and responsibilities, if they chose *italianità*.

2 Power and Justice

Although it was not her intent, Luigia Barbarovich Paulovich tested the bounds of fascist success in molding new citizens and inculcating *italianità* in the borderland. In 1931, while the Paulovich case was winding its way through the halls of Italian justice, Minister of Justice Alfredo Rocco was boasting of fascism's success in the "Transformation of the State." From the March on Rome in 1922 to 1925, he claimed, "Public spirit had matured through the complete abandonment of antiquated judicial and political forms through the advancement of political and moral education." Educational reform had "laid the foundations for a system of schools to educate not only the intellect, but also [to mold] character." These schools had inculcated "national spirit" instrumental in shaping "the modern Italian."[1]

After 1925, Rocco identified the beginning of the second phase of reform, constitutional reform "to give structure to the Italian state."[2] Yet, Rocco's confidence that the "public spirit had matured" to accept fascist visions was misplaced, at least in some cases. Paulovich's unwillingness to accept surname Italianization indicated that much work remained for the regime to effect the widow's "political and moral education" and to ensure that Italians had sufficiently imbibed fascist national spirit.

Aldo Pizzagalli's handbook for surname Italianization, published in 1929, warned that some might balk at restorations, but ascribed individuals' objections to "egotism, sentimentality, fears of economic or patrimonial damage, or preoccupation with their solid reputation." These reasons should "melt before the tide of national sentiment." Resumption of a proper Italian name instilled pride ample to compensate for any inconvenience or to overcome hesitation.[3] Paulovich's sense of fascist public spirit proved insufficient. She had not succumbed to fascist enticements and could not accept the nationalist surname restoration that she felt to be an affront to her as an Italian and an indignity to her family.

Paulovich's insistence on keeping her married surname and her determination to annul the name restoration was incomprehensible to fascist officials convinced of the superiority of Italian civilization and culture. They believed that surname Italianization should be welcomed as an opportunity to erase the "taint" on people living in territories that had been ruled by for centuries by backward or barbarian peoples. For them, Italianization was a sign of modernity. It indicated the triumph of civilization and culture in the borderland.

Transforming the State

Italian Minister of Justice Alfredo Rocco was renowned as the "jurist of the [fascist] revolution." The architect of the juridical, legislative, and economic reforms of the fascist state from 1925 to 1932, he was a committed nationalist who turned to fascism out of disappointment with the liberal state. Like many, he traced the defects of liberal society to emphasis on individualism and materialism and, in particular, to the promotion of individual rights over collective interests.[4] His commitment to national solidarity led him to support a form of national syndicalism in the wake of World War I, a philosophical position shared with others like "proletarian" nationalist Enrico Corradini and "hero of Fiume" Gabriele D'Annunzio.[5]

Best known for economic restructuring and development of the fascist corporative state, Rocco's reforms also reconfigured the Italian legal state. An unabashed elitist, Rocco's vision did not rely on the use of "charisma, intuition, or terror." Rather, he sought to enforce order and adherence to national standards through legal reform and strict enforcement of the law.[6] In this respect, the proper functioning of Rocco's legal state relied on the success of the Gentile's nationalist education. Persuading Italians that the health of the nation relied on their willingness and commitment to place the benefit of the societal "organism" above that of its individual "cells" was at the core of fascist philosophy and legal praxis.

Rocco's policies, inspired by the philosophies of French syndicalist Georges Sorel, sociologist Emile Durkheim, and jurist Léon Duguit, stressed efficient production in a modern state to bring order—political, economic, and legal—to the fascist state. In economic terms, this translated to support for "economic groupings" that functioned as the organizational bases for the corporative state. In legal and administrative reforms, Rocco relied on Duguit's notions of "social solidarity," according to which the law's validity rested on its ability to maintain social order rather than on its power as a "sovereign command" or on its "abstract authority of natural law or justice." This conception of the law recognized

an inherent flexibility in the law on account of which "acts done in violation of it cause social disorder and a spontaneous, almost a reflex, movement towards readjustment."[7]

In Rocco's view, the law protected individuals when "they use[d] their
powers to further social solidarity."[8] He saw solidarity in organic terms.
Society was paramount, an "imperishable organism where life extend[ed]
beyond that of the individuals who [were] its transitory elements."[9] His
reforms promoted the health of the "state organism" over the needs of
individual cells.[10] This organic view meshed with conceptions of the
"nation" as "the subject of vital and spiritual processes," a body that
should be protected "in all its biological, economic and spiritual, religious, moral, cultural values," espoused by fellow legal professionals like
Francesco Orestano. An Italian jurist and philosopher trained in liberal
jurisprudence in Napoli and philosophy in Leipzig prior to World War I,
Orestano's writings on law and legal development in the Italian state published from 1915 to 1940 encapsulated the liberal legal perspectives that
characterized the thinking of Rocco and men of his generation.[11]

Rocco's approach relied on the application of modern ideas of governance based on currents of thought in the political and behavioral sciences that had emerged with the development of the social sciences at the
turn of the century. Acting in the nation's best interests required "deep
study . . . [of] social needs" to determine how to meet the needs of Italians as constituent members of the nation and as cells of the state.[12] This
perspective served as the basis for the evolution of fascist policy in the
second decade of the *ventennio*. In 1934 fascist politician and journalist
Giuseppe Bottai (who served as Mussolini's minister of education from
1936 to 1943) echoed Gentile and Rocco's organic metaphor of the state,
suggesting that fascist society was ideally made up of individuals each of
whom, having eschewed the individuality of the liberal man, "aspires to
totality" and "ascends from his individual being to the unity of the state."[13]

Fascism claimed to transcend the limitations of the liberal state. Rocco
turned a blind eye to the means the fascists employed to take power and
to exercise control, but he did not eschew liberal foundations or traditions
in the law. Orestano explained the law's function, under both liberalism
and fascism as the means to govern the "necessary and elective relations
among all the members of a consociation of humanity." His emphasis on
the law as dependent on a "category of relationships" and "relational"

understandings was common to western European legal relations and integral to the Italian legal system.[14] From this perspective, ideas of legality and illegality reflected a particular institutional state of mind rendered valid in the public's eyes by tradition and practice. In the reform of the Italian legal system, Rocco adapted such conceptions to fit fascist exigencies and render fascist notions valid.

Within this conceptual framework, Rocco relied on a rationalist, legalistic formula to restructure all branches of the fascist government. "Politics" was a science designed "to organize [the state] in the best way" to insure efficiency and to meet the general interest. At the same time, it functioned as an art "of ruling the people and of guiding them to the level of great civil power."[15] To lure workers away from socialist and communist politics that had seemed particularly threatening to Italy in wake of the "red biennium" of 1919 to 1921, Rocco sought to adapt and reconstruct Italian legislative and judicial bodies to enforce legal and administrative standards and to discipline "unruly" elements, enabling them to serve better the interests of fascism and the new governing authorities. In this respect and in his belief in the educative and guiding responsibilities of the elite, Rocco's reforms meshed with Gentile's emphasis on education and discipline as building blocks of the new Italian nation.

Despite fascist criticism of the liberal state and emphasis on building a new Italy, Mussolini did not rule, as Hitler would later in Germany, in the "vacuum of a state" dispossessed of its monarch and set adrift from its prewar institutional moorings.[16] The monarchy, traditional liberal parliamentary parties, working-class political parties, and the Church maintained influence over Italian society, and, at least early on, Mussolini had to consider their power in his attempts to expand the reach of the fascist state. In August 1924, in the wake of the Matteotti crisis, he named a Commission of Fifteen (including five senators, five deputies, and five scholars) to study the relations between legislative and executive powers, and between the state and labor.[17] The commission was also to examine the relationship between fascist government and such institutions as the press, credit institutions, secret societies, and international parties. Mussolini charged the commission to make recommendations for reform and to "harmonize" Italy's liberal constitution with corporative legislation to strengthen fascism's ability to retain and expand the power of the state.[18] Reorganized and expanded the following year to become the Commission of Eighteen, with Giovanni Gentile as its president, the commission grafted Mussolini's corporative perspective onto the existing government structure.

The commission included an eclectic mix of old nationalists, leading fascists, journalists and university professors. Among them were Arturo Rocco, a professor of law and penal procedure and brother of the Minister of Justice Alfredo Rocco, and Santi Romano, the respected legal scholar and president of the Council of State from 1928 to 1944 who oversaw the Administrative Court at the time of the Paulovich hearing. Fulvio Suvich, a Triestine politician, also served on the commission. An irredentist of the old order, his perspectives formed of experience in the Adriatic frontier zone meshed with those of nationalist syndicalists.[19]

Gentile argued in his philosophy of fascism, "freedom can only exist within the State, and the State means authority." He rejected liberal notions of liberty, arguing that liberalism had set "the individual against the State and liberty against authority."[20] However, he did not advocate reform to install a totalitarian or authoritarian system. Gentile's position reflected his association with Alfredo Rocco and Enrico Corradini's brand of Italian nationalism espoused in the periodical *L'idea nazionale* prior to World War I and his support for maintaining power in the hands of traditional elites. Labor, fascism's most tenacious political and economic opponent, was the primary target of the reformers' efforts. Reform to disenfranchise labor required a philosophical reorientation of the juridical and legal energies to decrease the emphasis on individual rights and equalities (prized in theory if not always in practice) in the liberal Italian system.

Heavily influenced by existing institutions and laws, Gentile's commission's recommended reforms failed to please Mussolini. Administrators on the Grand Council, more sympathetic to fascist revolutionary tenets, reformulated the commission's recommendations prior to passing them into law.[21] As was the case later for Nazi Germany, the Italian fascist state justified reforms and changes to professionals' recommendations as necessary to preserve and defend Italian society. Socialist leader Tito Zaniboni's attempt to assassinate Mussolini in November 1925 proved serendipitous for the fascist cause in this respect, as it proved that opposition posed a real threat to the government and fueled fascist fires, justifying the passage of exceptional legislation.

Still, attempts on Mussolini's life continued. In April 1926, the month the new "Rocco laws" for economic restructuring took effect, Violet

Gibson, a British Catholic shot Mussolini lightly wounding him. In September 1926 Gino Lucetti, an Italian anarchist, threw a bomb at his car. Mussolini escaped unharmed, but by October 1926 the fascists dissolved the Socialist Party and suspended the publication of its paper, *La Giustizia*. Another anarchist assassination attempt by fifteen-year-old Anteo Zamboni that followed led to the violent repression of all perceived opposition.[22] The November 1926 legislation restricted public employees' associations and membership in organizations. The Council of Ministers passed strict measures to punish disloyalty in the party ranks.

The December 1926 laws allowed for strict punishment of functionaries deemed hostile to the regime and further restricted the freedoms of the press. Although the only attempt on Mussolini's life by a foreigner had been at the hands of mentally unstable Violet Gibson, who acted alone and likely out of anger related to Mussolini's religious stance, the fascist government increased border patrols and engaged additional security forces to protect against infiltration by dangerous foreign elements.[23] Deflection of the threat to the borderlands exacerbated tensions already evident in relations between the South Slav State and Italy and between Italians and Slavs in the Adriatic provinces.

Protecting the State

Rocco's laws for the protection of the state included measures reinstituting the death penalty, strengthening the political policing powers of the state, and establishing the renowned fascist court the Special Tribunal for the Security of the State.[24] The measures abrogated the privileges of the Western liberal social contract developed in the tradition of Rousseau that had been incorporated into the Italian governing system since the Risorgimento. Rocco's reforms emphasized duties to support the moral and material health of the state organism over individuals' responsibilities to participate in governing society according to the "general will." Individual "egotism" constituted a threat that could and even had to be eliminated, in some cases, by force.[25]

In Rocco's view, fascism promised to create "a State of truly sovereign authority dominating all the forces in the country which at the same time is in constant contact with the masses, guiding their sentiments, educating them and looking after their interests."[26] His rational legal system, designed to discipline the state and the populous, maintained power in the hands of the elite best suited to understand, protect, and carry out national interests. This elitist perspective meshed well with Gentile's emphasis on the government's responsibility for citizens' education.

The prefect of Trieste's commitment to the protection and promotion of society over the interests of individuals brought him into conflict with the widow Paulovich engaged in safeguarding her rights as an individual and citizen of Italy. Fascist officials saw nationalizing legislation developed in the Gentilian spirit as a means to reinforce the nation and incorporate new citizens into the national organism. Local officials in Trieste viewed surname restorations and corrections as "exquisitely political" acts "in the national interest."[27] In the methods of execution, application, appeal, and judicial review outlined in the surname measure, the prefect of Trieste recognized the imprint of Rocco's belief in the marriage of a rational legal system to an elite political authority.

Government representatives were to serve as learned guides to prompt the public to understand and accept the process of Italianization. Article 3 of the surname legislation gave the Ministry of Justice administrative oversight of the measure's execution and application, placing it in the purview of administrative and judicial authorities rather than the police. Although the measure passed for Trent came in January before the regime concentrated on dictatorial measures later in 1926, the subsequent passage of authoritarian measures cast it in an oppressive tone. In the eyes of some borderland inhabitants, including Paulovich, the surname measure became a tool of oppression in the hands of overzealous provincial authorities and a measure that robbed individuals of their civil rights.

The new Penal Code of 1930 criminalized actions judged to constitute a threat to the state's security and also extended officials' powers to consider acts as potentially threatening to the state's "personality."[28] According to Rocco penalties were "not made only for delinquents." He viewed them as psychological disincentives "to hold in sight of all citizens a threat of consequences." Their primary aim was not to reform individuals but to enforce social discipline.[29] While Paulovich challenged the prefect's authority to issue the surname restoration to her, she did not act in an undisciplined manner toward the state that would have been punishable under the criminal codes.

Policing and judicial authorities severely punished challenges to Italian authority in the borderland. From the fascist government's inception,

"Slavic treachery" had been a constant theme of rhetoric and an excuse for repression and violence in the Adriatic provinces. After 1922 populations considered "insufficiently Italian"—including those in the Adriatic, Brenner, and even western "French" borderlands, as well as in the colonies—were singled out for persecution. The Special Tribunal for the Security of the State functioned as a judicial body from 1926 to 1943, but its primary task was not to adjudicate and interpret the laws, but to destroy opposition and dismantle antifascist networks.[30] Those arrested on charges under the jurisdiction of the Special Tribunal were incarcerated and not entitled to parole.[31] Ordinary rules of evidence were suspended. The accused had no ability to collect evidence to mount a defense and the time for examining the state's evidence was an abbreviated eight days.[32] Alleged members of socialist, communist, and republican political movements were the most-often targeted.[33]

By January 1927 laws for the protection of the state threatened refugees and exiles in Italy with the loss of citizenship and sequestration of property.[34] Over the period from mid-1927 to 1930, the Organization for Vigilance and the Repression of Anti-Fascism (OVRA) or secret police—a political policing organization with aims analogous to the Special Tribunal in the judicial sphere—developed under the eyes of the Head of Police Arturo Bocchini. Like the Special Tribunal, OVRA clamped down on elements that appeared to threaten the state, but its methods were considerably less bureaucratic than the court's.[35]

A disproportionate number of the Tribunal's cases dealt with "Slavic" treachery—antifascism, anticommunism, and disloyalty. Many of the accused were associated with Italian communist or worker political organizations suspected of receiving support from sympathizers abroad. The first proceeding directly involving an allusion to Slavic threat involved Slovene Stefano Leban of Slivia in the Province of Trieste. In late June 1927 the stonecutter charged with "wide diffusion in Trieste of communist newspapers, among them *Delo* in Slovenian" was given five years and six months for spreading communist propaganda.[36] In March 1928 Francesco Plegnik, a worker from the Servola district of Trieste, a suburb of the city on the Muggia road and home to industrial workers, received a four-year sentence for membership in the Communist Party and distributing subversive propaganda. He was arrested in possession of antifascist handbills in an inn in Trieste.[37]

By 1929 the prosecution of groups operating in the borderland—Istrian Slovenes and Triestines and Venetian Republicans—ranked second only to the prosecution of communists (always in the majority of cases brought before the Tribunal). In February Stanislao Cok, a Triestine trader from Longera was charged with "activities damaging to national interests" for purported association with the "irredentist Yugoslav organization *Orjuna*." He was sentenced to ten years imprisonment. The first person to be condemned to death by the Tribunal, sentenced on October 12, 1928, was a Tuscan communist from Pistoia responsible for killing two fascists and wounding a third in an attempt to foment antifascism. The second was Vladimiro Gortan, an Istrian accused of being the head of a group of terrorists bent on creating havoc to undermine the security of the fascist state. In Pola, the proceedings against Gortan and four other accomplices who received thirty-year sentences, were hailed as a move against "Slavic terrorism."[38]

By 1930 it became clear that one of the major preoccupations of the Special Tribunal was the struggle against populations fighting against violent fascist denationalization or Italianization policies in Venezia Giulia and the eastern border areas.[39] The first sentencing of the year, on February 25, involved the case of thirteen Istrian farmers from Maresego and nearby Villa Decani and Cesari arrested on a variety of charges, including homicide, terrorist acts, subversive organization, aid to antifascists (*soccorso rosso*), arson, and so on. Their punishments ranged from three to twenty years imprisonment, with four acquittals.[40]

The Power of the Prefect

Even in this climate of suspicion and violence, the Paulovich widow's conflict with the prefect over surname Italianization remained an administrative rather than a criminal matter. Paulovich's appeal of the surname restoration went against the local policies supported by the Fascist Party, challenged the prefect's authority, and questioned the judgment of the local commission the prefect had appointed. As the prefecture was the most powerful unit of local administration in the national fascist system, Paulovich's appeal was a challenge to the national representatives overseeing the local bureaucracy.

Prior to the fascist takeover, the liberal government generally appointed prefects on the basis of their support for the government or their skill at obsequious mediation. Parliamentary leaders promoted those who curried favor with elements important to the state rather than competent leaders who acted with independent initiative. Although the liberal prefect might have enjoyed considerable prestige, the national government's political machinations and general unwillingness to intervene forcefully to check local elements acting in their own rather than in national interests limited his power. An embittered Nasalli Rocca, dismissed from his post as prefect of Venice prior to World War I, warned of the weaknesses of leadership and the precariousness of the prefectural system, "When in lacking a skilled engineer, one trusts the construction of a building to a master builder. There should be no reason for surprise when the building crumbles."[41]

Mussolini's authoritarian instincts enabled him to recognize the power of the bureaucracy and its utility to the state. He maintained that the bureaucracy constituted "a continuous and daily force of the state," functioning like "a gigantic motor" that sometimes needed adjustment. Once he gained power, he announced his intention to maintain the bureaucracy but to "proceed by steps, by pieces" to transform it into a "bureaucracy of black shirts."[42]

Prefects were among the first to feel the effects when the liberal building "crumbled to ruins" and the fascists gained control of the Italian government. From the March on Rome in October to the end of 1922, Mussolini's new government transferred, recalled, retired, or appointed sixty-two prefects, among them the prefect of Trieste, to underline the transition from liberal to fascist power.[43] The fascists bolstered the prefects' prestige and power and gave them the title "excellency," elevating their position in the order of ceremonial protocol to one commensurate with high-ranking officials of the courts and military.[44] Mussolini also increased their responsibilities, which had been defined by practice, precedent, and "bit by bit in an arduous and still uncertain elaboration of doctrine and jurisprudence."[45] A circular of January 1927 "solemnly reaffirmed" the prefect's position as the "highest authority of the state" in each province."[46] Fascist prefects enjoyed considerably greater policing powers than their liberal predecessors in their ability to marshal national forces to maintain public order and protect public interests (predictably interests dictated by Rome). They also had expanded administrative powers to promote a rational and uniform rule through sound local and municipal administration. Included in the prefect's expanded responsibilities, which were introduced in the circulars of 1926 and 1927 and codified in the reform of 1934, was the duty to lead in molding "new Italians." The fascist government expected the prefect to oversee, "by a steady political education and discipline on the part of the state," the development of trust and respect for authority that had been eroded in Italy by centuries of foreign rule.[47] This included repression of threats to the government and also support for proactive initiatives and policies to strengthen society and improve the quality of moral, social, and legal life for those in his prefecture.[48]

The combination of unrest in Trieste and tensions between various factions in Rome resulted in several swift changes in local leadership in Trieste from 1924 to 1929. From November 1922 to June 1924, local civil servant Francesco Crispo Moncada served as vice commissioner for Venezia Giulia and then prefect of Trieste. The fascists transferred him to the post of head of local police, and Amadeo Moroni, a career civil servant appointed by Prime Minister Francesco Nitti, who had already served a stint in the eastern borderlands as the civil commissioner of Zara from 1921 to 1922, replaced him. A hardline fascist who quickly ran afoul of local leaders and commercial elites, Moroni was recalled in December 1925 to be replaced by Giovanni Gasti, an Italian police agent and criminologist turned politician, who served but a year.[49] Gasti was the first prefect of Trieste to be involved with the surname legislation. In January 1926, shortly after his appointment and after the surname measure was passed for Trent, Gasti wrote to Rome to request that it be extended to his province.[50] Gasti's request was an invitation for Rome and the fascist Italian government to take a stronger hand in integrating and nationalizing the province, a reflection of his preference for cautious execution of legal policies over violent, repressive tactics. In December 1926 Rome recalled Gasti, replacing him with Bruno Fornaciari, a lawyer and career civil servant, who was also a moderate but more committed to the fascist line.

By July 1929 Ettore Porro took the helm as the prefect of Trieste. Prefect Porro, a lifelong civil servant born in 1874 in Novara in the Piedmont region, was responsible for the conduct of Paulovich's case. Porro, who studied jurisprudence and then entered the service of the Italian Ministry of the Interior in 1899 to serve there until 1921, followed the typical carrier trajectory of those who entered into the civil service under the liberal government. Drawn from the professional and political classes, career civil servants aspiring to the position of prefect were generally well familiar with the halls of the government. They often shared the outlook of ministers and superiors, but they also knew that in order to advance, they needed to please their superiors.[51] Porro's first appointment as prefect in 1921 was in Catanzaro (Calabria). From Catanzaro, he moved to Messina and Genoa before transferring to Trieste, where he served as prefect from July 16, 1929, to January 15, 1933.[52]

In August 1931 Mussolini required all the prefects of Italy to be present at Rome's Campodiglio, or Capitoline Hill, for the centennial celebration of the establishment of the Council of State. Established by an edict of Charles Albert of Sardinia in August 1831, the Council of State was a venerable and respected institution of the Italian government. Mussolini presided over the festivities surrounded by the highest echelons of the fascist civil and military hierarchy in the renowned Sala degli Orazi e Curiazi, signaling the state's emphasis on the Council of State's role in the "unitary organization of the state."[53] For the prefects stationed throughout the country, the pomp and circumstance on the hill with broad vistas of Rome revealed by recent demolitions of nearby buildings underlined the primacy of Rome under fascism. Recently excavated Roman ruins around the Capitoline Hill and in the city center drove home the centrality of Rome's history to Italian visions of the state and its power.[54] Mussolini took advantage of his speech on the occasion of the centennial to emphasize the prefects' role as "the direct representative of the State" in the various provinces, with the implication in the august surroundings that the fascists' intended to use administrative and legal means to co-opt provincial officials and stifle the independent exercise of power.[55]

The prefect's powers and influence grew so much under fascism that antifascist exiled intellectual Gaetano Salvemini, admittedly an outspoken critic of authoritarianism, labeled the system a "prefectocracy."[56] Yet, the constitutional and legal reforms that emphasized central power created jurisdictional confusion in the evolving fascist system. The transfer of power from locally elected officials to nationally appointed representatives, particularly evident after the mayoral and provincial reforms of

1928, altered the balance of power developed over seventy years since Italian unification.[57] In Trieste and the territories had been under Habsburg sovereignty until the end of World War I, the effects of the administrative upheaval were particularly acute. Special regulations and separate administrative jurisdictions lingered well into the first decade of Italian rule, and the laws of Italy and the Italian system were not firmly established. Full legal integration into the Italian provincial and legal systems came after the fascist imposition of dictatorship, but the memory and traditions of Habsburg provincial autonomy remained strong.

In theory, by the time Ettore Porro reached Trieste in 1929, the prefect's power as supreme representative of the national government was uncontested. Struggles between the prefects and local party bosses or *federali* that had characterized the early fascist years had been played out. The prefects' ability to govern by legal means under the oversight of the Ministry of the Interior had triumphed over the *federalis'* use of violence and intimidation to serve the interests of the Fascist Party.[58] Of the 443 prefects who served the government in the fascist *ventennio*, less than one-third (103) came from party ranks. Career civil servants were in the majority.[59] However, prefects had to be circumspect in discharging their duties. Officially, the prefect bore responsibility to "harmonize the activities of the Party in their various manifestations."[60] But, the party hierarchy reported directly to Rome and maintained control of the secret police, who routinely reported on the state of local affairs. As a result, in some prefectures relations between the prefect and party secretary were strained, marked by hostility and jealousy.[61]

Over the course of the three years from 1926 to 1929, with the help of the moderate local Fascist Party Secretary Giuseppe Cobolli Gigli (Cobol prior to the application of the surname measure), Triestine officials made significant strides to harmonize provincial and Party politics. Francesco Giunta, at the head of the Trieste *fascio* from 1919 until he was called to Rome after the 1922 March on Rome, and other hard-line fascists prone to violence and excess yielded to more moderate figures. In March 1927 Cobolli Gigli became the local party secretary. A "skilled engineer," both literally and figuratively, Cobolli Gigli was a technocrat who had joined the party in 1922. Known for his ardent irredentism and voluntary service in World War I, he was a committed nationalist who preferred to mediate between local economic interests and the government rather than serve revolutionary party interests. Party zealots criticized his moderation, and under fire from the national party leadership and local extremist factions in January 1930, he was forced to step down and was replaced by Carlo Perusino, an avid fascist who could be counted on to "keep the *squadrista* spirit alive."[62] Although the party apparatus no longer held a place for him, Cobolli Gigli's brand of fascist nationalism continued to hold sway.[63] Paulovich launched her appeal of the surname restoration in this "tormented political terrain."[64]

Published on August 5, 1926, under the signatures of Minister of Justice Rocco and Minister of Finance Giuseppe Volpi, the guidelines for the application of the surname measure named the prefect (in 1926 the prefect of Trent, but prefects in all areas that subsequently became subject to the legislation) as the Ministry of Interior's designee to enforce the measure. As the local agent responsible for administrative oversight and for coordination and supervision of security forces in the province, the prefect's duties with regard to the legislation included:

1. Compiling a list of surnames and noble titles to be restored to an Italian form;
2. compiling a list of families bearing these surnames or titles;
3. preparation of individual decrees for all members of the families, except those who were living with the head of the family (their names could be listed on the head of the family's decree, even if they had reached the age of majority);
4. notification of the heads of families affected;
5. dissemination of individual decrees;
6. notification to city and village officials responsible for maintaining the civil registries;
7. notification to clerics responsible for certifying marriages and births (including those who had performed these duties during the Austro-Hungarian period); and
8. notification to judicial and prison authorities.

City and village officials assured that restored Italian forms appeared on conscription, electoral, and jury lists and on provincial and communal tax, public school, and welfare rolls. They were responsible for notifying postal officials and consular offices for those who had emigrated but maintained official residence in affected provinces.[65] Only in cases where the name in question related to a noble family would it be referred outside of the prefecture, to the Council of Ministers' Heraldic Administrative Office.[66]

Paulovich did not seek to discredit the local leadership, but to remedy what she felt to be a misapplication of legislation that affected her family. Throughout the *ventennio*, reforms designed to discipline and "fascistize" the state spurred debate regarding the nature of law and the bases for individual rights. Liberal jurists, among them Vittorio Emanuele Orlando, clashed with syndicalists, like Sergio Panunzio, over the bases and foundation of laws and rights and the role of the government in organizing and administering society.[67]

The differentiation in Italian law between *constitutional rights*, rights related to the state as constituted (or the legal state), and *juridical rights*, those related to outcomes that arose from the activities of the state as it carried out its duties, was important to the adjudication of the Paulovich case.[68] Paulovich believed that the surname restoration violated her rights, but she did not question the law itself. In legal parlance, her complaint pertained to an administrative act and dealt with an individual's "interest aggrieved thereby."[69] This placed her complaint in the jurisdiction of the Administrative Court of the Council of State rather than in the hands of criminal and civil courts like the Court of Assizes. The various courts contested the boundaries of their jurisdictions, but in her case article 3 of the surname measure laid any question to rest by specifically identifying petition to the Council of State or to the king as appropriate avenues for appeal.[70]

The Workings of the Administrative Court

Established by an edict of Charles Albert of Sardinia in August 1831, the Council of State was a venerable and respected institution of the Italian government by the time Paulovich's case came before the court.[71] According to the Italian constitution, the Council of State was an official administrative body supervised directly by the head of the government. In the modern Italian state, three of its five sections held consultative powers related to matters of law and the functions of the various ministries of government. The other two sections formed the judiciary branch. Established by an act of 1889, the judiciary branch protected individuals' *interests* with respect to the administrative functioning of the state. An act of 1916 extended the administrative judges' jurisdiction to include cases that involved the protections of individuals' *rights* with respect to the actions of the administration.[72]

The Council of State survived World War I and into the fascist period intact, functioning as the highest court for the mediation of conflicts involving various state agencies' exercise of power. Acting within carefully prescribed boundaries, it did not agitate for or make laws, nor could it overturn them. Rather, its justices ensured that administrators followed the laws and properly administered legal measures with respect to rights and interests of the parties affected by them.[73]

At the end of 1923 the fascists began to curtail the court's consultative and juridical powers. A decree of October 1925, augmented by an Emergency Decree of January 1927, allowed for the dismissal of councilors "for reasons of incompatibility" with the regime.[74] The 1927 Fascist Charter of Labor called on the regular courts of appeal to act as labor tribunals in the resolution of labor disputes.[75] This extension of the regular courts' powers did not affect the Council of State's judiciary powers, which remained intact in Sections Four and Five, the arms of the Administrative Court. Fascist centralization and corporative reforms as well as efforts to legalize dictatorship affected the workings of the council, but its judicial and administrative skeleton remained intact.[76] The criminal courts and the judiciary of the Special Tribunal functioned as arms of repressive fascism; the Administrative Court remained a forum dedicated to the protection of citizens' liberties and interests. In 1930 the court functioned, as it had for nearly a century, as an arbiter of state authority with the power and authority to police organs of the state. Although supervised by the head of the government, administrative justices ostensibly exercised their powers "with full liberty and independence of judgment" in matters under their jurisdictional authority.[77]

The Council of State's centennial celebration, at which all Italian prefects were present, took place just four months prior to the Administrative Court's hearing on the Paulovich case. On that occasion, Mussolini as head of the government had assumed the minister of the interior's functions, and with respect to the council, had become directly responsible for the appointment of councilors. He cast this move as part of the fascist effort to discipline and modernize the state and sought to reassure the audience of his benevolent intentions and respect for Italian legal traditions. "A regime of authority like this fascist one has a tremendous interest in making an organ of control, consultation and justice like the Council of State function consistently," he stated.[78]

The survival of the Administrative Court that in the prefascist era had been the bastion of the "forces of legalistic individualism," a body responsible for protecting individuals against arbitrary administrative actions by the government, seemed to contradict the strictures of dictatorship.[79] Yet, the court's continued functioning into the period of dictatorship was consistent with the regime's broader legal approach. Fascist juridical reforms were not generally radical innovations. Rather, they advanced liberal legal trends and tendencies toward modern state control while at the same time slowly eroding individual rights.[80] In his speech in 1931, Mussolini justified the reforms affecting the Council of State as a way to reduce the risk of interference in deliberations and to prevent corruption. However, the government's motives were not so noble. In 1932 measures that required Fascist Party membership for civil service appointments demonstrated the fascists' intention to restrict the freedom of the court and to exercise greater oversight over the entire bureaucracy. The law restricted the pool from which appointees to the Administrative Court could be selected and forced potential appointees to tow the fascist line.[81]

In the late 1920s and early 1930s, jurists and legal theorists in Italy engaged in heated and intense debates over the development of public law under fascism and the extent and breadth of change necessary to bring the Italian system of jurisprudence into line with the needs of the fascist state.[82] Councilors often considered sensitive issues relating to the clashes between traditional legal privileges and protections and new laws related to professional organizations and collective contracts introduced under the fascist corporative system. Further, as contemporary commentators noted, fascism's commitment to social revolution resulted in "perpetual movement," particularly in the "field of social legislation" where "new studies and proposals" subjected women, in particular, to seemingly daily changes.[83] In the early 1930s, at the time Section Four considered the Paulovich case, fascist reforms were just beginning to filter down to influence the court's decisions.

Over the period from 1931 to 1935, as the power and reach of the dictatorship expanded, Sections Four and Five of the Council of State became

less inclined to exercise independent prerogative and hand down decisions against representatives of the national government.[84] In Section
Four, the court that considered the Paulovich case, the number of appeals
related to the jurisdiction of the state administration increased from 493
in 1931 to 664 in 1935, but the number of successful appeals against state
administrators dropped from 111 (22.5 percent) in 1931 to 58 (8.7 percent)
in 1935.[85] The decrease in complainants' success testified to the court's
increasing hesitance to support individuals questioning the government.
In Section Five, the branch that handled complaints against public administrative entities not directly tied to the functioning of the state, the
rate of petitioners' success was considerably higher. Of the 939 petitions
brought in 1931, 310 (33.0 percent) were granted. Of 906 brought in 1935,
444 (49.0 percent) were granted.[86] These figures indicate that Section
Four became less tolerant of complaints against those directly representing the state, but Section Five increased its support for complaints against
administrators in quasi-statal organizations. The shift in the pattern of
decisions indicated the regime's use of the court to bring to heel those who
engaged in state business but who were not directly under its control.

Despite the increasing reach of fascist control and the extension of
the fascist government and the legal reforms, court personnel were not
purged. Sheltered and segregated from the general public, councilors remained legal scholars and, even under the thumb of Mussolini, retained
considerable latitude in rendering their opinions. From the justices' perspective, upholding fascist laws related to dictatorship did not present an
ethical dilemma. Maintaining principles of the Western legal tradition
handed down from the liberal period, they claimed to separate moral
judgments from judicial responsibilities in efforts to uphold extant laws
in the name of a just and legal society. Eminent jurists focused on their
duty to maintain the state of Italy as a "State of Law," and this meant adhering to the constitution and laws. Interpreting the intention of the laws
and mediating relations among the executive, legislative, and judicial
branches of government with respect to administration of the laws remained their primary function.[87] Court officers sought to adhere strictly
to codes of law and to rule on the basis of precedent, much of which was
inherited from the liberal period.

Fascist legal scholars argued that while in theory a system of balances of
power and checks and balances was desirable, the importance of upholding
this principle had to be measured against the need for the state's action to

be "straightforward and uniform." They diverged from Western traditions in their support for the notion that it was "a necessity that one power stand as preeminent above the others." Naturally, under fascism this supreme power was invested in the executive of the national government in Rome. "Represented by the King and the Cabinet" but, in fact, centered in Prime Minister Mussolini's hands, the executive power was to have "absolute predominance over the others powers, if one wanted to realize a State of united, uniform, and straightforward action: the legal State."[88] Discipline trumped commitment to democratic ideals.

Members of the Council of State acquiesced in the elevation of the executive, but, at the same time, retained a reputation for prudence and courage that made them difficult for the fascist executive to control entirely.[89] Santi Romano, president of the Council of State from 1928 to 1944, was among the many functionaries involved in the process of reform who followed a relatively moderate political line. Romano became a member of the Fascist Party only months before his appointment to the council, and he strove to carve out a niche for the Council of State as the government's consultative body for administrative and technical matters. Ignoring the broader implications of the fascist takeover and the reform measures' broadening of the scope of executive power, he sought to reserve the council's power in a manner similar to the way in which the Grand Council exercised its functions as the consultative body for political matters after the constitutional reform.[90]

In fact, throughout the fascist *ventennio*, piecemeal and narrowly targeted reforms, as well as competition among various levels of government, contributed to making the law and fascist interpretation of it dynamic rather than static. The fascist government did not exercise censorship as "a monolithic and tightly coordinated machine of repression," nor did it use administrative justice solely as a repressive instrument. Censorship had many faces and its enforcement passed through "different phases" in the same way that administrative justice functioned with some flexibility and independence within its sphere of competence. In much the same manner that the fascist apparatus for censorship and enforcement of censorship laws allowed for a variety of cultural products and press debate, the fascist judiciary in the administrative courts enjoyed interpretative power and, like censors, "neither shared precisely the same perspective nor imposed their beliefs with complete consistency."[91] In the case of censorship, the fascists sought to educate cultural producers.[92] In the case of nationalizing policies pertinent to the Paulovich case, they sought to educate national citizens to assist them in understanding appropriate standards of Italianness.

Commitment to the rule of law, of liberal or fascist origin, allowed the Administrative Court to continue to function as the judicial body responsible throughout the *ventennio* for overseeing and enforcing jurisdictional boundaries within the government bureaucracy. In the climate of dictatorship where the court proved willing to accept and incorporate fascist laws into the Italian justice system, this power to adjudicate might have seemed limited or trivial but, in fact, the court provided a forum for administrative debate. Its deliberations on cases like Paulovich's indicated that the lines of dictatorship were far from clear inside the halls of the fascist government.[93]

The majority of cases Section Four considered were brought by individuals complaining about the treatment at the hands of officials in the Ministry of War or the Ministry of Education with respect to issues related to professional status. Those challenging the minister of war typically sought compensation for unjust punishment or dismissal, failure to be promoted, or inadequate pay or pensions. Cases against the Ministry of Education often related to the changing circumstances for teachers, particularly women teaching at the elementary levels who were affected by fascist policies to reduce women's employment. Other matters were related to individuals' complaints against local administrators. The Paulovich surname case against the prefect fell into this category, but much more common were cases related to expropriation of land and seizure of property or the granting of local licenses for professional activities or regulated commercial activities (like the running of pharmacies).

The court even considered cases against the minister of justice, and the administrative justices did not hesitate to rule against decisions of their peers when they felt that the law had been violated. Cases brought against the minister of justice in 1931 by two former judges, Francesco Fiorenzano and Vincenzo Pelaggi, revealed the depth of the magistrates' commitment to the rule of law. In 1926 the Ministry of Justice dismissed Fiorenzano and Pelaggi from their posts on charges that they had violated the law of December 24, 1925. They had "continually expressed sentiments hostile to the regime," "publicly criticized the acts of the government," and the "gravity" of their actions proved that "these political attitudes would persist" and their hostility would continue. In 1931 their appeal came before the Administrative Court. The government's representative justified the judges' dismissal charging that their opposition to the regime had impeded their ability to carry out their duties and had caused a lack of public confidence in their abilities. No one contested the judges' vociferous and public opposition to fascism. However, lawyers for Fiorenzano and Pelaggi pointed out that their opposition, voiced in 1924 and 1925 (likely in response to the Matteotti crisis), was public before the dictatorship measures of December 1925 required unquestioning obedience. Since the 1925 measure could not be applied retroactively, the judges had been illegally dismissed. The Administrative Court magistrates sided with Fiorenzano and Pelaggi. They ruled that no documents or evidence produced in the case proved the gravity of the infraction or that the judges' public opposition continued after 1925. The Ministry of Justice's application of the law of December 1925 and the appellate court in Catanzaro's affirmation of the ministry's action were incorrect.[94]

Fascist officials in the Ministry of Justice often warned local authorities of the limited scope of their authority and the importance of acting within the specific requirements of the laws. A memo from Minister of Justice and Cultural Affairs Rocco directed to the prefect of Trieste on the extension of the surname legislation in April 1927 warned specifically of the narrow applicability of the measure. Rocco reminded Triestine officials to observe "the strict formalities" prescribed for restorations and corrections. The minister underlined that article 2 allowed for petitioners to request surname corrections and simply afforded an option to individuals. He warned the prefect that it was "inadvisable to resort to propaganda or to use the press to coerce or play on the spirit of interested parties" to induce people to come forward to request name corrections.[95] The prefect was bound by his official duty "for reasons primarily historical or of opportunity" to protect the rights of all individuals and strengthen the nation through the proper application of the surname law.[96]

While fascism increased local prefects' authority in their own jurisdictions, the nature of fascist rule and the hierarchical bases of fascist governance placed them in fierce competition for national attention and resources. Prefects relied on the minister of the interior's good graces to keep their offices and win promotions. Throughout Italy, prefectural officials magnified their efforts to shine in the execution of centrally driven initiatives in hopes of furthering their careers.

In the eastern borderland, local officials, who often felt (and even complained) of being ignored and isolated on the periphery of the nation, saw the surname legislation as a rare chance to impress superiors with their zeal in the faithful and diligent application of legislation that was in effect only for the New Provinces. While they recognized that the success of nationalizing policies including surname restorations and corrections relied on popular acceptance or acquiescence to the measures rather than on repression or threat, they were eager to affirm borderland citizens' Italianness and loyalty to the nation. Acting on the prefect's behalf, local civil servants interpreted broadly their responsibilities related to the surname measure and encouraged widespread surname alteration. Paulovich's insistence on her individual rights and obligations as a citizen of Italy pitted the prefect of Trieste, engaged in zealous enforcement of nationalization measures, against the central government seeking to rein in local power, modernize the state, and enforce uniform standards across the nation.

3   Legislating *Italianità*

In Trieste, the winter of 1929 was exceptionally harsh. The month of February was bitterly cold, with the average temperature below freezing.[1] The *bora*, the famed east wind originating in the interior plains, swept through the city at record velocity in February and March, topping at some 90 miles per hour.[2] As the frigid wind blew through the city, a bureaucratic whirlwind stirred behind the closed doors and shuttered windows of the prefect's office in Trieste. The committee of linguists, glottologists, jurisprudence experts, and appointed officials who had worked together since the summer of 1927 issued a flurry of surname restorations and corrections. Under the crystal clear blue skies left in the wake of the *bora*, they swept the city clear of the detritus of foreign surnames—restoring them to their original Italian or Latin forms or correcting those that failed to reflect Italian, Roman, or Venetian influences consonant with a petitioner's national sentiments.

The surname restoration campaign began after years of policy formulation to smooth enactment of the measure. The legislation reflected the "nationalist aspect" of fascist law which, in the words of a contemporary legal critic of the regime, was "essentially a means of maintaining, preserving and advancing the greatness of the Italian people."[3] Extension of the surname legislation to the eastern borderlands provided a policy arena in which local nationalists and party officials could act in harmony with the central government's educational efforts to promote what the same critic referred to as the belief in the "organic unity of the Italian people, past, present and future, of its reality transcending the mere aggregate of human beings alive at any particular moment, and consequently of the superiority of its claims to those of any particular human beings."[4]

Italianization under the surname measure was extensive. Of some 900,000 people in the northeastern provinces of Venezia Giulia, as many 100,000 had their names altered under the legislation. Many petitioners sought corrections but the overwhelming majority was subjected to restorations by fiat.[5]

Nationalist Naming in the Adriatic

By the early twentieth century, nationalist naming was familiar to Europeans. With its roots in the radical secularist phase of the French Revolution, nationalist naming was in some cases a spontaneous, voluntary reaction by individuals wishing to demonstrate nationalist affiliations or political loyalties. In Italy in the wake of the Risorgimento, nationalist naming manifested in the choice of given names. Names based on cities became popular. For example, nationalists commonly chose derivatives of Rome, like Romano. The second most popular forms recalled Trieste (Trieste, Triestina and Triestino), reflecting the irredentist sentiment spurred by the failure to redeem Adriatic lands. After 1882, derivatives of Oberdan, commemorating the Guglielmo Oberdan (or Oberdank), executed by a firing squad for treason due to his involvement in a foiled assassination attempt aimed at the Habsburg emperor, also indicated strong irredentist support and antipathy for the Habsburgs and their rule in the Adriatic.[6]

By the turn of the twentieth century, the understanding that names served as markers of nationality and that name change could serve as a means of assimilation (forcible or voluntary) led nationalists throughout Europe to encourage or require name changes. Toponyms as well as personal names were subject to scrutiny and manipulation. Fresh in Triestine memory was the extensive Magyarization that followed Hungary's separation from Austria in the wake of the 1867 Compromise, particularly the repressive and intimidating nationalization under Hungarian Prime Minister Dezsö Bánffy from 1895 to 1899.

The fascist surname measures, although the most extensive and repressive, were by no means the first attempt to rename populations and territories to promote national sentiment and patriotism in the Adriatic provinces. From the Risorgimento in the mid-nineteenth century, Italian sympathizers and irredentists in the Habsburg Adriatic Littoral supported the work of linguists and geographers who uncovered the inherent Italian character of the Adriatic landscape. Tracing all place names or toponyms to ancient and Latin or Roman roots, these scholars employed what they asserted to be scientific and empirical research techniques to trace civilization in the Adriatic coastlands to the Italian influences of Rome or Venice, before the immigration of Slavs, who irredentists argued came in a state "of complete barbarity" intent on destroying civilization.[7] Attempts to cast Slavs (a term used generically to represent Slovenes, Croats, Serbs, and other European peoples involved with the pan-Slavic movement after 1848) as barbarian and backward ran counter to claims by Slavic nationalist, particular Croat and Slovene nationalists who linked claims to lands in the Habsburg Adriatic provinces to the Slav national awakening in Europe.

Nationalizing the Adriatic

In a diatribe against the enemies of Italy on the eve of World War I, Italian propagandist Virginio Gayda charged that Habsburg bureaucrats had worked in tandem with the clergy to Slavicize people's names. Gayda claimed that while Rome was aware of the priests' alteration of Italian names and promotion of Slavicization, authorities in Italy had no power or official means to counter it.[8] Once Italy assumed control of Trieste, these machinations became the basis for appeals to the government for name change.

Some evidence supported Gayda's claims, but the extent, contours, and effects of clerics' machinations were not clear. Links between the Church and naming were deeply rooted in the region's administrative history. Beginning in the mid-1600s, Habsburg officials recognized as legal names the names that local priests entered in parish registers. In the second half of the nineteenth century, disgruntled nationalists alleged that priests took advantage of poorly educated parishioners and deliberately altered the spelling and form of names to manipulate the ethnic appearance of local populations.

In the Adriatic Littoral, many priests were from the countryside or interior lands inhabited by Slovenes and Croats, and many clerics' links to nationalist movements were strong. In Dalmatia, the priests' Croat nationalism not only reflected ethnic proclivities but was also linked to their centuries-old stance in the defense of Catholics against the Turks.[9] After the mid-century, increasingly shrill irredentist and anti-Papal nationalist Italian voices, the contradictory attitudes of the Papacy toward Slavs, the Papal relationship with Russia, and the attitude toward the Eastern Church further complicated the local relationship with the Catholic Church. Particularly contentious was the clergy's encouragement of Slovene and Croat attempts to maintain a separate Catholic identity. In the monarchy that based ethnic identification on language of daily use, debates raged over the priests' use of the vernacular, ministering to their flocks in Slovenian or Croatian rather than in the Latin of the Church.[10]

Certainly, the politics of Bishop Josip Juraj Strossmayer, the Habsburg palace chaplain in the 1850s, who by the 1860s was head of the Croatian People's Party, encouraged the spread of romantic Croat nationalism in the latter half of the century. The Bishop's prominence, renowned faith, prestige, leadership, and promotion of Croat culture encouraged support for *trialism*—the further division of the dual monarchy of Germans and Hungarians to take into account the interests of a third group, the Slavs. Strossmayer's support for the united Slavic cause and for Croat nationalism, while at the same time remaining a firm supporter of the monarchy and a favorite of the royal family, typified the ambivalence and ambiguity of nationalist associations in the Habsburg lands.[11] It also stoked the fears of ethnic Italians who saw trialism, which promised to privilege Slavs, as a threat to their culture and well-being in the Adriatic Littoral.

In some areas of Dalmatia and along the southern Adriatic coast, evidence suggests that priests and recording church officials did Slavicize names. But, in most instances, naming practices and alterations likely reflected the clerics' level and languages of literacy, understandings of their parish duties, or the illiteracy of their parishioners in the rural areas rather than deliberate nationalist manipulation. Ethnically based name alteration was not official policy of the Habsburg government. In fact, under Habsburg law an individual's name was sacrosanct. An 1826 edict proscribed name change except in cases of conversion to Christianity or ennoblement. In this latter case, the explicit permission of the sovereign was required. Other cases, "those worthy of particular regard," went to the Ministry of State and the emperor reserved personal judgment. In 1866 as part of limited decentralization policies, Vienna granted provincial political authorities the power to make name changes.[12] Nonetheless, names remained closely monitored. A circular from the Austrian Ministry of the Interior in May 1883 directed the Lieutenant of the Adriatic Littoral to guard against changes made in registries without the express consent of the individuals involved. Habsburg officials warned priests not to alter children's names on entering them in the registers without the knowledge or against the wishes of parents.

The ministry's circular clearly responded to name alteration being practiced in some parts of the Littoral, but this did not mean that the name Paulovich had been deliberately stripped of its Italian or Latin associations. In 1883 the surname that appeared as Paulovich on earlier documents relating to Antonio became Paulovič on Luigia and Antonio's marriage certificate. The appearance of the Slavic *ič* form on their daughter Ines's birth certificate from Zara in 1885 suggested Slavicization. Yet, no evidence suggests that the family objected to the alteration from Paulovich to Paulovič at the time.

Emphasis on persecutory intent exaggerated the attention paid to name recording and ignored the likelihood that slight variations in spelling and form of names was a normal consequence of life in the multiethnic, polyglot Habsburg Adriatic provinces. Standardization of surnames or in Europe was linked to the rise of modern states, and generally surnames evolved from four different sources. First, they were derived from geography or topography including the place of habitation (as in the French name Dupont or "of the bridge"); from the region of origin (as in Genovese or from Genoa); or from the position of land holdings (parcel number or name). Second, surnames could be linked to professions, relations or relatives, or titles (as in the English names Chandler, Taylor, or Lord). Third, they could originate in nicknames or sobriquets reflecting physical traits or moral characteristics (for example, Little). Finally, surnames could originate as patronymics or indications of filial descent (as in Johnson meaning "son of John").[13]

Across Europe, the patterns and chronology of the adoption of legal surnames varied widely. In England, the legal use of surnames developed fitfully from the twelfth to the fifteenth centuries as a means of tracking property ownership, inheritance, tax collection, and registration.[14] In Sardinia, the binomial (given name + family name) system was established by the twelfth century, but the process of surname transmission was not patrilineal until the late seventeenth or early eighteenth century.[15] On the Italian peninsula the fifteenth-century Florentine *catasto*, a precursor to the modern state census, relied on nicknames, occupational designations, and personal characteristics rather than hereditary surnames to identify the Florentine elite. It did little to track the less privileged or rural populations.[16]

In areas removed from centers of control, place names and surnames were not rigidly defined until modern state bureaucracies took hold in the eighteenth or nineteenth century. Even Italian nationalists had to admit that Slavic names were common in Dalmatia well before the modern era, in records dating back to the tenth century.[17] Over time and certainly before the Napoleonic era, changes in spelling, phonetics, or form were as often spontaneous, inadvertent or passive acts as they were active attempts at socio-ethnic engineering. Even after names became standardized, individuals continued to use different names in civil, social, and economic contexts.[18] Across several generations, nicknames or unofficial names could exist alongside legal designations.[19]

In twentieth century Italy, prior to the fascist takeover, some petitioners sought name changes simply to eliminate confusion and regularize the form and spelling of a particular surname. In April 1922 a Triestine calling himself Antonio Baiz wrote to local authorities assuring them he did not seek a change of his name for "political reasons," but rather to "stabilize" his surname in the form *Baiz* to "avoid errors in transcription." He claimed that the multiple forms of his name including Bajes, Bejc, and Bajo had been the cause of "inconvenience and embarrassment."[20] After the fascist legislation took effect in 1927, a man petitioned for surname correction under the measures complaining, "even I don't know anymore what I am supposed to call myself." In another case, a man born in Trieste asked prefectural officials to "transform the name in whatever way it pleased them." His mother's name was Maria Sadkovich. On entering military service under the Habsburgs, he was enrolled as Giuseppe Zadhovich. All of his subsequent tax documents and other documents related to his professional life as a barber referred to Zadhovich, but on seeking a marriage license, he was informed that his surname was Sadkovich. In October 1927 he emerged with the Italianized form Zatti.[21]

Zadhovich / Sadkovich's experience spoke to the inconsistencies of national identification in the borderland, but did not suggest deliberate tampering. Propagandists like Gayda had interpreted the experiences of those in the frontier zones through their own lenses to tap into currents of anti-Habsburg popular rhetoric and belief. In a June 1919 request to the occupation government of Venezia Giulia, engineer Carlo Marinig summed up prevailing notions in a request that he be permitted to "cleanse his name" and return it to its correct version *Marini*. Citing the prevalence of names ending in the suffix *ic*, he charged that the "former Austrian government put all kinds of obstacles in the way of those who wanted to rectify their names when they wanted to assume a pure Italian form, while they instead tolerated the reverse in the Slavicization or the Germanization of names." In July 1919 Maria Vittoria Segré, the widow Lussich and her son Giorgio Lussich cited the Austrian regime's encouragement of the "notorious mania for Slavicization," in are request to assume their "original surname," Lussi.[22] The tone and rhetoric of these early name change requests provided fodder for the fascists' propaganda mill and set the stage for surname restoration.

Place Names and the Defense of the Territory

From the Risorgimento, irredentists and Italian nationalists had sought to extend Italian sovereignty in the north and to win the Brenner provinces for Italy. On the eve of World War I, avid Italian nationalist Ettore Tolomei proposed Italianization measures for South Tyrol. Born in Rovereto, a village in Trent, Tolomei admitted the necessity for "cohabitation" of Italians and Germans, but his philosophy of co-habitation was far from generous. He stressed the need for the state to aid the "Italian element to return and take back its ground."[23] Efforts to "take back ground" included the Italianization of the territory through creative administrative toponymy that painted an Italian landscape.

During World War I, irredentists called for the revival or revaluation of Italian toponyms in the Adriatic lands to honor Italians fighting for their liberation.[24] Naming alterations formed part of the plans for the annexation and redemption of the Habsburg territories, and Tolomei, the "creator of Alto Adige," was largely responsible for developing the process for the Italian renewal of local toponomy.[25] Antifascist Gaetano Salvemini called Tolomei's efforts to discover Italian or Latin roots for names in South Tyrol the "harmless diversions of a provincial scholar," but Tolomei's toponymic work was well-regarded and taken seriously in Italian institutional circles. In 1916 the Royal Italian Geographical Society published Tolomei's *Prontuario dei nomi locali dell'Alto Adige*.[26] In 1917 a similar publication, the *Prontuario dei nomi locali della Venezia Giulia*, followed for the Adriatic territories, introduced by historical geographer and member of the Italian Geographic Commission Carlo Errera.[27] Both books were based on Tolomei's schema for "restoration, substitution or creation" of names to reflect inherent *italianità*. On Italian takeover in 1918, Tolomei was nominated to the Commission on Language and Culture in the Alto

Adige, a body funded by the Geographical Society and specifically designed to promote Italianness in the new borderland.[28] His renaming schema served as the basis for fascist policies and procedures adopted after 1922.[29]

Place name change was a common weapon in nationalizing authorities' arsenal after World War I. Onomasty tied the new provinces of Venezia Tridentina and Venezia Giulia to the indisputably Italian Venezia Eugenea (Venice proper, the Veneto, and parts of Friuli joined to Italy in 1866) with the three areas forming the Tre Venezie or Three Venices. The term *Tre Venezie*, coined during the Risorgimento by Gorizian linguist and glottologist Graziano Ascoli, underlined the regions' common histories and language, painting them as indissolubly linked to Italian culture and ethnicity, and spiritually bound to Venice.[30]

From 1918 to 1921 renaming places was common practice in Venezia Giulia, but the process was haphazard and created considerable confusion with various public entities assigning and using different names. In 1921, to rein in the confusion, Prime Minister Giovanni Giolitti appointed a commission including representatives of national government, local government, military and civilian geographical societies, and the Italian Touring and Alpine clubs to determine the official lexicon of place names for cities, villages and districts in the new territories.[31] The administration in Trieste substituted patriotic Italian names in place of names associated with Habsburg rule.[32] The substitution of Habsburg for Italian or Latin names and names honoring Italian heroes or history created a greater Venetian or Italian space in the newly constituted Tre Venezie, emerging from World War I and, according to Italian nationalists, recovering from the ravages of centuries of foreign domination.

With the fascist takeover in 1922, the commission's work to nationalize toponyms became more deliberate. By December, the new government urged the committee for naming in Venezia Giulia to work vigorously not simply to systematize but to Italianize place names even in small districts and parts of cities.[33] In Venezia Tridentina and Venezia Giulia as well as old border areas of less conspicuous Italianness like Val D'Aosta, where French names were in common use, the fascists assigned place names to assert *italianità*.

To assert the superiority of Italian civilization, the fascist government often tied name alterations to modernization schemes. For example, the government undertook to refurbish the Adelsberg caverns site, a tourist attraction that hosted 40,100 Habsburg visitors in 1913. A name change accompanied the face-lift. First, Grotte di Adelsberga was proposed, but this was rejected in favor of Postumia, recalling the Roman name and settlement Arae Postumiae (and, although the fascists failed to mention it, closer to the commonly used Slovenian Postojna). In 1929 more than 200,000 visitors flocked to the Postumia grottoes. Approximately 127,000 were Italians attracted by government incentives to bring tourists from the peninsula to familiarize them with the redeemed territories.[34] Other government sponsored trips visited battlefields, natural sites, monuments and Roman ruins to reinforce Venezia Giulia's history of Italianness and remind visitors of the local populations' sacrifices in Italy's name.

In Venezia Giulia, government officials took pains to justify the imposition of new Italian names, appealing to history, linguistics, and the "science" of naming. At the same time Pizzagalli's surname commission toiled, a toponym commission led by Professor Enrico Rosamani, a philologist and dialectician at the Società Alpina delle Giulie (Giulian Alpine Society) worked to Italianize the landscape to ensure that "in its countryside nomenclature" the new territory offered "the most eloquent manifestation of national character."[35] The toponym change process inspired local irredentist and historian of Istrian origin Nicolò Cobolli, a member of the Trieste surname commission, to write a three-part series of articles that emphasized the ancient Roman roots and Latin origins of place names in Trieste and Istria. His articles, published posthumously in *La porta orientale*, emphasized the work of nineteenth-century Triestine historian and early "archaeologist" Pietro Kandler, who just decades before had been denounced by Italian nationalists as an Austrophile. Under the fascists, Kandler was reborn as a man of science who sought to uncover the truth of the mixture of populations and to explain the realities of the situation for those inhabiting Latin regions.[36] Italianization extended beyond simple translation to fit Italian or Latin linguistic patterns. Local nationalists called for sensitivity to the developments of topographic names in Italy. "In the choice of synonyms, to proceed accurately, it is not enough to consult dictionaries and nomenclature of the national language and botanical texts, but [it is necessary] to consider also lists of rural toponyms of the various regions of Italy to understand the vitality of given voices in the popular toponomy."[37] The fascist commission used Kandler's work to justify the choice of ancient Latin or pre-Roman place names to replace names commonly used when the lands were part of the Habsburg monarchy. Members also cited cultural and historical arguments, military necessity, and reasons of security and defense to support Italianization in the region. As late as 1931, local commentators complained that failure to adopt new names created a public menace, causing difficulties for the military which found itself confronted by "insuperable difficulties during tactical exercises in the Upper Isonzo, the Carso, and the Upper Timavo due to topographically illegible maps."[38]

Appropriating Forenames

In 1932 *La porta orientale* continued with its theme of onomastic articles in a two-part forename series by Angelo Scocchi touting the ancient Roman and Latin roots of the eastern border peoples.[39] Restrictions governing the choice or use of first names went into effect in March 1928. The fascist forename policies reflected a long European tradition of granting nationalist-inspired first names. Unlike inherited surnames, given names reflect parents' tastes and choices. Sometimes based on specific and idiosyncratic events or chosen in recognition of specific well-known persons of an era, they are products of the social and cultural environment.[40] As Marc Bloch, the noted historian and founder of the *Annales* commented in interwar France, "The choice of baptismal names, their nature, their relative frequency . . . suitably interpreted, reveal currents of thought or sentiment to which the historian cannot remain indifferent."[41] Nor could contemporary governments remain indifferent.

The fascists tightened controls on first names to civilize the population in the same way that they had civilized the landscape through place name changes. The given name policy fit with linguistic reforms, promoted the fascist language and style, and encouraged veneration of fascist leadership and uniformity consistent with fascist ideals.[42] The 1928 given name law aimed first and foremost at names that implied foreign or antifascist political sentiments. It also prohibited "surnames as given names" or names "ridiculous or shameful or which are an offense to public order or to national or religious sentiment or that are geographic names of places."[43] Unlike the surname law, which was confined to the new territories, the forename law affected the entire population of Italy. It impinged on parents' traditional rights to choose newborns' names. It also allowed authorities to change names already in registered in church and civil rolls. The policies affected most those aged six to twenty, who were pressured by school officials or military conscription officers to conform to fascist expectations.[44]

The regulation of given names, a reaction against imported "exoticism and foreign vocabulary" as well as a means to rob the regime's opponents of an arena for "symbolic acts of resistance," was selectively applied. Such names as Oberdan, Garibaldo, and Azeglio commemorating heroes of the Risorgimento continued to be accepted despite the prohibition on using surnames as given names. Unification era battlefield names and place names also remained in use. The government acted to eliminate such names as Anarchio, Liberto, Libera, Comunardo, Ribelle, and even Soviet, typically associated with sympathy for the workers' movement. The selective nature of enforcement was evident in the experience of a Livornese woman, Anita Repubblica Trieste, who became Anita Maria Trieste in 1928. She retained Anita, popularly associated with Anita Garibaldi, wife of Risorgimento hero Giuseppe Garibaldi; switched Repubblica to Maria eliminating the reference to democratic politics in favor of a reference to the Church and conservative tradition; and kept Trieste with its irredentist and nationalist connotations.[45] The fascists distinguished between classical Greek and Roman names dismissing the former, including names like Achille, as associated with democracy and foreignness and promoting the latter, including names like Romano, as linked to the progenitors of modern Italy. For example, a man in Massa Marittima named Ateo Robespierre became Angiolo, forsaking the atheist, revolutionary and Greek-inspired names for a derivative of angel, the messenger associated with Catholicism and God.[46]

In the newly annexed borderland, the given name policies had a greater impact in ethnic than in political or historical terms. The law of 1928 effectively upheld a Habsburg law that remained in force, which prohibited names deemed "immoral, ridiculous or offensive to religion." Liberal application of the Habsburg law had enabled officials in the eastern borderlands to enforce Italian naming standards well before 1928. In the era of World War I Gayda and other commentators portrayed Croat name choices as reflective of the barbarous or uncivilized cultures of the Balkans. During the fascist period, the state's reconciliation with the Church and Italy's expansionist ambitions complicated the discussion. Linguists like Angelo Scocchi insisted that great care had to be taken to correctly identify the derivation of seemingly Slavic names to differentiate those of eastern, "Yugoslav," or "Serb" importation from those of western Christian or Latin derivation. "Research in the Latin language is not enough to find the key to the etymology of some Roman names," Scocchi argued. He advocated more extensive research in Etruscan, Latin, and other tribes' names. Slovene and Croat names that testified to the triumph of Catholicism over the "eastern Byzantine" world were to be welcomed as a symbol of the "territory irradiated after all in the light of western civilization." The Serbs' Yugoslav or Orthodox influence was the foreign import and overlay from the east.[47]

The Surname Campaign

In some cases, the surname alterations were tied directly to place name changes. As Scocchi pointed out, "Several villages of recent formation are known by the surname of the group of families that live there." Commissions charged with rectifying surnames in each prefecture had to make sure that in the process of name alterations they maintained the proper name correspondences.[48] Due to similarities in the fascist authorities' procedural approaches, the similarity of linguistic assumptions that guided committees charged with executing name campaigns, and the overlapping duties of fascist personnel, many linked place name and surname alteration campaigns. They both originated in nationalizing impulses, but they differed, to some extent, in their intents and legal implications.

The fascists' procedural approach to surname alteration embedded in the 1926 and 1927 measures had its roots in Ettore Tolomei's proposals for Italianization for South Tyrol laid out in a speech in Bolzano in July 1923. Tolomei's plan had included more than thirty prescriptions, only one of which was a provision for the return of "Germanized" surnames to their original (that is, Italian or Latin) forms using the process of "restoration, substitution and correction."[49] Despite surname alteration's resemblance to forename and place name Italianization, it differed significantly in legal terms. Because the surname served as a marker allowing the state to track individuals, it was legally sacrosanct.

After World War I in successor states throughout Europe, officials encouraged name changes or engaged in renaming campaigns to reinforce cultural legitimacy. In some cases in the former Habsburg lands, petitioners sought Slavicization, Magyarization, and Germanization of their surnames to acculturate more quickly into their newly chosen or adopted homelands. Officials in Belgrade, Budapest, Linz, and other cities notified Triestine officials of name changes accorded to people born in the Italian lands of the Adriatic Littoral who had chosen to make their homes outside Italy. In other instances, the work of governments was heavier-handed. As an Italian official defending the prefect of Trieste's name restoration process put it: "It is not only Italy that proceeds in this fashion: in Yugoslavia a law similar to ours provides for the rendering of Italian and German names Slav; in Hungary surnames become Magyar in their spelling; in Greece, under the law, Slavic names become Hellenic; each people tends naturally and logically to put its onomasty in harmony with its national character."[50]

Name change was also part of the process of secularization and modernization. As part of the Kemalist reforms, the new Republic of Turkey passed a surname law in 1934 requiring citizens of the republic to adopt and register Turkish names in the span of two years. Here, adoption of Turkish surnames served at least two "civilizing" functions: to promote the state's nationalizing efforts and to compile accurate records for bureaucratic purposes.[51]

In the confusion of the transfer from Habsburg to Italian sovereignty, Italian military occupation officials in Trieste changed some three hundred surnames. Using the Austrian law, they interpreted the transfer of sovereignty as "a circumstance worthy of particular regard" (clearly in a manner contrary to the legal intention). With the support of the local nationalist press, they liberally Italianized surnames from 1918 to 1919.

Civilian officials proved much more reticent than military occupation authorities, and after 1920, although they wished to adopt a policy "inspired by liberality in the tendency to favor Italianization of surnames," they were concerned with upholding the law and maintaining administrative standards and hesitated to allow alterations that skirted the laws requiring direct transmission of patrilineal surnames.[52] In the some areas particularly in Istria, pressures to conform to "Italian" standards remained strong, but prior to the fascist takeover involuntary Italianization was localized and depended on micropolitics rather than national policy.[53]

From 1922 to 1926, the fascist government granted a handful of surname changes that indicated their sympathies for surname modification
and their willingness to skirt traditional laws that made name alteration
difficult. In 1923 authorities acceded to Count Salvatore Segrè's request to
add the maiden name of his wife, born Baroness Paolina Sartorio. Asking
for an exception to laws that prohibited taking a wife's name, Segrè pointed
out that the baroness was the last descendent of the prominent Sartorio
family that had contributed much to the patrimony of Trieste, including
art collections donated to the Museum of History in the city of Trieste.
He called on fascist authorities to recognize the family's generosity and
what the name meant to Triestines and to allow him to add the name to his
own to ensure the line's survival.[54] The count's position and influence as
well as his appeal to the national and community spirit of Triestines
clearly swayed officials serving the fascist government who permitted
him to become Count Segrè-Sartorio.

In some cases, the civil servants working for the fascist government
accorded requests for surname changes denied by liberal authorities. In
1919, authorities denied a surname change request from the Cociancich
family in Castellier di Visinada.[55] The family petitioned again in 1921 on
the third anniversary of the Italian occupation, pointing to their desire to
change the name "in part [to conform] to Italian sentiments" and also to
mark the family's pride and "eliminate the common homonym," to differentiate themselves from other families bearing the name Cociancich.
For nearly two years the request languished, until in July 1923 fascist authorities permitted the family to adopt the name Cossiani.[56] Such name
changes served as precedents for widespread application of the surname
measure. Under the fascist surname statutes Cociancich later took on
a variety of forms including Canciani, Canziani, Coceani, Cociani, Cos-
ciani, and the above-mentioned Cossiani.[57]

The fascist measure for surname restoration retained the trappings of
prefascist administrative legislation and nodded to liberal laws and policies in force prior to World War I. The fascists maintained that surname
restoration respected core principles of justice in that it sought only to
remedy injustices perpetrated by "foreign oppressors." Aldo Pizzagalli,
head of the surname commission in Trieste, admitted in a nod to Habsburg
justice that Austrian officials had attempted to curb forcible Slavicization

and Germanization, but he repeated the familiar accusations against local clerics, claiming that their deformation of surnames in church registers necessitated the fascist measure.[58]

The 1926 and 1927 Surname Measures

According to the Ministry of the Interior special name restoration and correction legislation was necessary, because Italian law reserved the power to grant name changes to officials in the Ministries of Justice and the Interior and required petitioners to bear the administrative costs and pay a tax. *Restoration* or *correction* set the nationalizing process apart from name *change*, allowing officials to skirt extant name change principles, laws, and precedents. According to the measure, surnames had to be restored to their Italianness, lost or subverted over centuries of "foreign" rule. The measure was limited in scope and application. Val D'Aosta and other border areas linked to Western or Latin cultures, even if not specifically to Italian culture, were not subject to the measures that amounted to an assertion of the triumph of Western or Latin and Roman culture.

Local populations and officials responded differently in the various provinces subject to the surname measure. In the new northern provinces of Venezia Tridentina, including Trent where the surname measures originated, despite Tolomei's efforts and zeal, the effects of the surname campaign were limited. Whether efforts to restore or correct surnames were quietly abandoned, a victim of the national government's turn to more important priorities with respect to Italy's relationship to Germany and Austria in the late 1920s (as Salvemini suggested in 1934), or the potential for destabilization of the local environment was too great, is difficult to assess.[59] Even Eduard Reut-Nicolussi, a staunch defender of the ethnic Germanness of Tyrol bent on recounting the evils of fascism, admitted in 1930 that the measures were an abject failure in the Brenner provinces. Aside from a few "voluntary reversions" that he claimed were made under pressure from the fascist authorities, Reut-Nicolussi noted, the "demand for the change of names had practically no results."[60] Fascist authorities resorted to more direct methods of Italianization, including the promotion of internal migration and relocation of Italians from the peninsula to Venezia Tridentina.

In the mid-1930s, the fascists revisited the subject of surname Italianization in South Tyrol. Italy's warming relations with Germany in 1936
spurred Tolomei to redouble his efforts and, with a missionary's zeal, he
published *Il lavacro dei cognomi* or *The Cleansing of surnames*. The link to
redemption and the religious allusion were unmistakable in the handbook
that purportedly used German sources to prove the Italian or Latin etymology of surnames in South Tyrol.[61] In the year following the book's
publication, Tolomei bragged that 4,000 restorations had been requested
or obtained, but the attempt at wholesale surname reform clearly failed.
Enforcement of surname Italianization seemed to be a low priority.[62]

The situation and response to the legislation in the eastern territory
of Venezia Giulia—which by 1927 had been divided into four provinces
including Trieste, Gorizia, Pola, and Fiume—presented a stark contrast
to that in the Brenner provinces of Venezia Tridentina. As required in the
legislative guidelines accompanying the fascist measure, on May 6, 1927,
Prefect of Trieste Bruno Fornaciari appointed an advisory committee to
compile a list of surnames and a list of noble predicates to be restored to
Italian form.[63] He placed Aldo Pizzagalli, an Italian nationalist and a civil
servant from Pesaro who came to Trieste in the wake of World War I at
the head of the commission. Known for interpretations of D'Annunzio's
prose and for his writings for children, Pizzagalli was a linguist and a relatively new member of the Fascist Party (Pizzagalli joined in 1926 when it
was expected of civil servants). He held a seat on the provincial committee for the Opera Nazionale Balilla (ONB), the fascist youth organization.[64] Pizzagalli saw the basis for Italian culture and the Italian nation
as tied to an affiliation with ancient Rome.[65] This emphasis on Italian
culture and heritage dovetailed with irredentist perceptions of Italianness
in the borderland and with fascist encouragement of aggressive border
fascism to assert Italy's influence in the Adriatic. His work with ONB and
in children's literature testified to his focus on education and his interest
in preparing children to be proud Italian citizens.

Enforcing the Surname Legislation

No racial or ethnic litmus test could be applied to determine fitness for
surname correction or restoration. The Triestine Commission interpreted

the legislation broadly and applied extensively the requirement to restore surnames to their Latin or Italian roots. Using lists of local names that authorities in each city of the province sent to Trieste, the name restoration committee began its work on May 16, 1927. In some cases, the committee took into consideration the names Italian occupation authorities and liberal civil servants had granted to petitioners in the immediate aftermath of World War I. Authorities transformed Bassich to Bassi for three petitioners in 1919. On Pizzagalli's list, the names Bass and Bassich both became Bassi.[66] In 1920 authorities translated Giovanni Golob's surname to Colombo. On Pizzagalli's list Golob, Golobig, and Gollob became Colombi.[67]

Several criteria guided decisions that certain names were "indubitably of Italian origin." If the committee judged a surname's "philological and etymological elements" indicated Italian or Latin origins, the name was restored. If the spelling of the surname could be rectified to an Italian form by "the removal of the suffixes 'ich, cich and vich,'" (generally meaning *son of* in South Slavic usage), it was often considered a candidate for restoration.[68] Dissecting the name Paulovich convinced the committee that the surname was related to the name Paul, well-documented in the Roman usage as Paulus and linked to the Catholic religious tradition with the apostle Paul. In its modern Italian form, the named appeared as Paolo. In the fascist nationalist climate, the committee's instinct to rescue the name from its heathen form (indicated by the *ich* suffix) and return it to its pure Italian form Paoli was irrepressible.

The "Table for the reduction of Slavic forms [or *voci*] with alteration of their sounds to Italian spelling" guided the commission in choosing Italian forms. Prepared by linguistic experts, the table instructed committee members that the letter "'c' sounded like the Italian 'z' in 'forza' . . . and should be written in Italian as such to maintain the sound unaltered." The Slavic š had a "palatal sound" as in the Italian *sc*, while the simple *s* (without the "double accent") sounded like the Italian *ss* as in the word *messa*, and the Slavic z corresponded to the Italian s as in the word *rosa*. An accompanying "Table of Correspondence" simply listed:

v in Italian u
š in Italian sc, s, ss, zg, zl, zn
zr in Italian sg or sgh, sl, sn, sr, and so on.[69]

The explicit instructions in the table gave the impression that careful scientific, linguistic consideration guided standardized and impersonal procedures. However, the listed equivalences were highly selective and offered little more than a nod to linguistic sciences. In theory, all deformed names—German, Slovene, Hungarian, Croat, Serb, Turkish—fell equally readily to the fascist pen. But, given the preponderance of ethnic Slovenes and Croats in the region and the fascist insistence that clerics serving in the Habsburg lands had deliberately Slavicized names that were originally Italian, Slavic names commanded the commission's attention. Old irredentists and ardent Italian nationalists predominated on the Triestine committee and the recent history of conflict between the autochthonous populations fueled fires of prejudice. At the same time, the prefect evidently did not consciously consider the implications of anti-Slav attitudes and their effect on the surname process in forming the committee in May 1927. Rather, only after it began its deliberations did Prefect Fornaciari add Slavicist Umberto Urbanaz (later Urbani) in late June. Born in Capodistria and trained in philology in Graz, Urbanaz was a product of the polyglot borderland. An avid Italian nationalist jailed by the Austrians for irredentism, he was a translator and language teacher specializing in Croatian and Slovenian.

Pizzagalli's committee took twenty months to compile the list of names subject to restoration.[70] In March 1929 the prefect approved it, setting the stage for the restoration of over two thousand surnames. The compilation of the list was the first phase of the administrative process. Officials in the prefect's office then began using police and census records as well as demographic data supplied by mayors of small surrounding villages to compile a list of individuals and households affected by the legislation. In the spring of 1929 the Triestine daily *Il Piccolo* began to publish the list of names subject to restoration beginning with those starting with the letter A. It took several months for the newspaper to reach the letter P. So, sometime in the late spring or summer of 1929, the Paulovich family became aware of the prefect's intention regarding their surname. By the late autumn or early winter of 1929 to 1930, the prefect began the arduous task of issuing decrees to each individual or family officially notifying them of "the restoration to an Italian form." The *Gazzetta Ufficiale*, the kingdom's official record of legislative proceedings, announced all restorations, and civil servants noted them in official registries.[71]

While the surname list had been compiled and restoration decrees were beginning to be issued in great numbers by 1929, the committee's work in formulating names was far from complete. The bulk of committee members' subsequent tasks related to surname corrections. From its passage in 1927, the surname legislation generated a flurry of requests for name correction. Each petition that reached the prefect's office had to be researched and considered on its own merits to ensure compliance with the statutes and adherence to the surname correction guidelines.[72] Beginning in early 1928, well before the restoration lists were complete, the local press began to publish periodic columns detailing the surname commission's decisions on each correction petition.[73] The government portrayed the crowd of petitioners as "motivated by pure instincts of national pride and political loyalty." In a show of officials' supposed moderation and commitment to the voluntary nature of the name correction, Pizzagalli enjoined those seeking to correct their names under article 2 to "take their time." After all, he noted, "to change a surname, is not like changing clothes or brands of cigarettes." Nonetheless, he touted requests for "correction" by the "impatient crowd of petitioners" as a "calm and solemn" plebiscite in favor of the surname campaign.[74] Those seeking surname corrections ranged across the spectrum of nationalist fervor. Some were ecstatic at the prospect and obsessively sought Italianized surnames to demonstrate "enthusiastic adherence to the surname convention" or to rid themselves of names "barbarously distorted over the centuries." Others claimed to want to rectify the spelling of names to make them easier to pronounce. Many sought corrections out of a sense of pragmatism, hoping that the patriotic act would enhance their economic, social, or political position.

Although officials cast all requests for corrections as evidence of a desire for Italianization, in some cases they were nothing of the sort. Despite the Ministry of Justice and Cultural Affairs' insistence in April 1927 on the voluntary nature of the reforms and its emphasis on the legislation's intent to "right past wrongs" and on protection and promotion of Italian society, the crowd of petitioners included many pressured by employers, officials, family, friends, or even acquaintances to seek Italianization of their names. Party officials and other local fascist elements applied considerable pressure. In Trieste, the provincial secretary of the Fascist Party personally initiated a campaign by political organizations, including the syndicates and the Dopolavoro, to support and assist individuals to correct their surnames.[75] Functionaries serving the party structure or *federale* referred Triestines and supplied petition forms to facilitate individuals' application for name correction, if their names did not appear on the list for restoration. The school directorates for Trieste and Zara issued circulars in 1928 urging local school inspectors to be persuasive in their efforts to encourage teachers to be among the first to request name correction. In 1929 they pushed teachers to participate in the surname initiative and to persuade their pupils' families to do so as a "way to serve the fatherland and fascism."[76] Other public employees—including officials working for the post office, customs, and the local Port Warehouse Authority, many of whose applications were forwarded under the auspices of the Fascist Party—were among the first to come forward to request surname corrections. Employees of large firms reliant on state contracts including, perhaps most notably, Trieste's large shipping and ship building firms followed closely on the heels of civil servants. By the early 1930s, in the climate of increasing corporatization and economic centralization, individuals like licensed professionals and small business owners who counted on state patronage led the ranks of those who sought name correction. Fascist encouragement of name corrections was similar to subtle intimidation and persuasion employed to encourage writers' and artists' cultural cooperation.[77]

Directives that charged officials to define particular forms for names restored under article 1 enjoined them to maintain a disinterested stance in regard to petitions filed under article 2. The application of consistent (if undefined) standards guarded against interference in or manipulation of the scientific or empirical process grounded in linguistic principles. Pizzagalli warned civil servants in his employ to guard against interference by individuals who acted out of personal ambition or desire for personal gain. For example, no individual could petition for a name that belonged to a famous family in Italy. "National sentiment should prevail over any egotistical consideration," he noted.[78] Officials were not to bow to the wishes of petitioners who sought to minimize the alteration to a name to avoid a new sound or those who sought to link the sound and spelling to the past form of their names. They were also to resist acceding to the wishes of those who sought total eradication of their surnames. Individuals who sought to modify a name for egotistical reasons, because they felt detached from their past, or wanted to adopt a wholly new Italian identity were not be rewarded with a form that did not conform to fascist naming standards designed to benefit the community.[79]

Inconsistencies, Loopholes, and Uncertainties

Despite Pizzagalli and other officials' commitment to apply so-called scientific and neutral principles in the application of the surname measure, as Orestano observed, interpretations and the practice of law were often "motivated by considerations of political necessity or of economic convenience."[80] The list that the committee produced and the processes that evolved to deal with restorations and corrections were haphazard and based on committee members' judgments. Despite its *ich* suffix, Paulovich's maiden name Barbarovich was never included in the list of names for automatic restoration, and therefore remained untouched throughout the entire restoration conflict. The reason for its absence from Pizzagalli's list can only be guessed at. It may have been related to the name's rarity in the registers in Trieste or to officials' failure to take notice of it. Luigia Barbarovich was already married by the time she arrived in Trieste. Under Italian and European law, on marriage a woman assumed the name and nationality of her husband. Unlike in many countries such as France, Great Britain, and the United States, where the woman's family name was lost completely, in Italy, it was customary for the man's surname to be added to the woman's name.[81] However, the widow did not appear under the name Barbarovich as the legal head of a family. That privilege was reserved to her husband, the deceased Antonio Paulovich. There is no indication that any member of her extended Barbarovich family was in Trieste area or became involved in the dispute. Thus, the name may simply have escaped the notice of the commission members who compiled the restoration list.

The absence of Barbarovich from Pizzagalli's list may also have been linked to the name's association with the name Barbara in the Venetian context. Barbarovich was likely a derivative of Barbara, a name that was diffused throughout the Venetian dominions and associated with Saint Barbara and with a leading Venetian family.[82] Luigia Barbarovich's family's heritage on the Dalmatian island of Brazza pointed to Venetian lineage. It is also possible that fascist linguists did not consider the name

Barbara, despite evidence of its diffusion in ancient Rome, as linked to a Latin heritage. Its etymological root in *barbarian* may have been an overriding consideration, and while the name *Barbato* was recognized as among the Latin names "venerated by the Church as part of the saints and martyrs of the Christian faith," the name *Barbara*, unlike Paul or Paulus, did not appear on Pizzagalli's list.[83] Perhaps a number of factors were taken into account.

Members of the local population continued to maintain overlapping or competing identities characteristic of the borderland despite fascist attempts to eradicate competing associations. In 1938 typographer Vittorio Tence filed a petition asking his surname be corrected to Tenze, "as it would be read in the Slavic language." Fascist authorities seeking to Italianize the population found unacceptable his request to change the spelling to encourage native Italian speakers to pronounce "properly" the name with foreign roots. They responded offering an alternative "Italian form." He refused it, insisting on his original proposition. At an impasse, the authorities simply filed the petition and made no change. Such requests, filed as late as 1938, indicated the failure of fascist education to win over the local population to national conceptions of Italian citizenship and belonging.

Even among officials overlapping or competing identities remained a source of debate, and civil servants in the various borderland provinces debated the extent and scope of the surname law as well as its applicability to specific individuals or names. When the members of the Cian family, nobles in Venezia Giulia, petitioned for their name to be corrected to Ciano, national officials at the heraldic commission denied the request for "reasons of state" and responded that the name Cian was "perfectly Venetian." While the excuse was ostensibly based on linguistic etymology, the response reflected officials' political pragmatism and recognition of the surname Ciano's association in the national context with the prestigious Ciano family in Rome.[84]

Despite the legislation's obvious nationalist intents, civil servants denied petitioners' requests to alter names to forms that recalled their patriotic associations but did not derive directly from the foreign surnames. They denied, for example, a request for the name Premuda, in honor of the unredeemed Dalmatian island near which the Austrian battleship Saint Stephen was sunk in World War I. Officials also denied petitioners who desired to take names that recalled their geographic origins, such as names of towns or villages. In their estimation, such alterations constituted "changes," not "corrections" and therefore fell outside the scope of the legislation.[85]

Although the legislation required return to a Latin or Italian form, officials seemed to have lost sight of the importance of Latin roots by 1935. In the case of one petitioner who wished to relinquish a hyphenated Slavic-French name, the official blatantly flouted the laws. He allowed the petitioner to drop the French name and Italianized the Slavic name, violating both the Latin name principle and the prohibition on changing names.[86]

Guidelines specifically prohibited officials from correcting names derived from local dialects, which reformers saw as important to maintaining the richness and diversity of Italian culture. Friulian names, ubiquitous in the Adriatic provinces, were considered Italian in origin and could not, therefore, be tampered with.[87] Pizzagalli's agents were particularly careful to delineate a name's specific status in cases where they refused correction. In the case of a woman who asked for the correction of the name Tomadin, the official noted, "The surname is already Italian." On review of the case, an official crossed this out, and in a nod to the perceived importance of local dialects substituted, "the surname is not foreign."

By the 1930s tolerance and encouragement of regional diversity would wane. In 1932, Mussolini's rejection of literature written in dialect signaled a shift in official policy and attitudes. Yet, censorship of the use of dialect and attempts to marginalize works written in dialect were never successful.[88] In the same vein, standards for Italianness and national cultural belonging were not consistently or exclusively defined. Surname restoration and correction procedures were never amended to reflect the shift in priorities. Local civil servants sought to balance erasure or erosion of onomastic markers that were useful for local differentiation with standardization of surnames to conform to the state's modernizing and nationalizing aims.

When the surname legislation came into effect, prefects had the power to dismiss local employees whose activities and attitudes they saw as incompatible with fascist political aims. But until 1933 local functionaries were not required to be party members.[89] The nationalizing campaign offered Triestine civil servants the opportunity to advance their careers by *translating* specialized local knowledge encoded in particular surnames that was unintelligible to national authorities.[90] Authorities promoted the restoration and correction campaign as a means to ensure the more efficient function of the bureaucracy. At the same time, the campaign made local civil servants indispensable to representatives of the national government who required assistance to navigate the renamed environment. Local officials involved in the process neither sought nor desired national interference in their renaming work, a task that gave them particular knowledge and control of the local citizenry. The Pizzagalli commission's meticulous outline of the policies and procedures may have reflected a commitment to efficiency, fairness, and scientific administration. But, Pizzagalli's thoroughness and the formality of the name handbook's production were intended also to impress his superiors and to establish Pizzagalli's as an unrivaled name restoration expert.

Most complaints relating to the surname measure reflected an individual or family's dissatisfaction with the new form of the name, the spelling or sound of it, or the contention that it constituted a misunderstanding of the surname's root and therefore a mistranslation. Functionaries at the prefect's office working on the name restorations considered each complaint, referring many to Pizzagalli for his comment. Pizzagalli dealt with the vast majority at the local level, either certifying the correctness of the individual's assertion and making an alteration or denying the supplicant's claim. Placing the responsibility for the promulgation of the surname law in the hands of the prefect and a committee of academics and political appointees clearly indicated that the surname campaign was a matter of bureaucratic and administrative concern. The administrative nature of the surname alteration process and the specifics of the law that placed responsibility for it with the Ministry of the Interior's administrative offices for territorial governance and the minister of justice suggested that nationalization, not defense, was the measure's priority. Nowhere did the measure refer to the Interior Ministry's Head Office of Public Security.[91] Had the fascist government intended the act to be putative or aimed to use it to root out enemies of the state, responsibility for carrying out the measures would have involved the *carabinieri* or eventually the fascist OVRA, the secret police that used repressive techniques to keep the population in line. The appeals process too reflected the administrative nature of the measure. Power would likely have been shared by the fascist militia, in particular special units of the MSVN charged with ensuring security of the border areas, had the government intended the measure to have teeth. Failure to comply would certainly have subjected the offender to punishment harsher than the levying of a fine, no matter how steep. Trieste (along with the Tre Venezie, Lombardy, Piedmont, Val D'Aosta, and Liguria, considered border areas) was located in the first zone of OVRA created in 1927 and seated in Milan under the control of Francesco Nudi. Nudi's background was in the Ministry of the Interior, where from 1900 he built impressive credentials as an investigator, studying socialist and communist movements to root out elements threatening the State. By 1929 OVRA had begun to build its network of agents, and while still in its infancy in 1930, the secret police and Special Tribunal made their presence clearly felt in Trieste.[92]

Few whose wishes were not granted by the prefect or Pizzagalli had the energy, the means, the conviction, or perhaps the courage to bring their cases to Rome. Certainly, those who challenged the prefect and local authorities representing the authoritarian regime incurred, or at least perceived, a risk in the prospect of drawing attention to a complaint against government officials. Taking that complaint to the national level was even more daunting. Yet, the widow was not intimidated. Dissatisfied with the dispositions of the prefect and authorities in Trieste, Paulovich sought higher justice. Seeking to validate her position as a loyal citizen and Italian nationalist and as an honorable widow and mother, she appealed to the national level in a complaint that pit government-appointed officials in the prefect's office in Trieste against officials in the Ministry of the Interior and magistrates of the Administrative Court of the Council of State.

4   The Family in Question

Luigia Paulovich insisted that it was her duty as a widow to maintain her married surname in the form used by her husband to honor his memory and his family. This type of forbearance and spirit of sacrifice, even in the face of opposition, was the burden the fascists expected widows to bear. Self-abnegation in the name of family and children was expected of women like Paulovich in European society. But, as Italian novelist and journalist Matilde Serao wrote in 1916, "It is more difficult to be a noble widow, a good widow, than a true spouse or a real husband."[1] Paulovich's defense of her family—what the regime saw as her primary moral and political responsibility—lay at the heart of her protest of the surname restoration.

Fascist ideologues recognized the family as the bedrock for Italian society. The Italian family structure was rooted in a hierarchical, patriarchal system of family management traced to the Roman family and traditions. Under Italian civil law, the conjugal home and conjugal relationship constituted a single legal familial unit.[2] Rocco and elites were eager to see that under fascism the family maintained its structure, cohesion, and centrality to Italian society.

In a 1929 speech before parliament, Rocco identified the "legal family" as a "social and political institution" that was "the primary cell of the nation." He thus extended the metaphor of the nation as an organism composed of individual, subservient cells to include the family as a core component.[3] In metaphorical terms the nation was a family. "At its base, the interests that tie together the single members of the family and the spiritual affinities that distinguish one family from another delineate the single components which distinguish one from the other" and define familial roles and responsibilities in the nation.[4]

The prefect's decree issued on June 26, 1930, restored the name of "Luigia Barbarovich daughter of Antonio widow Paulovich born in Milna on Brazza (Habsburg Monarchy) on May 14, 1854." It did not aim at her as an individual, but as the head of her family, a legal status conferred on the death of her husband.[5] The surname decree also named two of her children, despite their being well past the age of majority.[6] Her daughter Ines and son Ernesto were also subject to the restoration to Paoli.

The prefect's office understood that for families surnames held sentimental value and importance as "a history." As Pizzagalli suggested, "[A] surname holds within it infinite memories and long traditions; it is the inheritance of a glorious past; often it represents a moral patrimony conquered with honored deeds and transmitted with considerable fortunes, its just rewards; always it is a signal of an existence in itself, as in a delicate or bright metal, each manifestation of its conspicuous activity for good or bad, it illustrates or obscures, glorifies or defames."[7]

Yet, officials expected Paulovich and her children to submit to the naming commission's judgment and to obey the government. Certainly by 1930, in encounters with the fascist government, most chose acquiescence to authorities.[8] The widow's protest launched in defense of her husband's honor and in remembrance of his family's loyalty and support for Italy came as an unwelcome surprise to those who sought to welcome loyal families into the fold of the nation through surname Italianization.

Questions of Jurisdiction

Members of the Paulovich family signaled their displeasure at the prospect of their surname's restoration before the prefect issued the name restoration decree in late June 1930. On June 9 the prefect of Sondrio, a province of Risorgimento Italy along the Swiss border, wrote a confidential memorandum to the prefect of Trieste asking that the Pauloviches be spared the effects of the surname legislation. Prefect Stefano Pirretti's particular interest in the case lay in the name restoration measure's effect on Luigia Paulovich's son Ernesto, a civil servant working under his direction. Ernesto had taken advantage of the civil service opportunities available to Italians in the New Provinces and, by the late 1920s, had moved to serve the Italian government in "old Italy" in a post at Sondrio. Aware of the inclusion of the name Paulovich on the prefect's list in Trieste and of the imminent issuance of the restoration decree, and in response to an official's discussion with Luigia Paulovich regarding the name, Ernesto sought his employer's intervention on his family's behalf.

Like Prefect Porro in Trieste, Prefect Pirretti in Sondrio was a career civil servant. Originally from Matera, he transferred from his post as prefect of Aosta to become prefect of Sondrio in July 1929.[9] Known for his anti-Bolshevism and rigid adherence to discipline and order, Pirretti evidently hoped that his intervention might sway one of his peers.[10] In his memo to Trieste, he questioned the surname legislation's applicability to the family on the basis of the surname's Slavic (he asserted) etymology and on the basis of the family's demonstrated allegiance to Italian causes and the Italian nation. Pirretti relayed Ernesto's agitation and "heartbreaking regret" that the name Paulovich appeared on the list for restoration.[11]

Ernesto Paulovich saw his surname as "tied to unforgettable memories, which testified to his family's exquisitely patriotic Italian traditions and sentiments." The restoration constituted "a refusal, even if unintentional, to recognize these traditions and sentiments." Likely at Ernesto Paulovich's prompting, Pirretti asserted that the surname Paulovich was "not of Italian or Latin origin" nor was it "disfigured from an Italian form." To its original form Paulovič, the Venetians had added the "h" as a mark of the family's loyalty to the Republic. Pirretti assured the prefect of Trieste that Ernesto "demonstrated true Italian sentiments, discipline and zeal," and reminded him that Paulovich had volunteered "in the Italian army during the 'war of liberation,'" and that his brother Enrico had been "imprisoned in Austria for having publicly called for the victory of the Italian Army" while Trieste remained under Habsburg rule.[12]

Porro replied to Pirretti with an explanation of the technicalities of the surname restoration process. Obviously aware that the name Paulovich appeared on the local list for restoration and knowing of the official intention to issue a restoration decree, Porro somewhat disingenuously offered, "The local Registry Office [in Trieste] has not required the mother or the son to change the surname to an Italian form." Triestine officials had contacted the widow as a courtesy on account of the petition filed in 1928 by her elder son Enrico and his surname correction to the Italian form Paolucci. According to the prefect, an official had asked Luigia Paulovich in the spring of 1930 if she preferred to adopt Paolucci, the form Enrico had chosen rather than the form that appeared on the restoration list. "The interested party responded in the negative," Porro said. He added, should the widow Paulovich persist in her objections to the restoration after the prefect issued a decree, she was free to follow the appeal procedures outlined in the legislation.[13]

Porro's curt dismissal of Pirretti's questions did not mean that he saw the matter as closed. Even before receiving the letter from Pirretti, he had somehow been alerted to the Paulovich family's dismay and intention to fight the restoration. In March 1930 he had contacted the prefect of Zara, the province of the family's origin, regarding that office's handling of the surname Paulovich. Various prefects could consult one another freely, but the legislation and administrative guidelines made no provision for the coordination of surname restoration lists or of specific procedures across prefectures. On March 26 Prefect Marcello Vaccari—the youngest prefect in Italy, a political appointee from the party ranks, and a protégé of Galeazzo Ciano—responded, "In Zara, the surname Paulovich does not appear on our list as subject to restoration under the terms of the statute."[14]

Clearly, this was not the answer that the official in Trieste had hoped for. But as the prefectural system and the provisions of the legislation left the specifics of execution to the competence of jurisdictional authorities, decisions in Trieste did not have to coincide with those taken in Zara. Conformity across prefectural boundaries would have been desirable (and perhaps strengthened the Triestine prefect's position), but naming authorities in Trieste decided to maintain their assertion that the name Paulovich had Italian or Latin roots and remained subject to restoration.

Luigia's son Enrico Paulovich's request for Paolucci in 1928 had come before the naming commission had begun the process of restoring surnames. His petition for correction under article 2 was not in any way unusual. The prefect's office interpreted it as a patriotic act. Pizzagalli had counseled, "If a restoration to Italian form for a listed name is requested by an interested party prior to the prefect's decree authorizing the restoration, then it is logical and opportune that the request be immediately granted."[15] Paolucci was not the official form listed for the restoration of Paulovich, but it did conform to the general linguistic formulas developed to facilitate application of the surname measures. In fact, in its translation of Paulovich (son of Paul) to Paolucci (little Paul), it was, perhaps, a more accurate rendition than the commission's Paoli (simply a derivative of Paul).

Had Luigia Paulovich accepted the prefect's offer to restore her name to Paolucci, officials would have understood her willingness to follow her son. It would have reinforced their traditional patriarchal notions of the state and men's superior position in the family and affirmed that within the widow's nuclear family Italian sentiments were strong. The prefect claimed that he had approached the elderly widow to see if she wanted to adopt her son's name Paolucci out of respect for Enrico, recognizing his responsibilities as a dutiful son to oversee the nationalist interests of his widowed mother after his father's death. He had acted with confidence that the elderly woman would wish to stand alongside Enrico at the vanguard of nationalization in the borderland and would consider officials' willingness to facilitate the correction to Paolucci a favor.

In many cases, petitioners used the correction provisions in article 2 as a means to assert control over the fate of their surnames. In November 1927, a petitioner expressed the desire to correct his name to Bonelli, because on the basis of an article by Francesco Babudri published in the local Catholic periodical *L'era nuova*, he understood that his surname, diffused throughout Istria, would be converted to a very popular Italian name. Officials granted his request.[16] Through suggestion of a specific form for an "exotic" name, he distinguished his family members among the many families who would receive the official restored form.

Prefectural officials did not intend to undermine the distinctiveness of families or to standardize names in a manner that erased familial ties. To the contrary, maintaining familial distinctions promoted stability, facilitated surveillance, and simplified record-keeping. However, in many cases, Pizzagalli's commission traced various different names to the same Italian root and gave them the same Italianized form. The surname *Paoli*, already common on the peninsula became the Italian form of the surname for families bearing the "deformed" surnames Paolich, Paulakovic, Paulic, Paulich, Paulichievich, Paulisic, Paulissich, Pausler, Pavaletz, Pavlic, and Pavlovcic.[17] In 1928 Enrico's desire to maintain a distinctive name could have influenced his request for Paolucci. The effect of his early correction was to set him apart from the sea of newly created Paoli families. Luigia Paulòvich and her other children could have chosen to follow his lead to preserve the family's distinctive heritage and name in the Italianized form Enrico had chosen.

Knowledge that women often sought name corrections with the support of brothers, uncles, or husbands would have reinforced the prefect's certainty that the widow would be amenable to the name correction to Paolucci. Officials routinely granted women's requests for surname correction when they conformed to requests by male family members or when they were supported by husbands, brothers, or fathers. For example, officials granted a correction to the surname Taurini to a woman who petitioned at the same time as her brother and his wife. A sister and brother who filed separate petitions, at the same time, asking that their surname be corrected to the Italian form Valori, both received instead, the Italian correction to Cambi, which officials deemed a better translation from the original German. In fact, women often assumed that official corrections or restorations given to nuclear family members automatically extended to them. Such was the case of a married woman who wrote to officials in 1941 asking for correction of her maiden name to Antonini. Although married since 1919, she assumed that the Italianization afforded her father and brothers in 1930 would extend to her. She had waited more than a decade to request the name correction. On behalf of their wives, husbands routinely asked for and received corrections of both maiden and married surnames. Such was the case for a woman whose husband's name became Zaghi. Although her father did not seem to be involved, her maiden name was transformed too, to the Italian form Galassi.

Officials also frequently restored the names of widows and fulfilled requests from widows who sought to have their married names and the surnames of their children Italianized. In one case in 1935, officials' alacrity to restore the name of a widow and her thirteen children became a cause for debate when the official in her village of Postumia pointed out that the widow and one of her sons had both died in 1931 and that seven of her children and several grandchildren lived abroad. The local official asked for the reissuance of the decrees to affect only those who were alive and resident in the village.[18]

Triestine authorities in the prefect's office saw Paulovich as vulnerable and in need of the state's protection and guidance. Their moral guidance extended to assistance to help her to choose how to nationalize her surname. Prefect Pirretti, acting on Ernesto Paulovich's behalf rather than on Luigia Paulovich's behalf, would not have been swayed by such sentiments. His approach to the restoration would have been from a more critical, male legal stance.

In addition to questioning the decree's advisability on the basis of etymology and of the family's history, the prefect of Sondrio questioned the decree's applicability to Ernesto Paulovich. As a civil servant in Sondrio, Ernesto had established official residence outside Italy's New Provinces, and, born in 1891, he was well above the age of majority. To clarify his posi-tion on this point of residence, Triestine Prefect Porro once again sought advice from the prefect of Zara, who once again disappointed him. Vaccari maintained that the legislation applied only to those currently resident in the territory in question. The legislation covered the populations of Zara (the Paulovich family's province of origin) and of Trieste (the widow's official residence), but not of Sondrio. Therefore, in Vaccari's estimation, Ernesto should not be a candidate for surname restoration.

Recognizing the importance of family ties and the role of the family as a building block of the fascist state, Porro and Pizzagalli included household members like Ernesto on restoration decrees whether or not they actually lived in the province of Trieste. They justified inclusion of these family members on the grounds that the Ministry of Justice's guide-lines called for notification of "postal and consular officials" for resto-rations granted to "official" residents living outside the territory. Their interpretation of the ministry's instructions hinged on the contention that Trieste was Ernesto's official, if not actual, residence in Italy. It also mani-fested in practice with their willingness to correct surnames of Italians living outside the province or even abroad. For example, Triestine officials readily acceded to a request from a submariner living in Taranto, in the southern Italian region of Apulia, to have his name corrected to the Ital-ian form Debrazzi. In 1930 an artist of Triestine birth living in California succeeded in having his name corrected to Severi on the basis of a peti-tion filed with the prefect of Trieste through the offices of the Italian Consulate.[19]

The Fascist Family Unit

Porro's suggestion that Luigia Paulovich might consider adopting the name Paolucci was not merely a matter of administrative expediency or national-ist sympathy. It reflected fascist understandings of the family, its cohesion and functions, and legal standards favoring the maintenance of consis-tency in family names.

In 1931 Giuseppe Bottai's polemical periodical *Critica Fascista* placed "each family unit's" intimate acceptance of the "integration of fascist so-ciety with the Nation" at the heart of success of fascism.[20] Yet, the family's legal status and its role in the fascist system remained open to debate. The 1865 Italian Civil Code (the so-called Pisanelli Code), based on the traditions of the turn of the nineteenth century French Code Napoleon and the 1837 Sardinian Albertine Civil Code, did not define the family as a legal entity. Instead, the first book of the code "of persons and of the family" in 455 articles referred to the "'relations of the family', to the 'familial patrimony', to 'crimes against the family' etc."[21] In practice, since the founding of the modern Italian state, the family had maintained a particular and peculiar juridical position between civil law with regard to the individual and statutory law with regard to the political community.

After the fascists took control, Italian jurists like Antonio Cicu, a legal expert whose writings on family law were published originally in 1914, manipulated traditional values and ideas to fit individuals' new relationship to fascist totalitarian society and the fascist family. Considering the family as a superior cell or primary social unit undermined the primacy of the individual and individual rights articulated in Western liberal legal assumptions and assumed in aspects of the civil code. However, liberal law remained in force, and the fascists did not legally abrogate individual rights in favor of family rights. Nor did they seek to change the boundaries between the family and the state in public law.[22] They did not make substantive changes to the family law until 1942, more than a decade after the Administrative Court considered Paulovich's case. Even then, in the "Bill of Rights" related to considerations on reform of the judicial structure of the state, produced in Pisa in 1943, the family remained "the fundamental nucleus of national society," with basic rights to be protected by the state.[23] Instead of actually changing the law in the reforms of the late 1920s, Rocco shifted the Italian gaze, highlighting the family's civic function in such a way as to elicit each member's complicity in the compromise of his or her individual rights.[24]

As Cicu explained, the interests of the family superseded those of its members as the interests of the state superseded those of its constituents. Adhering to basic political principles grounded in the Enlightenment and to Rousseau's ideas of the general will and the social contract, the fascists should have maintained individual rights. But, Cicu argued, because "sovereign will" should not be arbitrary, it should not bend to the "individual will."[25] This view of the primacy of the "sovereign will" and subordination to the state differed profoundly from the paternalistic hierarchical notions of the *Führerprinzip*, or *Führer* principle, under which the Nazis defined the family and its members as subordinate to the supreme leader.[26] In the fascist case, it was the exercise of the sovereign will that served the general will and the greater needs of the society.

The fascists' understanding of the relationship of the individual and family to the state reflected fascism's syndicalist approach to societal organization. As the fascists expected workers to subordinate individual needs to the efficient functioning of the state, to the nation's needs, and to the realities of production, they expected family members to subordinate their needs and feelings to the efficient functioning of the family as a building block of the nation.[27] In 1933, in *Critica Fascista*, journalist and ideologue Manlio Pompei insisted, "The family is and must remain the mother cell of fascist society."[28] Such notions shaped later fascist racial policy as a manifestation of the extreme nationalism of the state in which man was "considered under law to be part of a particular political society (citizenship), part of a particular domestic society of which he carries the name (family), and part of a particular ethnic group (race)."[29]

The fascists relied on the family as a structure to mobilize Italians and ensure a productive population and as a tool of social control. They attempted to manipulate individuals' socio-biological commitments within the framework of the family to ensure support for policies to strengthen the state.[30] Through Rocco's reform of legal and administrative structures, the fascist government attempted to blur the boundaries between *civil* society and *social* society.[31] But, it did not seek to alter the structure of the family or abnegate liberal family law. Interwar Italians were well-acquainted with social theories that traced the decadence of society to the breakdown of family structure. As Italian economist and social scientist Ferdinando Loffredo, one of the foremost fascist ideologues of social policy explained, "Demographic decadence derived exclusively from the decadence of the institution of the family."[32] Capitalism led to the breakdown of the Italian family, the moral decadence of Italians, and the demographic decline of the state. The shift away from stable habitation and rooted families to mobility characteristic of urban, apartment-style living and tenancy was at the heart of the problem.[33] The success of the state relied on the restoration of the traditional family.[34]

Under fascism, each individual had a specific role contributing to the family. Extralegal familial responsibilities included contributing to the greater collective as a citizen of the fascist state. In socio-biological terms, the family's duty was to meet its responsibilities to "the collective needs of the stock" as outlined in Mussolini's Ascension Day speech in May 1927 promoting the health of the Italian people and race and the demographic campaign.[35]

These biological responsibilities were matched by moral expectations promoted and policed within the family on an individual level. The precepts "believe, obey, and fight" guided each individuals' contributions to the regime.[36] In this respect, the fascists insisted that women take an active role in shaping the future of the nation, disseminating fascism's "moralizing discourse" that "through practical examples" taught the fundamental principles of the family."[37] It was the woman's duty to set the tone as the domestic pillar of the family and "to remain steadfast in her mission in the life of the people" understood as "the mission of mother."[38] Her acceptance of this mission constituted her primary contribution to the "larger organism" of society.

Loffredo's "Christian-warrior family," "the only nuclear family in which numerous future sons of the Patria could be born and grow," encompassed socio-biological and moral imperatives.[39] In the first two chapters of his *Politics of the Family*, Loffredo took on the capitalist order and called for "combat" against individualism and materialism. In the third, he turned to the strengthening of Italian society through the strengthening of religious sentiment. Loffredo identified religion as a cornerstone of the state, and he called for intensification of the relationship between the fascist state and the Catholic Church. Loffredo's religious approach, traditionally soundly rejected by Italian leadership as in opposition to the secular Italian state, kept with popular cultural sentiment in Italy. It also found resonance in aspects of Italian law. As Orestano and other legal philosophers recognized, "religious or moral interests" affected state systems of justice.[40] The Napoleonic legal code's delegation of responsibility and authority to the male head of household combined with Risorgimento insistence that the family formed the cornerstone of the Italian society. As the Catholic Church affirmed in 1930, men remained at the head of the family and it was women's responsibility to maintain traditional roles that assured the "right ordering and unity and stability of home life."[41]

The husband and wife's maintenance of their roles and responsibilities in the family assured "the conservation and propagation of the human race."[42]

Church and Family

Loffredo's call for "precise collaboration" with the Church was consonant fascist demographic policy in the late 1920s and with the fascist state's position vis-à-vis the Church after the signing of the Lateran Pacts in 1929.[43] In the Treaty of Conciliation of the Lateran Pacts, Mussolini agreed that Italy would "revise its legislation in so far as it concerns Ecclesiastical matters." He promised to reform and reintegrate its laws in the spirit of the Concordat "in order to bring them into harmony" with those of the Holy See.

The Lateran Pacts specifically addressed the importance of the conjugal relationship between husband and wife, which constituted "the foundation of the family," as the basis for cooperation and formulation of common interests of the Church and State.[44] As racial theorist Giulio Cogni explained, "In matrimony, the individual usually undertakes the most important act of his life. . . . from this act arises, not superficially but in substance, the family, the society, the state and the world."[45] Tying the fundamental unity of the family to the ties of humanity associated with the Church, the state aided the family "in carrying out its civil functions in the same way that the Church aided it in carrying out its religious functions."[46]

The National Organization for Motherhood and Childhood (Opera nazionale maternità e infanzia) (**ONMI**) founded in 1925 had assured a "fruitful collaboration between the state and the family." Such statements as one issued in celebration of the Festival of the Mother and Child in 1933, "Each woman is a mother not of one child, but of those which multiply in the future generations and in this sense each woman is Eve, because she reproduces the miracle of generation and multiplication," tied biological aims for women as mothers to responsibilities for both state and Church.[47]

The family's role in the political and legal hierarchy and its acceptance as a legitimate "political and social institution" cemented its place as the "cornerstone" of the pronatalist, demographic policies of the regime.[48]

According to Loffredo, the "totalitarian state" was responsible for enact-
ing and maintaining a juridical substratum based on totalitarian moral
and economic concepts grounded in the restoration of religion and the pursuit of "superior motives" of political demography.[49] In fact, Mussolini tied
the demographic campaign directly to family politics and the Church.[50]

Pope Pius XI's December 1930 *Casti Connubii* affirmed the "primacy of
the husband with regard to the wife and children" and called for "the ready
submission of the wife and her willing obedience," not as an unthinking
and uninformed minor, but as a "companion," reasoning that in the "body
of the family," the woman was the "heart" and the man was the "head."[51]
Such statements and beliefs accorded well with Italian law and fascist
expectations. In legal terms, the marriage of Church and State recognized
Catholicism as the "confession of the great majority of Italians," and acknowledged that it had contributed "in history and in fact, precious and
incorruptible spiritual direction" to the state. On this basis, the fascist
state pledged to "obey the religious conscience of the Italian people."[52]
While Mussolini's hopes to harness the Church in the interest of the state
were dashed, the pacts did formally establish a concordance of interests,
particularly with respect to the family.[53] Metaphoric reference in the papal encyclical to the woman and man as parts in the whole of the family
body and the emphasis on the reciprocal relationship between head and
heart stressing their partnership in the functioning of the family echoed
in fascist conceptions of the family's role in the body of the nation.

The role of the Church and the Church's attitude toward the family
and its moral functions were particularly important in the borderland,
where the entire process of annexation to Italy was linked to religious
imagery and destiny. Religious symbolism and allusion, consistent with
right-leaning agendas, permeated the irredentist and nationalist movements into the fascist years. The annexation and occupation of the New
Provinces was referred to as the *redenzione* or redemption, a metaphor
that served well the purposes of those on the peninsula seeking to promote the idea that Western Catholic values and "civilization" had triumphed over "barbarity." But, it did not translate well to the religious
realities of the Adriatic borderland. In southern Alpine districts of the
Habsburg lands, Südmark propaganda included calls for importation of
German Protestants to promote "Germanness" at the expense of the
Catholic Slovenes. In the Adriatic borderlands, religion could not be used

to distinguish between ethnic communities or to promote one ethnic group or agenda over another.[54] Catholicism promoted conservative and traditional social agendas, but it did not separate Italians from Slovenes or Croats. Rather, Catholicism had served historically as a unifying force in the monarchy and a means of differentiating Habsburg peoples from Balkan, Ottoman, or Orthodox populations.

Surnames and the Family

While religion did not separate the various ethnic groups along the Adriatic coasts, traditions related to Western notions of inheritance, honor, and familial devotion as well as expectations for family structure did. Modernization and urbanization had a profound affect on societal life in the eastern Adriatic over the course of the nineteenth century, but vestiges remained of the South Slavic family structure or *zadruga*, the family or clan unit that formed a basis for communal structure in the Ottoman and Habsburg Balkan territories.[55] In the Habsburg era, the *zadruga* had formal legal status in the codes of the Military Border of Austria and Civil Croatia.[56] While these communal *zadruga* arrangements had eroded by the twentieth century and *zadrugas* were uncommon in Slovenia, they remained "the object of passionate discussion on the part of the writers of economic history" in the interwar period. Western scholars observed the *zadruga* with curiosity. Some saw it as the basis for utopian models of familial engagement. Others denounced it as a communist or socialist societal structure, anathema to fascism and the Italian western household-based Roman law family model.

According to the demographer Haskel Sonnabend and like-minded Italians *zadrugas*, a "communistic form of the large family," posed a threat to the western social structure.[57] In the communal unit, headed by an "elected" or group-appointed leader (normally male, but in some cases female), inheritance was not based on the male line but on communal customary agreement, an arrangement that ran counter to Italian and fascist beliefs in the primacy of the father or male head of household. Further challenging to Italian notions of the primacy of the male line and the importance of blood ties was the *zadruga's* reliance on a complicated and varied organizational structure based on complex and intricate biological or adopted kinship relations.[58]

Traditions of the *zadruga* affected the form and transmission of surnames in the Adriatic provinces, a fact that fascist officials had to confront
in their campaign to Italianize surnames in the 1920s and 1930s. Although
Italian officials did not make specific mention of it (nor perhaps completely recognize it), renaming those bearing Slavic surnames actually
had the effect of restructuring the South Slav family to conform to western European and Italian traditions.[59] In many areas of the eastern Adriatic territories, surnames were associated with the vestiges or the memory
of specific clans.[60] Patronymics related to members of the *zadruga* could
represent personal characteristics or be markers of particular relationships (such as wife of or son of) with other members. Family names were
often derived from the given name of a famous ancestor.[61] Surnames also
linked individuals to towns and villages that bore names of the ruling
zadruga or leading family. Writing of the Poljica parish, scholar Ante
Kadić recalled the specificity of names in the small villages along the
Dalmatian coast between Omiš and Split. "All villagers with our family
name lived near our house. There was not a single man with our last
name in any other place . . . When anyone in Poljica, from Dolac down to
Podstrana, uttered our name, he knew that meant the clan which lived in
the middle of Krug, neither at the top nor bottom of the village, but a little
above the church."[62] The restoration of Slavic surnames to an Italian form
dissociated individuals from a family or clan's past and erased markers of
unique local and family ties, kinship networks, and hierarchies.

In the interwar period, Europeans recognized well the association of
Western-style patronymic surnames with the promotion of modern, urban, industrialized civilization and the emphasis on the nuclear family
unit. The Turkish surname law of 1934, a deliberate attempt by reformers
to bring Turkey into line with the western European nation-state model,
was likely based on an international article of 1924 that identified the introduction and standardization of family names as an important component in building "social and national solidarity."[63] Upholding Italian
naming laws and legal precedents remained important to fascist officials,
even those consumed with the nationalization project. While Italianization was desirable, it should not interfere with familial responsibilities and
traditional interpretations of duties and rights under family law.

In granting Enrico Paulovich permission to adopt the name Paolucci in
1928, the Triestine prefect created an anomaly that officials felt compelled

to address when automatic restoration came into effect. In the spring of 1930, members of the same nuclear family bore two different surnames, Paolucci and Paulovich. Fascist preference was to maintain consistency in the family's name in line with preferences inherited from liberal predecessors and laws designed to maintain the integrity and even the sanctity of the family. Inconsistency of surnames among family members was an administrative nightmare for officials seeking to maintain civil records.

Emphasis on consistency and the maintenance of the patronymic was more than a matter of administrative expediency. It served as a means of social policing. No matter what the ethnic sonance of the parental names, petitioners could not adopt a maternal surname in place of a paternal surname. The patrilineal name was a sign of legitimate birth. Officials in Trieste were quite careful to ferret out individuals who attempted to use the name restorations and corrections campaign to subvert Italian laws and paint a façade of legitimacy on illicit relationships or illegitimate births.

Officials routinely refused petitions brought by women trying to use article 2 to acquire the name of a lover or longtime companion noting simply, "The surname is that of her lover." No further official action or comment was necessary. Attempts to acquire fathers' names for illegitimate children were similarly denied. "The name of the child needs to be regularized by marriage or through official recognition. This is an issue for the magistrate, not the prefect," officials responded on such occasions. Illegitimacy did not affect eligibility for nationalization through surname correction or restoration. Officials did not refuse individuals of illegitimate birth who presented themselves to correct a legal surname (generally the mother's maiden name). Guardians could request corrections to bring the surnames of orphans and children under institutional care into conformity with Italian norms.

Even if the stigma of illegitimacy remained very real under the fascists, the regime, in the effort to increase the birthrate and promote Italy's strength "in numbers," moved away somewhat from the liberal government's harsh stance. Italian law prohibited women from adopting or giving their children the name of a lover but, in cases where women sought to take and to give children the surname of a father who had died prior to marriage in the line of duty to fascism, the "father-in-law" or (grandfather to the children) could request permission or support the woman and her children in adopting the Italianized form of the deceased's surname.[64] Such dispensations fulfilled fascist aims by recognizing fascist heroes (or martyrs) and, at the same time, validating and strengthening family units by making their children appear legitimate.

Patrilineal name transmission took precedence over nationalizing aspirations. The fascists encouraged petitioners to request correction of foreign names, but refused permission to those who sought to replace a father's exotic name with a mother's Italian one. A father's foreign name could be corrected, but the mother's Italian name could not be adopted in its place.[65] Officials maintained that the law provided only for the restoration or correction of a surname; it did not allow for its replacement or change.[66] Using the public records at their disposal, documents presented by petitioners, and also any information available in the local police files, local officials assiduously explored the background and status of each individual involved in a surname correction request. They sought to insure that each correction fit the stringent requirements set out in the legislation and guidelines.

Anomalies of Surname Restoration and Correction

Despite local officials' recognition of their nationalist duties and their administrative responsibilities to the state, the surname restoration and correction legislation could not be harmonized with desire to maintain onomastic integrity. The eastern borderland presented particularly thorny problems to officials seeking to evaluate the status of individuals and rename families. According to the census of 1931, the eastern Adriatic provinces of Venezia Giulia and Zara had the highest rate of "irregular families" (those in which one of the members was born out of wedlock or of illegitimate unions) in the country. Likely related to inconsistencies between Austrian laws in force until after World War I and Italian laws, in particular to Italy's failure to recognize religious marriages as civil marriages prior to Mussolini's Concordat with the Catholic Church in 1929, the prevalence of irregular families and differing legal traditions made determinations regarding those eligible for name restoration and correction complicated.[67]

Italianization was consistent with fascist nationalist aims, and officials believed that surname correction aided those wishing to integrate fully into the new Italian society. They assumed that children, even those who had their own families, would follow their fathers' lead. However, they were forced to recognize, by families like the Pauloviches, that family members' attitudes within or across generations were not consistent. In addition, loopholes and inconsistencies in the legislation undermined officials' attempts to maintain consistency. The handbook for Italianization recounted the case of a forty-year-old man estranged from his father and brothers on account of his decision to Italianize his German surname. The lack of harmony in the family was "regrettable, but seemed unavoidable." Officials fulfilled their duty in trying to mediate among family members, but ultimately they were not responsible for the decisions of those involved or the family's failure to choose uniform Italianization.[68]

In Paulovich's case, the father to whom the sons owed allegiance was deceased. The widow's role as the leader of the family may have been uncontested in the private realm, and the sons owed her respect as their mother, but the role of protector and protectee was murky. Fascist officials expected Paulovich's sons to act for her or at least on her behalf. Enrico desired Italianization and altered the name to Paolucci. Ernesto fought to maintain Paulovich. The two sons contested, as equal partners, the bounds of familial allegiance and the meaning of familial loyalty; there was no father to decide which course of action was more appropriate for the family.

The "Privilege" of Italianization

Inconsistency in familial surnames could result from family discord or administrative oversight, or it could be a consequence of an official's refusal to restore or correct the name of an individual deemed unworthy. Pizzagalli and his commission treated Italianization as a privilege to be granted only to worthy citizens. Weeding out undesirable citizens from the garden of the nation, or excluding them from surname correction was an administrative priority. Individuals of "bad moral and political conduct," as certified by the police and determined according to political and legal standards, were denied surname Italianization. Poor conduct was not based in ignorance (which could have been attended to through officials' educational effort) but was a mark of willful and organic lack of fitness at a basic level that precluded inclusion in the national community.

Notions that some were organically unfit reflected nineteenth-century perspectives on criminality and degeneracy pioneered by Cesare Lombroso. His works *Criminal Man* (1876) and the subsequent *Criminal Woman* (1893) written with Guglielmo Ferrero, set the tone for studies of criminology that focused on innate characteristics and genetic predisposition to crime.[69] Fascist officials and particularly social scientists like the linguist Pizzagalli judged petitioners who had been convicted of criminal acts or deemed to be of "bad moral and political conduct" unfit for name restoration or correction. These petitioners routinely found that their requests "could not be fulfilled" even in cases where the surname correction had been granted to parents, brothers, uncles, and unmarried sisters and aunts.[70]

Despite the naming commission and the prefect's insistence on adherence to scientific and legal standards, in the maze of bureaucratic regulation and legal wrangling, individuals and officials saw the process of surname alteration as subject to negotiation. Frequently, individuals seeking corrections under article 2 made requests for specific forms. In many cases, officials rejected their requests on linguistic, nationalist or political grounds. Yet, they often offered other forms. If the individual agreed to one of the proposed forms, the name was duly modified. Where an official offered the petitioner a choice of corrected forms, none of which the supplicant found acceptable, often the Italianization was simply abandoned. The frequency of petitioners' failure to follow suggests that they did not fear punishment or retribution. An official record of the request remained, and suggested that the petitioner had been motivated to seek name correction for personal, rather than strictly patriotic reasons. Nonetheless, if no form of the name could be mutually agreed upon, neither party bore the blame. There were no evident repercussions to allowing a request to languish or simply be filed away without definitive action.

Even annulment of correction decrees could be negotiated without penalties in certain circumstances. In 1933 a man wrote to the authorities asking for permission to revert to the use of his foreign name. On its face, the request seemed risky. If officials were bent on enforcing the surname campaign and requests for nationalization were evidence of support for and loyalty to the regime, then the man's request could signal an improper attitude or lack of loyalty and patriotism. However, his petition was obsequious and made clear his "purely economic" and "practical" motivation. Citing his international licensing and reputation as reasons to revert to the foreign form, he emphasized his fear of appearing to be "an undisciplined citizen," and noted his "preoccupation" for his son who "wished to use the Italian diction" and to grow up under and adhere to the "new directives." In this case, the father reverted to the foreign form, and the son kept the Italianized version.[71]

The businessman's international experience and contacts weighed in his favor. Allowing the man to revert to the old form made economic sense in his individual case, and it was politically savvy on the part of officials to affirm the regime's benevolent intentions in international economic circles. Further, the specific language used in the man's letter likely persuaded officials that he was genuinely committed to Italy. He emphasized discipline in the name of the nation, referred to his responsibilities to his son, and insisted that the younger generation in his household wanted to "adhere to the regime's directives." His plea indicated recognition of his responsibilities at the head of an Italian family and affirmed his desire to be an upstanding fascist citizen.

Families, Loyalty, and Resistance

The fascist regime's recognition of the strength of family ties and reliance on the family and on familial associations was actually a two-edged sword. Family formed a convenient means for fascist intervention in society and an instrument through which the state could act to protect or oversee its citizens. The notion of family as a constitutive part of nation was so ingrained in the Italian national ideal that OVRA and other of the regime's repressive police organizations exploited vulnerabilities related to close family ties and networks of family loyalty. Family associations provided a means to clamp down on opposition or dissent through intimidation or threats aimed at members of elaborate family networks.[72] Antifascist activism often followed familial lines with women associated with antifascism acting in concert with male family members. Due to their political marginalization, women were, at the same time, particularly useful in antifascist networks and particularly vulnerable to political manipulation and violence.[73]

Luigia Paulovich's petition did not appear as an act of resistance against the nationalizing impulses of the fascist regime. The widow's protest launched within the confines of the Italian legal system actually had its roots in objections raised by her son Ernesto and voiced by his employer, the prefect of Sondrio. It appeared merely to challenge the application of a legislative measure. The avenues available to the Paulovich family to voice objections to surname Italianization in the early 1930s demonstrated the fascist government's intent to uphold the state of law and willingness to acknowledge citizens' administrative rights within the framework of the state. While the prefect of Sondrio's argument on behalf of the family did not persuade the Triestine officials to stay the decree, Porro and local authorities in Trieste willingly relied on the legal system to mete out justice. They took seriously their responsibilities to adhere to the law.

The decree issued to the Paulovich family in late June 1930 included both Ernesto and Ines. However, Ernesto no longer lived in Trieste with his mother, and in fact, as Pirretti had pointed out, the son's duties (according to his appointment by the national government) required official residence outside the new territories, in a province whose population was not subject to the legislation. Despite his family's origins in Dalmatia and his long residence in Trieste, Ernesto no longer qualified as a citizen of the borderland. This argument that his inclusion on the decree was inappropriate on the basis of his legal residence in Sondrio prevailed. On January 15, 1931, officials in Trieste voided the June 26, 1930, restoration decree and issued another, assigning the name Paoli only to Luigia Barbarovich Paulovich and Ines.

If officials in the Triestine prefect's office thought about Luigia's Paulovich's complaint beyond the necessity to deal with it administratively, they likely attributed her reluctance to accept Paoli to a failure in her political education, to her innate weaknesses as a woman, or to her confusion as a widow robbed of the counsel of her husband. Her case required the regime's firm but gentle guiding hand, not the harsh fist of punishment or oppression.

Had Paulovich family members accepted the prefect's execution of the surname measure, after January 1931 three different surnames would have divided Luigia's nuclear family. The widow and her daughter were given the name Paoli. Enrico was Paolucci. Ernesto alone (ironically the only family member to have left the eastern borderland) would have continued to bear the name Paulovich. This inconsistency alone might have given Luigia Paulovich pause. Her belief in her family, her memory of her deceased husband, and her desire to venerate Antonio Paulovich's name and family encouraged her to pursue appeal. The decree issued on January 15, 1931, to Luigia and Ines that further divided the family in onomastic terms offended Paulovich's sense of justice. It set the widow on the road to Rome.

5   A Citizen Seeking Justice

On April 6, 1931, three months after the prefect of Trieste issued the revised surname restoration decree, Luigia Paulovich filed her petition for its annulment.[1] Her protest against the name restoration pertaining to her and her daughter Ines was a complaint regarding the prefect's treatment of the Paulovich family, a questioning of government officials' actions with regard to a citizen of the state. Despite the fascist state's authoritarian tendencies, the complaint did not offend authorities. As Piero Calamandrei, Italian jurist and professor of law in Italian civil procedure at the University of Florence from 1924 to 1956, explained:

> Sometimes litigiousness is a sign of morbid anti-social instincts. At other times it is the result of a holy desire to protect society against malefactors and is evidence of an abundant faith in the administration of justice.
>
> To litigate may mean . . . to have faith in the effectiveness of the State.[2]

Calamandrei went on to suggest that "the State finds its highest expression in protecting rights, and therefore should be grateful to the citizen who, in demanding justice, gives it the opportunity to defend justice, which is the basic *raison d'être* of the State."[3] The prefect of Trieste may not have been "grateful" for the opportunity to defend the justice of the Pauloviches' surname restoration decree, but he respected the family's right to pursue redress. Luigia Paulovich did not exhibit "morbid antisocial instincts." She had faith in the Italian state and Italian justice.

Paulovich's first appeal to the prefect's office had resulted in a modification that removed her son Ernesto's name from the restoration decree. Subsequent pleas to vacate the decree for all members of the immediate family failed to move the prefect to further action. By 1931 the prefect of Trieste had overseen the processing of thousands of name restorations. The vast majority had accepted Italianized name forms without comment. The Paulovich's decision to pursue an appeal meant swimming against the tide. The widow and her daughter found the prefect unyielding in the decision to Italianize their surname. Bent on pursuing her case,

Paulovich consulted her notary in Trieste who turned the matter over to special solicitor Giulio Morpurgo to be filed in Rome. The Council of State stepped in as the appellate court to adjudicate the controversy between a citizen and representatives of the government. The case fell within the purview of Section Four of the Administrative Court, the branch that dealt with cases involving state administrations.[4]

The Legal Process and Administrative Justice

Section Four of Administrative Court of the Council of State adjudicated the dispute as an administrative disagreement between Paulovich and the prefect of Trieste that centered on questions of jurisdiction and procedure. Paulovich's was not the first appeal relating to surname restorations. The Administrative Court had considered the first case relating to the surname restoration measure, an appeal from a petitioner named Nicolich, in early 1931. The Paulovich case in December 1931 was the second. In the entire period from 1931 to 1935, only eleven appeals were brought.[5] Fascist officials insisted that the population's quiescence proved that Italianization was a spontaneous and largely voluntary process that was a considerable success.

Many thousands in Trieste had their names restored to an Italian form by 1931, but, according to the state's attorney Petrilli, only four had sought recourse through article 3 of the legislation before Paulovich's solicitor filed her petition. The number *four* was certainly misleading. It likely referred to the four individuals involved in the Nicolich family's case adjudicated by the Administrative Court in the spring of 1931 and implied that all others had approved or even welcomed name restorations. To further undermine Paulovich, Petrilli added that no other families whose name was restored to Paoli had complained.

The rarity of challenges to the surname measure, however, could not be ascribed to the population's acceptance or acquiescence. Article 3 of the Ministerial Decree of August 5, 1926, placed few restrictions on individuals' rights to appeal, but those affected faced very real impediments and deterrents to lodging complaints regarding objectionable or uncomfortable restorations or corrections. Economic, political, or cultural circumstances rendered many unable or unwilling to protest. Those whose political past was checkered, who were already under suspicion for disloyalty, or who felt the sting of Italian subjugation or oppression in the borderland were unlikely to call attention to themselves or their politics by voluntarily petitioning a fascist court, even if cases related to surname restoration were treated as administrative and not criminal matters. Paulovich had no cause to fear political censure as she could easily prove her family's devotion to cultural Italianness and willingness to fight and sacrifice for the Italian cause. She had both the political capital and economic means to engage a lawyer and pursue the case. The involvement of her solicitor Giulio Morpurgo proved decisive in her ability to move forward and oppose the will of the prefect.

Giulio Morpurgo's willingness to take Paulovich's case and prepare the appeal did not suggest sympathy for political complaint or protest. Appeal through the prescribed channels of the Ministry of the Interior and on to the Administrative Court was standard procedure in both liberal and fascist Italy. Even after the reform of 1934 (enacted more than two years after the decision in the Paulovich case) granted the prefect extensive emergency powers, the Ministry of Interior and the Administrative Court remained valid avenues for appeal.[6]

Italian Lawyers and Fascism

Morpurgo's work on Paulovich's appeal was consistent with lawyers' traditional role as *mediators* who maintained the balance of interests between the government and society.[7] It conformed to their role as trustees responsible for applying their legal knowledge to negotiate the bounds of political power.[8] Waxing poetic about his chosen profession in a fascist panegyric to lawyers, Luigi Gianturco explained, "If it is true that the laws are *the word of honor of a nation* we have the honor to be its custodians and defenders."[9] Legal theorists suggested that the State functioned as "the supreme organ for the political, juridical, and social protection of the universal interests" in the society under its sovereignty.[10] From this perspective, Morpurgo sought, in the name of all Italians, to protect the Paulovich family's interests from illegal encroachments by the state.

Lawyers in Italy participated actively in government. Since the unification of the modern Italian state, law had offered a road to politics. Led by the politician Camillo Cavour, lawyers served as architects of the state, planning administrative frameworks and constructing the bases for

government institutions. In the liberal period, they were the chief proponents of the governmental system and played a predominant role in
government offices and parliament.[11]

Mussolini called on lawyers to take an active role in the fascist revolution and, by referring to them as "Collaborators in Justice, social forces,
pillars of the Regime," sought their support in upholding the state.[12] Many
lawyers counted among the early supporters of fascism and, in the elections of 1921, of the 81 fascist candidates standing for election, 16 were
lawyers. All of the 16 were elected to the legislature that included 245
lawyers, who made up more than 42 percent of the total delegates.[13] Lawyers also dominated the leadership ranks of the state's civil service. Of the
103 prefects drawn from party ranks during the fascist *ventennio*, all but 36
had degrees in law.[14] Fascism's promise to rectify the crisis of professionals and its use of nationalist agendas to elevate professionals above the
masses proved attractive to many.[15] Particularly susceptible to fascism's
siren call were young lawyers looking to fascism to secure their futures.

Among the young lawyers elected in 1921 was Francesco Giunta, a
Siena-born fascist hard-liner who served as deputy for Paulovich's home
city of Trieste from 1921 to 1939. Giunta's fascism was particularly aggressive and extreme. After the Italian government put an end to D'Annunzio's
adventure in Fiume, Giunta led an attack on the Free State of Fiume in
March 1922 that forced Riccardo Zanella's autonomist government to flee.
At the head of the *squadristi* in Trieste during Mussolini's March on Rome
in October 1922, he went on to serve in a variety of national posts, including a stint as vice president of the Chamber of Deputies during which he
played an instrumental role by defending the new fascist government's
actions in the face of Giacomo Matteotti's accusations that the fascists
acted illegally.[16]

Giunta's extremism was far from the norm, but adherence to the fascist
government did not present a particular moral or ethical dilemma for
most Italian lawyers. Jurists were caught between impulses to maintain
and protect the traditional rights of Italian individuals as citizens and
propensities to uphold the law as it was being defined and redefined by
the fascist state, but generally they adhered to principles inherited from the
liberal government under which they had been schooled and trained.
They remained attached to the concepts of the legal state and to the importance of upholding the law of the state (be it fascist or liberal) against

abuse.[17] This commitment to upholding the law allowed for flexibility, but also resulted in myopia with respect to the particulars of fascist politics and policies.

By the time Paulovich's case came before the Administrative Court, after the syndication of the legal profession, the establishment of the Special Tribunal, and the legal reforms of 1928, most lawyers were Fascist Party members. However, in the first decade of fascist rule, fascistization of legal professionals had progressed slowly. Many were aware of the rather heavy-handed, if not lawless, tactics that Mussolini had employed to bring fascism to power. They were not oblivious to the climate of intimidation and threat particularly in the early years after the March on Rome that had allowed Mussolini to maintain and strengthen his hold on the state. Many listed in the lawyers' professional rolls had simply ignored the first calls to join the fascist syndicate.[18] Most eventually succumbed as a pragmatic choice. Lawyers' ability to practice their profession relied on government licensing. Ideologically, they were able or convinced to support the regime and overlook fascism's "shortcomings."[19] Their path was common to many intellectuals. For example, Giuseppe Prezzolini, a leading intellectual, conservative nationalist and propagandist prior to and during World War I, overcame his initial skepticism of fascism to become one of Mussolini's leading proponents abroad from his post at the Casa Italiana at Columbia University in New York. In 1926 he declared, "fascism is all for hierarchy, tradition, and respect for the law."[20]

Prezzolini's attitude mirrored that of Alfredo Rocco, who even as he oversaw the fascist reform of government, clung to conservative and traditional liberal elements and incorporated them into the new administrative system. Rocco recognized the dilemmas of those engaged in the legal profession. The "mass of practicing jurists preoccupied by the necessity of their office to study the law *as it is* have been won over by the changes in legislation," Rocco observed. "But," he suggested, "theories have not had the power to remake their culture." Adherence to the fundamental principles learned "at their school benches" remained a part of lawyers' ideological make-up.[21]

Reinforcing authoritarian tendencies of the fascist state, Rocco abrogated the power of parliament. He maintained that the "general reform of the State did not alter the characteristic institutions of administrative justice." Instead, it gave those institutions "new authority and vigor in the

Fascist State" which, "as it aims at being strong," still remains "within the law, that is to say, a legal State."[22] Rocco also retained the structures of royal power. As he claimed, "Ministers must enjoy the confidence of the King." Adherence to the concept of royal power provided Mussolini a legitimate avenue through which to exercise his authoritarian will. Although authoritarianism characterized Mussolini's regime for most of the *ventennio*, the legal retention of royal power ultimately proved fascism's demise. Royal prerogative provided the legal means for Mussolini's removal and the fascist government's downfall in 1943, eight years after Rocco's death.

Magistrates of the Council of State maintained the responsibility to oversee adherence to administrative law, of particular importance to the Paulovich case. Administrative law was one of the two major branches of legal study in Italy dating from the modern state's inception. In 1861, of nine university professorships in law, six were in constitutional law and three in administrative law. Over the course of the liberal period, as the bureaucracy grew and the legal system matured, administrative law overtook constitutional law as the leading specialization in university training, and a third area of study in public law emerged. By the fascist takeover in 1922, law faculties in Italy boasted four professorships in public law, fifteen in administrative law, and thirteen in constitutional law. Fascism significantly increased the concentration in public law at the expense of constitutional specialization. As a result of fascism's emphasis on lawyers' involvement in the public practice of law and the functioning of the legal system rather than in debates of the philosophical bases and interpretations of the law, only four posts in constitutional law remained 1932. One had been added in administrative law for a total of sixteen, and public law had grown substantially to fifteen posts, of which seven were devoted to corporative law introduced in accordance with the fascist syndicalist reforms.[23] Increased attention to administrative law and administrative science was characteristic of interwar efforts at legal reform and administrative transformation in conservative, authoritarian regimes. One of the first areas to which the Nazis turned their attentions in 1933 was the revision of legal curricula to increase emphasis on administrative law.[24]

Throughout the *ventennio*, lawyers and magistrates saw themselves as engaged in protecting individuals' civil liberties. But, upholding the legal state was synonymous, at least for most of the interwar period, with upholding the laws of the fascist state. In this respect, even magistrates serving in the infamous Special Tribunal remained committed legal professionals upholding the legitimate laws of the state. Their support for fascism or at least their ambition to rise within the fascist system was evident in their willingness to accept their posts, but their investigations, deliberations, consultations and recommendations made outside of the famed Hall IV (where sentencing was carried out) revealed a commitment to legal procedures, legal language, and even to judicial independence.[25] Dismissal of the government's case against Fiumian writer and journalist Leo Weiczen (Leo Valiani) known for his antifascist, leftist leanings and charged with possession of an antifascist newspaper illustrated the magistrates' adherence to the letter of the law. In 1928 Weiczen invoked his legal status as a stateless person (in the wake of the Austro-Hungarian collapse) and as a member of the Hungarian Socialist Party (not the Italian Socialist Party which was officially dissolved) to win the dismissal of his case. The justices agreed with his assertions that he had not participated in a banned organization, as the Hungarian party was not banned, nor had he acted as a disloyal citizen, as he was not an Italian citizen.[26]

Well into the 1930s, the cases of a significant number of those arrested by security forces and referred to the Special Tribunal never made it to trial. On investigation and examination, the court ordered the release of the accused for lack of evidence. Lucia Minon, the Triestine wife of an exiled anarchist, was freed. A cache of communist leaflets found in a search of her home in 1927 precipitated her arrest and referral to the Special Tribunal. After several months in jail, the court absolved her of wrongdoing for lack of evidence. In 1934 the Special Tribunal dismissed a case against Natalia Beltrame, a housewife from Udine, arraigned with a group of sixteen others for anti-Italian propaganda and criminal participation and association.[27] The arrest and jailing of suspects followed by dismissal of their cases was certainly a deliberate tactic of intimidation. Arrest and imprisonment could be a strong deterrent to those considering opposition to the regime. However, policing authorities, not justices, were responsible for arrests. The court's judicial officers carefully followed prescribed legal processes to maintain the legality of the proceedings.

The primary function of the Administrative Court of the Council of State was to protect against arbitrary state actions. President of the Council of State Santi Romano explained the court's role to act on behalf of "the public interest and legitimate private interests with very cautious juridical elaboration." The court's responsibility was to "encourage the maintenance of the respective boundaries of executive and judicial power."[28] It functioned as both an investigatory and an adjudicating body. Operating under the "inquisitional principle," the court was bound to take "positive action;" it had the right and duty to investigate cases and to seek out evidence to use in its deliberations.[29] As jurist Nino Pappalardo explained, the administrative justice's role was like that of "a good medical specialist" who has "constructed his armament of instruments, his whole system of rules of practice, which help him to formulate a diagnosis." The court's work required "a profound juridical sense and agile mentality" exercised by "practical men of the administration" whose job was essentially to examine a dispute and should a problem be uncovered, to diagnose it and suggest an avenue for rectifying it.[30]

Officials of the court in Rome began their investigations of the Paulovich case in May 1931 with a request for documents relating to the restoration of Luigia Paulovich's name. The prefect of Trieste responded on May 12 forwarding a copy of Luigia Barbarovich's birth certificate, a copy of the list of surnames subject to restoration in the province, and other information relevant to the decree. Attached was a note assuring Rome, "Nothing special has been done in making the restoration of the surname Paulovich to Paoli."[31] The name appeared on the list, and the prefect restored it according to the commission's recommendations. Prefect Porro believed that his office had acted in good faith—carrying out its general responsibilities within the purview of his duties. Morpurgo charged that Triestine officials had used excessive force, and had violated and falsely applied the law.[32]

In addressing the court, both Morpurgo and Deputy Attorney General Raffaele Pio Petrilli, a councilor of Pugliese origin representing the government's interests and the prefect of Trieste, employed tactics to appeal to the emotions of the magistrates. Such antics seemed designed to invoke the courtroom drama ordinarily reserved for public trials. They were wasted on the justices of the Administrative Court in fascist Italy. Morpurgo and Petrilli faced no jury nor were the proceedings public. They faced judges of the Council of State, members of the professional club, as typical professional legal elites committed to weighing arguments on their legal merits. At the same time, they addressed the magistrates as men of their time, influenced by the social, cultural, and political opinions typical of professional legal elites of the interwar period.[33]

Had the Paulovich case been subject to public trial, criticisms of the government would have been more difficult to launch and to debate. Under fascism, public court proceedings were carefully choreographed and scripted for the consumption of the press and the masses. In the Court of Assizes (the high court responsible for hearing criminal cases), Paulovich and her lawyer would have faced a panel including laymen (assessors) nominated by communal mayors (by then appointed officials) on the basis of their social, political, educational, and moral standing. The juridical reform of March 1931 required these laymen to pass through several layers of fascist bureaucracy to be appointed to their positions by the minister of justice.[34] Appointees to the Court of Assizes would have been less sanguine in the face of criticism of the local fascist authorities than were administrative judges, who were generally career civil servants who had risen through the ranks.

Questions of Legal Process and Applicability

In a brief submitted to the court in April 1931 asking for annulment of the name restoration, Morpurgo attacked the Paulovich's surname restoration decree on legal, moral, political, and national grounds. He intentionally adopted an irreverent tone casting civil servants in Trieste as incompetents serving in the peripheries. His tactic was to undermine the Triestines' authority, to present them as unthinking bureaucrats too engaged in overzealous and blind execution of their duties to recognize the limits of their authority and the illogic of their methods in applying the surname law. First, he pointed to several irregularities or technical violations that justified declaring the decree void on basic legal grounds. Morpurgo questioned the surname law's premise, contending that surnames were legally inviolable, an assertion consistent with legal precedent and practice in most European states. Pizzagalli's handbook had admitted "the principle of immutability of the surname is incontrovertible," but had emphasized the fascist contention that restorations and corrections were exceptional as they remedied earlier illegal changes.[35]

Morpurgo also challenged the name restoration on the basis of naming laws related to marriage and death. On her marriage to Antonio Paulovich, Luigia Barbarovich had assumed the surname Paulovich. When the marriage dissolved with Antonio's death, the law required that she resume the surname of her birth in all legal capacities. Therefore, for the decree to be valid, it would have had to rename her Luigia Barbarovich "the widow Paoli," not simply Paoli. Failure to insert the title *widow* effectively changed the name of a dead man, an action contrary to the law and one that violated not only legal principles but those of Italian and Catholic society. Petrilli countered that the law allowed reversion to a maiden name at the death of a husband, but did not require it.[36]

Finally, in a recital of officials' failure to pay attention to the technicalities of application of the legislation, Morpurgo argued that the woman named on the decree, "Signora Luigia Barbarovich widow Paulovich born on May 14, 1854, did not exist." The woman in question was born on June 26, 1856, he claimed. Therefore the decree could not stand because the widow was improperly identified. Petrilli easily countered this attack pointing out that the registry official in Brazza had furnished the date, and even if erroneous, it had been cited in many official documents issued to the petitioner over the years and had never before been the cause for question or complaint.[37]

In addition to the technical mistakes in referring to the widow and her birthdate, Morpurgo argued that the prefect's process violated the law and questioned the legislation's applicability to the Pauloviches' situation. The legislation of 1926 was limited in its purpose to "repair works of Austrian political agents if they were made as part of the process of denationalization of the unredeemed provinces." It only covered names affected by "overt or covert" attempts by Habsburg agents "to assure the predominance in the monarchy of their nationalities only: German, Slav, and Hungarian." The measure did not permit wholesale or blind nationalization. Morpurgo contended that the prefect could not prove that the surname Paulovich had a Latin or Italian root. No evidence suggested that the family's name was translated, "deformed" in spelling or altered by the addition of a foreign suffix.

Petrilli's countered that officials could not possibly process such information for each decree being issued. Requiring the prefect to offer specific proof for each case compromised officials' ability to carry out the surname nationalizing campaign and violated the spirit of the legislation. Petrilli defended the prefect's decree, pointing out that the committee of experts including glottologists had examined the surname and its spelling and had decided it was "indubitably" derived from a Latin form. They ascertained that it had taken on a Slavic form during the period of Slavic domination and included it on the restoration list as directed in the government's guidelines.[38]

According to Morpurgo, the contention that Paulovich derived from Paoli "lacked proof" and "defied logic." Using documents provided by the family, the widow's lawyer traced the family's use of the surname back several generations. Records from Dalmatia and the city of Zara proved that the Slavic forms of Paulovich and Paulovič predated the period of Habsburg control. A marriage license from one of Antonio Paulovich's ancestors dated the name to 1798. Since the groom would have reached the age of majority by the time the certificate was filed, the family had clearly been known by the Slavic form in Zara, even when the city was part of Venice's dominions between 1748 and 1797. "It is absurd to suggest that an Italian family of Dalmatian origin would give itself the Slavic form Paulovich under Venetian domination," Morpurgo contended. "An Italian name would lend a sense of nobility in contrast to the Slavic name. The thing to do would have been to Italianize the name, especially in Zara with its predominant Italian element."[39]

In light of Italy's conflicts with the South Slav Kingdom over Dalmatia and particularly over coastal lands claimed as Croat, dealings with petitioners of Dalmatian origins posed particular problems for fascist administrators in the interwar period. Deep-seated prejudices favored the history of Rome and the Venetian Republic over that of the medieval Croat and Balkan states in the territories along the eastern shore of the Adriatic Sea. Travelers and scholars had studied Dalmatian coastal settlements as part of Italian and Roman settlement at least since the Enlightenment, linking the cities of Fiume, Pola, Zara, Spalato, Trieste and others to ancient Rome and Italy.[40] Morpurgo reiterated familiar tropes when he explained the preeminence of the Italian element by suggesting that Zara, conquered in 1200 by Venice, had been called the "rock of Italianness of Dalmatia." The island was Italian "not only by culture, by civilization and by richness, but also politically, because Italian was dominant in Venice, while Slavs or foreigners were in an inferior and subjugated position."[41] Morpurgo's argument was consistent with the façade of inherent and long-standing Italianness that the fascists sought to maintain. The importance of asserting Zara as an Italian stronghold even led to focus on the city as an Italian cultural site in the Treaty of Conciliation of the Lateran Pacts between Mussolini and the Papacy. The Dalmatian capital was the only city specifically named in the 1929 treaty, as it became the seat for a new diocese to bring diocese boundaries into conformity with Italy's state boundaries.[42]

Despite fascist posturing, the history of non-Italian presence and control in the eastern Adriatic territories was obvious and lay at the heart of the surname measures and other nationalizing legislation. In the interwar period, the fascists continued to fight for control over Dalmatia, and the coastlands of the eastern Adriatic continued to be a target of irredentist efforts.[43] A cartoon in the Milanese satirical weekly *Guerin meschino*, interpreting the contest for its readers in the wake of anti-Italian demonstrations in Dalmatia in 1928, depicted an aggressive Venetian winged lion pulling along the papacy in its wake to assist its cubs against an equally aggressive Yugoslav winged pig. The lion calling for peace and the pig promoting war, each bore its message in Latin script.[44] Some sectors acknowledged Dalmatia's foreignness and used this as an excuse for Italian expansion or imperial control of the region. Italian nationalists like Attilio Tamaro balked at the 1929 fascist *Encyclopedia*'s recognition of Zara as a "principal focus of Slavic rebellion." The compendium of fascist thought had placed all of Dalmatia in the Balkan region.[45]

The tug of war over Dalmatia, while irksome with respect to Italy's foreign policy, had a more profound and immediate impact on borderland populations and on local interpretations of the intent of the surname legislation in the frontier zone. Claims for the spiritual, linguistic, and literary Italianness of Dalmatia were rooted in the voices of nineteenth-century writers. One of the most prominently cited in Trieste was Niccolò Tommaseo, a linguist and writer born in Sebenico who after studying in Spalato made his way to Padua to study law. From there his political activities led him into exile in Paris and Corfu. The fascists remembered him for his studies of the Italian language and contributions to promoting the Italian Adriatic. They attributed his "fanatic" attention to the details of the Italian language and devotion to the minutiae of grammar to his origins and obsession with the "contested" borderland, an obsession characteristic of those who felt the need to defend Italianness and were hyper-aware of language and its implications.[46] Although Tommaseo had devoted his life to support for Illyrian or Adriatic ideas of multinationalism or localism, nationalists and fascists in the interwar period appropriated his nineteenth-century observations to support Italy's continuing interest in and claims to Dalmatia.[47] In 1931 *La Porta Orientale* cited Tommaseo's support for the rights of Italian minorities in Yugoslav lands.

> Since when has the number determined the right? The enumeration of numbers enters only into the field of arithmetic, . . . The enumeration is an argument that one makes with one's fingers, and not with one's head and heart. History negates this arithmetic and humanity rejects it.[48]

Arguing on behalf of the Paulovich family, Morpurgo made use of this spiritual connection arguing that it arose from an impromptu and organic attraction to superior culture. He suggested that at its medieval height and even under Venice, Dalmatia remained "in great part Slav," despite the fact that numerous families like the Pauloviches became Italian in heart and mind and were loyal to Venice. For centuries, they had maintained their surnames without ever thinking that they could be offensive or indicate a lack of devotion to the "dominating spirit of Italy." Echoing Pirretti's assertion, Morpurgo claimed that to the practiced eye the Slavic-sounding surname held a hint of centuries of devotion to Italianness in its *-ich* (as opposed to *ič*) suffix, the final *h* being cited once again as a mark of loyalty granted by the Venetian Republic to differentiate local supporters from unfaithful or unreliable Slavs.[49]

Simultaneous claims that Dalmatian lands were and always had been Italian and that Italian minorities living among the preponderance of ethnic Croats required protection and cried out for Italy's civilizing influence posed a conundrum for Deputy Attorney General Petrilli. As it was his responsibility to defend the prefect's actions, Petrilli skirted the issue of recent control and simply traced his argument for the derivation of Paulovich back to the settlement of the area and the fall of ancient Rome. From a historical standpoint, he claimed, Dalmatia was "originally Italian" or populated by Latin speaking people, an argument that coincided with nationalist historians' expert opinions that emphasized the Roman and

Latin history and the subversion or transformation of Latin culture and names over time.[50]

Petrilli repeated Italian nationalist and government officials' oft-made charges of the Slavic clergy's "long tradition of hostility to Latindom." He claimed, "The majority of Slavic clerics have clung to this tradition throughout the successive centuries dispensing with the Latin idiom of the Church in each religious function and Slavicizing the Latin names of the faithful as well." After 1866 Habsburg Austria had "adopted a politics of denationalization—sometimes soft, sometimes violent—to the detriment of the Italians so that by 1914 not a single city rested in the hands of the Italians."[51] The nineteenth-century renaming of places in Istria was well documented. The Istrian Provincial Council had directed protests related to the Slavicization of toponyms to the Habsburg authorities in 1887, 1888, 1897 and 1899.[52] To Italy's chagrin, the Slavicization to the detriment of Latin influences and Rome had continued up to the present, Petrilli claimed. "Last year Yugoslavia erected a monument in the peristyle of Diocletian's Palace in Split to a priest of the tenth century whose sole merit was his opposition to the Papal Bull that prescribed the use of the Latin language in religious functions." He towed the official Italian nationalist and irredentist line touted since the late nineteenth-century, justifying the heavy-handed fascist surname Italianization as reasonable retribution. "All names deformed in Dalmatia by the addition of Slavic suffixes are subject automatically to the legislation as they have been altered under the influence of the Slavic and Slavicizing clerics," he reasoned.[53]

Petrilli tied the surname campaign to broader nationalization policies pursued in the borderland, particularly to restoration of the names of localities in Istria and other parts of the eastern borderlands that was part of administrative absorption, standardization, and rectification in the early years after the fascist takeover. The surname legislation had to be viewed in the broader political light of policies designed to promote geographical unity and to reconcile the history and politics of the borderlands with the rest of Italy. Measures for onomastic unification that contributed to ethno-linguistic unity were understood well in Gentilian educative terms. Striking a note of community responsibility to promote national character, Petrilli reminded the Court and the Pauloviches, "Foreign onomastics are not a negligible factor in Istria . . . they serve Italy's enemies abroad in their arguments that place in doubt the Italian character of our provinces."[54] Obliquely calling into question the Pauloviches' loyalty he noted, "All good Italians must consider the restitution of Slavic surnames to the Italian tongue a dutiful gift from the Patria."[55]

Morpurgo admitted that after Italian Unification and the inclusion of Venice and the Veneto in the Risorgimento state, nationalist politics conceived in terms of ethnic rights gained momentum and Slavicization occurred. Luigia and Antonio's marriage certificate of 1883 and Ines's birth certificate of 1885 attested to the Slavicization from Paulovich to Paulovič. Ines's birth certificate with the replacement of the final *ich* with *ič* demonstrated only what was "common knowledge." Clerics had transformed names on public documents in Dalmatia in the latter half of the nineteenth century. Prior to 1866, Austrian politics were not hostile to Italian elements. Italian Habsburg subjects in Dalmatia held the same status as Italian Habsburg subjects in Venice. He underlined that the "reduction" of the name to the "primitive" *ič* form was the only alteration the surname underwent at the hands of Habsburg officials. Paulovich had never been Paoli.

What Morpurgo did not mention, and perhaps did not know, was that fascist civil servants working on the surname campaign were equally guilty of creative respellings to facilitate name alterations that Italianized the population. In 1929 two sisters who listed their surname as Saitz petitioned for a correction to Sarti. The official in Trieste noted their official surname as Zaic and suggested a correction to Sai or Sassi, on the grounds that Sarti was linguistically "too far from Zaic." The sisters balked at the correction from Zaic, insisting that their birth certificates and school records listed the name Saitz, a name German in origin as they were from Wiener-Neustadt, and that the priest in Roiano had imposed the form Zaic on the family when they moved to Trieste. In essence, the sisters charged that officials executing the surname campaign had selectively chosen to transform the Slavic rather than the "original" German form, and in the process had mistaken the new Italian form. After some negotiation, the officials and the sisters settled on the new form Satti. It was clear that the fascist official had attempted to "shortcut" the process to transform a Slavic form that fit more readily into the prescribed correction schema.[56]

While Morpurgo might not have known of the specifics of civil servants' machinations in processing name corrections and restorations, he certainly recognized the malleability of conceptions of state, national belonging, and ethnic association. Arguing the Paulovich case, Morpurgo cited the difficulties in applying modern standards to historical phenomena and raised questions regarding the applicability of the modern state's conceptions and understanding of ethnicity and nationalism. Considering Venetian citizenship, loyalty, and ethnicity by contemporary interwar standards was anachronistic, he suggested. "Venice represented an Italian overseer [or ruler] but political belonging was not and could not be that which today one calls the Italian national conscience."[57]

Yet, he was suspiciously silent when recognition of malleability might weaken his argument. Given his attention to detail and alacrity to use the documents to prove the family's long-standing Italianness despite the Slavic sonance of their surname, it seems unlikely that he would have missed the fact that on the 1798 marriage certificate submitted to prove the surname's form in the Venetian period, the groom's name was listed as Paulovič while his father's was listed as Paulovich.[58] The change in spelling may have been a deliberate Slavicization in 1798. But, if that were the case, the recording official would logically have substituted Paulovič for both, entirely erasing Paulovich from the written record and covering the act of malfeasance. The more likely scenario, although it did not fit the lawyer's narrative or the family's contentions in the 1930s, was that the spelling change from Paulovich to Paulovič was made with the knowledge or even at the behest of the son, an indication of his acceptance of the political climate as the influence of the Venetian Republic waned of the end of the eighteenth century. It was also a testament to the malleability of names in the area and the ambiguity of identities and ethnic associations in the Upper Adriatic regions.

The Pauloviches' *Italianità*

Morpurgo carefully set out to prove that the Pauloviches, regardless of their Slavic sounding name, were "good Italians." He suggested that Luigia Paulovich's insistence on maintaining her husband's surname in its original form honored the sacrifices she, her husband, and her children had made and the hardships they had endured for their devotion to Italy. The family's Slavic surname, used for centuries "in its same phonetic and spelling form," actually preserved the integrity of the family by recalling members' patriotism and historic spirit of Italianness. This assertion that a name of Slavic sonance honored a family's Italian traditions turned Gentile's ideas of Roman heritage and Italian education at the core of Italian nationhood on their heads.[59] It called for reorientation of views of Italian spirit, locating sacrifice for the nation outside the trappings of Latin nationalism for which Gentile had been so keen.

Morpurgo pointed out that Paulovich and her family, had "taken an active part in battle for the Italianness of the redeemed territories," in Zara and Trieste. Antonio Paulovich was a life-long supporter of Luigi Ziliotto, a leader in Zara who fought against Austria "for the defense of Italianness." In Trieste, Paulovich's sons were committed irredentists. The Austrian authorities jailed Enrico for "singing hymns to the immaculate Victory of the Italian troops after Caporetto." Ernesto was an organizer of the secret society XX Dicembre (December 20) in memory of the Guglielmo Oberdan and a leader in other youth organizations including Giovane Trieste (Young Trieste) and the student society Concordia Vittoria. Purportedly on the instigation of his mother, Ernesto had deserted the Austrian forces to volunteer in the Italian army, joining some 2,000 Giulian and Dalmatian men who fought with the Italian forces and became heroes of the Italian nation.[60] Luigia Paulovich supported and encouraged her family's aggressive pro-Italian stance and suffered "persecution and outrages" at the hands of the Austrian police, according to Morpurgo's account. Her political conduct was above reproach, and her loyalty to Italy was genuine. Her motives for seeking to maintain the name Paulovich in commemoration of the family's indissoluble link with Italy should not be questioned. Ernesto's record of service to the Italian government continued into the interwar period, and by 1930 he held the civil service post in the prefect's office in Sondrio. His history of service certainly placed him in the ranks of loyal Italian citizens respected by the fascists.

Petrilli sought to demonstrate that the Paulovich family was less loyal than appearances suggested. His tone echoed the sarcasm of the prefect of Trieste who found it "strange that a family of Italian sentiments, seeing their surname of Slavic form transformed to an Italian form that no one can prove was not its original form, would not feel pride but instead regret." He attacked the idea that the family's attachment to the name made its correction an affront to their patriotic sentiment and sought to portray the prefect of Trieste as eminently reasonable in the face of a family determined to be noisome. Referring to Enrico Paulovich's successful petition to correct Paulovich to Paolucci, he argued that Italian law required all members of a family to maintain the same surname. The prefect had no difficulty granting the entire family the corrected form Paolucci and had even offered to do so.

Deflecting attention from the legal nature of the dispute to focus on sentimental issues, Petrilli suggested further that the family's protest seemed to demonstrate a lack of respect for fascist laws. "It remains, at any rate, a bit strange that the people who filed the petition claim to nourish strong and profound attachments to Italy and allege these sentiments as essential justification for their protest." This seems to imply, he quipped, that "only those who do not nourish Italian sentiments are bound to uphold and obey the fascist law."[61] Petrilli's comments resonated with the authoritarian view and reflected the attitude of the Fascist Party. Those whose names appeared on the list should feel themselves honored by the recognition of Italianness. Those who were not so "fortunate" could seek corrections given the Duce's well-known interest in the "onomastic harmony" of the new territories. Should they balk, they could not be forced, but "counseled," "persuaded," or "convinced" by party agents. Under the new legal system, the Fascist Party's duty included disseminating propaganda to "educate the Italian people politically and socially." The party acted as a kind of "civil militia" prompting the population to cooperate in the initiatives of the state.[62] This included the promotion of adherence to cultural legislation.

Nationalism and Fascism in the Borderland

The party-line view articulated by Petrilli failed to recognize the possibility that associations with *italianità* and support for Italian nationalism were not necessarily coincident with support for fascism. Morpurgo argued forcefully that the Paulovich family supported the nationalist aims of fascist Italy, but said very little about their support for fascism. Arguably, Antonio Paulovich's death before the rise of fascism left no possibility to establish support for Mussolini and fascism. However, mentions of Luigia

Paulovich's sons' Italian nationalist achievements do little more than nod in the direction of participation in fascist organizations or party functions. Despite her sons' adolescence and adulthoods in Trieste, with its active squads and ardent supporters of fascism, there is no reference to their direct participation in fascist politics.

While both Enrico and Ernesto were members of the Fascist Party and Ernesto was working for the government in Sondrio, their actions were directed more to irredentist and Italian nationalist causes in the Adriatic provinces than toward support for fascism *per se*. Enrico's request to correct his surname to the form Paolucci reflected clearly, although perhaps discretely, an adherence to the Adriatic irredentism and Italian nationalism of World War I. The choice in 1928 certainly brought to mind the exploits barely a decade earlier of Lieutenant Raffaele Paolucci. The naval surgeon from Abruzzi, celebrated as an Italian war hero and awarded the gold medal for valor, was renowned for his daring as one of the divers who, on the night of October 31, 1918, had attached mines to the Austrian battleship *Viribus Unitis*. On 1 November, the ship sank in the harbor at Pola (Pula), the naval port at the tip of the Istrian peninsula. [63]

The venture contributed more to the myth of Italian victory in the Adriatic than to actual success in fighting against the Austrian navy. The Habsburgs had essentially lost the war already. Hours before the mines were set, Janko Vuković-Podkapelski, an Austro-Hungarian naval officer of Croat ethnicity who served as the representative of the new Council of Croats, Slovenes, and Serbs had taken over command of the fleet at Pola including the *Viribus Unitis*. Vuković-Podkapelski, who had raised the Croatian flag over the ship, went down with the vessel. The incident's real importance lay in its paving the way for the Italian navy's triumphant entry into Pola on November 5 and its facilitation of American and Allied intervention in deciding the fate of the Austro-Hungarian fleet.[64]

Enrico Paulovich's choice of the name Paolucci, a decade later in 1928, honored the Italian war hero of the Adriatic but did not coincide with fascist political tastes. Raffaele Paulocci, the surgeon and decorated veteran, had made clear his political commitment to the conservative Italian nationalist cause and to the Italian monarchy, not to the fascist government. In 1921 he ran as a government supported candidate for Abruzzi, and the fascists drafted him as a representative for their autonomist list.

However, in 1923 he ran afoul of hardline fascists when he publicly expressed discontent with the treatment accorded long-time members of the Nationalist Party in the wake of the nationalist-fascist fusion. Roberto Farinacci and other hardliners effectively stalled Paolucci's government career in the years from 1924 to 1926.[65] Although Paolucci did not actively oppose the fascists, his divergence from the fascist line became evident when refused to take the fascist professional oath in 1931.[66]

Morpurgo's reference in 1931 to Antonio Paulovich's support for Luigi Ziliotto in Zara reflected a commitment to nationalist Italian sentiment and irredentism similar to Enrico's choice of the name Paolucci. Both reflected Italian nationalist allegiances characteristic of the frontier zone. Like Paolucci, Ziliotto was a hero for Italians in the Adriatic provinces with unimpeachable nationalist credentials. A lawyer and politician, Luigi Ziliotto was educated in Habsburg Graz. He led the Autonomous Party and won election to the municipal council in Zara in 1892 and to the Dalmatian Provincial Diet in 1895.[67] From 1896 to 1898, Ziliotto served as president of the Lega Nazionale or Italian National Association. In 1900 he became the mayor of Habsburg Zara.

Austria's concessions to Croat nationalists and the rapprochement between Italy and Austria in the Triple Alliance encouraged autonomists in Zara to seek Italian aid in the decades leading up to the World War I. By 1914 the Autonomist Party, which Italy considered to be the primary protector of Italians in Dalmatia, held seats only in Zara, where Ziliotto played a key role. One of the new generation of Autonomist leaders after 1891, Ziliotto did not place his faith in Habsburg Austria but saw the future in assistance from Italy.[68] However, his perspective on Italian nationalism and irredentism in Zara did not coincide with that of committed nationalists in Rome or Trieste.

Dalmatian autonomism was marked by two seemingly contradictory spirits, one in sympathy with Italian nationalism, the other guided by Dalmatian regionalism. Ziliotto was passionately committed to the defense and protection of the Italian language and culture and Dalmatians' Italian cultural identity, but he was not, at least at the turn of the century, a committed Italian nationalist devoted to separation from the Habsburg monarchy and annexation to Italy.[69] In fact, between 1908 and 1914, Ziliotto engaged in a political struggle against dissident autonomists including

Girolamo Italo Boxich and Raimondo Desanti, supported by prominent Italian nationalists on the peninsula including Luigi Federzoni and Enrico Corradini, founders of the Italian National Association who advocated maximal cession of Adriatic territory to Italy.[70]

Ziliotto saw this approach as brash and dangerous. He took a pragmatic stance and sought conciliation with the Habsburg supporters until the outbreak of war between Austria and Italy in 1915 forced the Autonomous Party to make its choice.[71] The impending collapse of the Habsburg monarchy left Italy as the alternative to assimilation in the Croat part of the new South Slav state. In 1919 Ziliotto flirted with D'Annunzio and the fascists in supporting Italy's annexation of Dalmatia, and Ziliotto was one of the senators in the Italian parliament who voted with the extremist wing of Italian nationalism against the Treaty of Rapallo for its failure to include the entire Adriatic territory in the Italian state.[72] But, by the end of 1920, with the political settlement signed into the treaty, attention in Zara returned to support for ethnic Italianness and links to Italy rather than irredentist activism for inclusion of all of Dalmatia in Italy. While Francesco Giunta led the fascist squads and garnered public support for hard line fascism in Trieste, Ziliotto led the Autonomist Party in Zara, concentrating on relations with the Italian government and establishment of a duty free zone to facilitate trade with the city's hinterlands assigned by the Treaty of Rapallo to the South Slav Kingdom.[73]

By 1922 Trieste had become a hotbed of fascism under the leadership of Francesco Giunta and other transplants from the peninsula, but the fascists had made fewer inroads in Zara.[74] While opponents of fascism and Italy contended that under the influence of Italian nationalists Zara became a hotbed of fascism, local alignments were complicated. Prior to his death in February 1922, due to complications from the flu, Ziliotto was absorbed in political fights against fascist candidates from the peninsula who sought control. Luigi Ziliotto's son Giuseppe maintained that, given the political climate, the Italian populace of the Dalmatian capital had no reason to openly oppose fascism, but he argued that his father and his friends along with many intellectuals in the city were "agnostics" with respect to fascism, reacting with a kind of critical "silence." Giuseppe's son Luigi, namesake of his grandfather Mayor Ziliotto, contended that his father Giuseppe's membership in the Fascist Party was more "formal" than "substantial." Giuseppe Ziliotto admitted to sympathizing with Mussolini before the March on Rome, having met him and shared his discontent over the signing of the Treaty of Rapallo and the, as he called it, "tepid nationalism" in post–World War I liberal Italy, but claimed that by 1922 he had begun to "tire" of the fascists, particularly of the aggressive tactics used to oppose his father in Zara. Giuseppe Ziliotto's participation in the Liberal Party Congress in Rome in 1926 testifies to the sincerity of his claims to disenchantment with fascism.[75] He did join the Fascist Party in 1933 at the same time as other professionals in Zara. But, he claimed, this was to support the local prefect and party secretary. As a lawyer, political pragmatism and economic concerns certainly guided this decision. No doubt, his recollections and those of his son Luigi were colored in their retelling by the subsequent history of fascist Italy, but evidence for a brand of Dalmatian *italianità*, distinct from that of Rome, the peninsula, and even Adriatic Trieste appears in their correspondence and actions of the period.

In 1931 Morpurgo's reference to Antonio Paulovich's support for Luigi Ziliotto recalled the politics of a bygone era. It placed the family's politics and understandings of Italian nationalism in the orbit of Dalmatia and Zara, the city they had left in 1905. Defense of *italianità* in Dalmatia represented support for the protection of ethnic rights and, in some cases, privileges. On the eve of World War I, it had promised triumph of the liberal Italian state over the traditional Habsburg monarchy.

By 1930, while evidence of fascism's hold was ubiquitous, the realities of fascist governance may not have intruded on Luigia Paulovich's daily life before the execution of the surname restoration decree. The overlay of fascism in new symbols appearing on local signs and buildings and the new architecture appearing in central Trieste were not apparent in the Pauloviches' neighborhood of Cologna, outside the business center and removed from the grand Piazza Unità around which the official buildings of Trieste and fascism were clustered. Cologna boasted monuments and buildings that served as reminders of the Italian patriotism of leaders of the unredeemed city at the turn of the century. Paulovich undoubtedly passed often by the bronze statue erected in 1901 at the entrance of the public gardens nearby to her apartment. The statue dedicated to Domenico Rossetti, one of the city fathers and a tireless supporter of public works to promote the Italian city under Austrian rule, was graced by the three figures—Justice, Poetry, and Archaeology—as a tribute to Rossetti's contributions as an Italian scholar of the arts, architecture, and archaeology.

Yet, the five pointed star affixed to the statue and understood as a symbol of Italian supremacy must have given pause to the elderly widow, who certainly remembered that it had been the cause of contention in Habsburg Trieste.

Before World War I, local Habsburg supporters, purportedly with the help of the police, had removed the star as an offending symbol. The city's public workers, ostensibly acting on noble sentiments and likely with a nod from the pro-Italian city council, replaced it. This cycle was repeated several times in a kind of tug-of-war over the monument. During the war, the Austrians removed the star and attached a plaque to the statute's base with a quote from Rossetti's work "The dream of Corvo Bonomo," that called for the creation of an independent Illyria with its capital at Ljubljana. The tablet bearing the quote, considered offensive by Italian nationalists, was removed by Italian authorities in November 1918.[76]

How much of this irony of nationalist representation Paulovich imbibed and how much this of this nationalist ambiguity she felt is open to question.[77] However, Paulovich family's attitudes were, perhaps, typical of recent immigrants to Trieste whose perspectives were not necessarily consonant with those of the leaders of Triestine nationalist circles closely associated with fascism. Some likely shared the nostalgia for return to Habsburg rule expressed in graffiti that appeared on the city's wall in the late 1920s, "Return, Francis Joseph: all is forgiven you."[78] Others supported different varieties of Italian nationalism and irredentism. In the early interwar years, a small left-leaning minority of Italian nationalists in Trieste aligned with the Italian Republican Party advocating a moderate pro-Italian stance that sought conciliation with minorities in the Italian state. Driven underground by the fascist government, such adherents of this faction as Gabriele Foschiatti served as local leaders of antifascist opposition and Justice and Freedom (*Giustizia e libertà*) cells that emerged and began, hesitantly, to cooperate with other local antifascist interests.[79] From exile in 1931, Gaetano Salvemini observed, the "burden of fascist rule rests not only upon the racial minorities in Italy, but upon the entire Italian population as well."[80] In Trieste, the many iterations of pro-Italian sentiment bred a variety of forms of Italian nationalism that reflected the complexity of the nationalist experience of populations of the Adriatic.

Enrico's choice of the surname Paolucci and the Paulovich family's history of irredentism and nationalism in Zara, coupled with Luigia Paulovich's willingness to take on the fascist prefect in Trieste, suggest that, while Paulovich's support for Italy and Italian culture was unwavering, she might not have equated loyalty to Italy with loyalty to fascism. Admittedly, the widow's struggle against the fascist directive likely sprang as much from personal motives as from her commitment to a specific brand of Italian nationalism and fascism or to her philosophical notions of justice. Yet, Paulovich's position as an elderly woman with established nationalist credentials made her a difficult opponent. Her conformity to the fascist image of the ideal Italian mother and widow allowed her the latitude to launch the name restoration appeal without fear. Her actions mirrored those of women celebrated by the fascists for their activism and sacrifice to promote and further the Italian cause in the name of their husbands and families.

6   A Fascist Woman?

"Justice," wrote Gina Lombroso, "is not the triumph of equality, liberty and absolute reciprocity, but the triumph of equality before the standard agreed on, the freedom to attain a certain goal and relative reciprocity."[1] Daughter of the famed Italian criminologist Cesare Lombroso—an accomplished writer, social critic, and popular scientist in her own right—Lombroso described the bases on which Luigia Paulovich sought justice. The substance of Paulovich's appeal and the tone of her lawyer's arguments recognized and accepted the widow's place in Italian society. Arguments made on her behalf played to societal expectations of women that had developed over decades in the modern state of Italy.

Lombroso identified the female archetype or the "highest type of woman" to be: ". . . among the sublime and unknown women who through their own efforts created the moral traditions that still govern us, the women who through their sufferings and sacrifices have won prestige and respect from which we still profit today, the women who managed to direct men and to inspire them to generous deeds, the women who have offered their all to advance an ideal, and who have buoyed up the falling, have soothed the suffering, and have smoothed the path for those who were fighting for the ideal."[2]

In 1930 Paulovich appeared as the model fascist woman—"a sublime and unknown" widow, who inspired her children to "generous deeds" in the service of Italy, and who suffered as a mother and as an Italian nationalist in the frontier zone. By 1930, in her seventies, Paulovich had adopted wholeheartedly the role of an elderly patriotic widow. However, she did not do it in the manner fascist officials expected. Rather than retire to her home and family, accepting the accolades offered to her as a "noble widow"—who had educated Italian children and encouraged them to accept the responsibilities of *italianità*, who stood alongside her husband in his irredentist activities, and who had suffered the loss of her husband— she asserted her patriotism and sought recognition of *italianità* on her own terms, not on the terms dictated by the regime that sought to restore her married surname to an Italian form.

"Difficult" Women and Opposition

At the head of the surname commission, Aldo Pizzagalli was prepared to face opposition. He singled out women, "discontented, difficult women" as most likely to complain about the surname restorations. This prediction reflected ubiquitous and deeply rooted prejudices of Italian and European society that saw women as "creatures of emotions," ruled by sentiments, not by reason, intellect, or logic in their approach to public and legal institutions.[3] Notions that women were fragile, emotional, and prone to act with raw "activity, passion and intuition" went hand in hand with biologically based theories that sought to explain women's natural inferiority.[4] Chief among the late nineteenth-century psychological interpretations of women's propensity to emotionality in Italy was *La donna delinquente*, published in 1893 by Gina Lombroso's father Cesare Lombroso. In the work that inspired his daughter, Lombroso melded physiological theories of gender characteristics with reigning ideas regarding masculine power and men's right to dominance. He portrayed women as inherently less intelligent and lacking in creative powers. Their inferior state was a natural, inborn one reflective of the female's reliance on the male for protection and survival in the animal world.[5]

Pizzagalli instructed his subordinates to adopt a rational (masculine and official) approach when facing "difficult women." He recommended advising these women to consider the name reduction "with mature reflection" and discuss it with (male) family members. If treated in such a manner, they would "return calmer and more quiescent."[6]

Pizzagalli did not anticipate Luigia Paulovich. The widow's opposition was neither irrational nor impulsive. She came forward with her son Ernesto and her daughter Ines to fight against the name restoration. A technicality of residence allowed Ernesto to escape the surname decree's effect. After the prefect refused to rescind the restoration and affirmed his intention to restore Luigia and Ines's surname to Paoli, the widow pursued her case through the offices of a lawyer. Proceeding in a rational and methodical manner through legal channels, she launched a measured appeal challenging the prefect's application of the surname law.

Paulovich's protest might seem to qualify her as an "unseduced mother" or "resistant female subject" of fascism.[7] But, Paulovich did not reject the government's desires or expectations. She embraced the state and put her faith in Italian justice. In Gina Lombroso's conceptualization, she understood justice according to "the standard agreed upon." Assumptions that men owed respect to elderly women combined with expectations that women were frail and "flighty" to make officials particularly tolerant of Paulovich's complaint. Local authorities in the prefecture and national magistrates saw the widow's appeal as a legal dispute, not as a protest against the regime. Paulovich's complaint did not threaten the "body" of the nation.[8] Officials felt no compulsion to intimidate her or to treat her harshly as they did women considered enemies of the state or perceived to be consorting with or supporting antifascist elements.

Antifascist propaganda harped on the particular cruelty meted out to women by the fascist regime, charging that Mussolini's government had, in such prisons as Trani, "brought back into the penal system . . . the worst barbarities of the Middle Ages."[9] During the *ventennio*, those found guilty of actions against the state and antifascism faced long jail sentences or deportation. Records of the Special Tribunal bear witness to the harsh punishment meted out to women associated with antifascism. Of the 15,806 individuals referred to the Tribunal, only 749 were women. Apart from those named as fascist enemies or coconspirators, many appeared as "sisters, wives, mothers, fiancées," —associated with political detainees as "clandestine militants."[10] In aggregate from 1927 to 1943, women were sentenced to more than 675 years in prison.[11]

The fascists viewed the borderlands with suspicion and disproportionately singled out borderland inhabitants as antifascists. Repression of ethnic "others," primarily Slovenes and Croats, fueled antifascist resistance that the fascists blamed on Slavs, despite evidence implicating Slovene, Croat, and Italian socialists. "Minority" repression produced a cycle of violence and retaliation. The fascists attributed antifascist activity to clandestine ties to Yugoslavia.[12]

The Fascist Woman and Complementary Nature

Even judged by the most rigid standards, Paulovich could not be classified as a resister or antifascist. In her comportment, achievements, and attitudes, Paulovich approached the fascist ideal for womanhood. "Humble and highest of creatures. The Mother. Creator, generator, bringer, former of life. The Italian woman is essentially a mother," explained Wanda

Gorjux, a leader of the *fasci femminile* in Bari and writer whose work on social and economic conditions and women appeared in a variety of publications including *Giornale della donna* and *La gazzetta del mezzogiorno*. Fascism's aim was "essentially to give women the conscience and knowledge of this mission [as a mother] on which the prosperity, the glory, the life, and the future of the nation depend."[13] By raising three children as proud Italians, the elderly widow had already made her contribution to Italy.

The regime's view of gender specificity in biology and nature that linked women's duties to their biological roles built on conservative notions of women touted in late nineteenth-century social science theories. In the years prior to World War I these ideas, spurred by Darwinist currents, echoed across the political spectrum. In *La donna delinquente*, Cesare Lombroso promoted visions of the dangerous primitive female.[14] He distinguished "normal" women from prostitutes on the basis of their actions, but noted that all women possessed inherent tendencies toward "wildness," particularly with regard to the defense of their children.[15] Futurist Filippo Tommaso Marinetti exalted women for their "animal value" or role in the reproduction of the species. Echoing traditionalist views of women's links to hearth and home, he emphasized their biological role as a responsibility "new women" understood as their means to serve the modern state.[16]

In the interwar period, beliefs that women's natural tendencies to innate emotionality made them well suited to motherhood and defense of their families in the name of the nation translated as well to general perceptions that they were poorly suited to assume men's responsibilities. Women's predilection to wildness, instability, and lack of restraint made them impure and prone to be hysterical and even dangerous. An anonymous letter to Mussolini in 1929 denouncing the Marquess Maria De Seta reflected perfectly the public's inculcation of these tropes. Describing De Seta as a seductress who captured the love of Undersecretary Michele Bianchi, a fascist leader and politician, the writer warned that Calabria had been "abandoned to the capriciousness and hysteria of a woman . . . a divorcée, whose shame finds no name, whose lovers cannot be counted." Government officials investigated this complaint and reported on De Seta and Bianchi's trysts on trains. They also considered accusations that the Marquess interfered in school examinations and manipulated grades in Calabria. However, while they acknowledged that her conduct "left something to be desired," they took no action against her even after Bianchi's death in 1930, and she continued to trade on his influence.[17] Authorities appeared resigned to her impropriety as a natural consequence of her mercurial woman's temperament and access to powerful men.

Paulovich's conduct offered no cause for concern. In fact, she exemplified the woman's attributes prized by the regime that saw women as complementary to men. Ideas of complementarity had developed over the first three decades of the twentieth century, to counter proto-feminist arguments for equality and concentrate on women's separateness and biological contributions. Gina Lombroso was among those who popularized notions of women's essential, organic differences from men. She rejected feminist claims that women's intelligence was the same as men's, arguing instead that "a woman's mind differs from a man's, not so much in quantity as in *quality* and *direction*." She suggested, "Woman has never fallen so low as when she began to try to imitate man."[18] She argued vehemently that "woman is not man's equal" for "aside from the evident physical and intellectual differences between man and woman," women were "alterocentrists" who centered their lives on people surrounding them not on themselves whereas men were "egocentrists" whose lives revolved around themselves.[19] Placing her observations in the realm of science, she observed that among animals as well as plants devotion and sacrifice were characteristic of females while egotism was characteristic of males.

Lombroso articulated her philosophy of women's separate propensities, impulses, and missions for a fascist audience in a collection of four women's autobiographies published in 1929 in a book called *Nuove vite*. The book, introducing women in four different European and Asian countries, intended to demonstrate the universality of women's experience by emphasizing three points: "the soul of the woman is the same in all climates and in all classes;" "national differences change the circumstances of [women's] lives, not their spiritual repercussions"; and "modern satisfactions mean less for the modern woman than she believes." Lombroso intended the collection to inspire women "to take immense delight in the simple and old-fashioned joys of love; more than the glory and independence conferred by a career and studies."[20] Margherita Sarfatti's intentions were similar in "The Joys of Woman" published in 1933 in *Augustea*, a review of politics, economy, and art. In her article, the Venetian art patron famed as Mussolini's mistress asserted, "The joys of the woman are above all altruistic joys reflected in others, [joys of] love, marriage, or motherhood."[21]

Such approaches played into the fascists' hands when they called on women to dedicate themselves to strengthening the state. Fascist ideologues, including Giovanni Gentile, celebrated women's complementarity building on the idea of natural biological differences to emphasize women's specific roles and their duties.[22] Men had a superior rational sense of order and ability to oversee the "chaotic" world, traits that made them the natural leaders in both society and the family.[23] Fascism encouraged women to embrace organic or biological differences and to eschew aspirations relating to the problematic modern woman whose selfishness and underlying masculine tendencies led her astray and distracted her from her responsibilities, detracting from her worth.

Mussolini's government disseminated scientific and medical research findings that supported notions of women's complementary existence. Gaetano Pieraccini's *The Woman in the Conservation and Perfecting of the Species*, published in 1931 in a series of *Biological Writings*, repudiated earlier notions of women's instability and weakness. Pieraccini rejected the suggestion that women represented the weaker sex. On the basis of scientific research, the medical doctor and instructor at the University of Florence found women to be biologically more resistant to debilitating organic threats, and therefore more suited physically than men to devote themselves to the conservation of the species' physical health. In Pieraccini's assessment, although more vulnerable to organic threats, the man maintained "dynamic" superiority to the woman, as the stronger "generator and distributor of physical and psychological energies."[24]

In the preface to Pieraccini's book, Luigi Castaldi, a professor at the University of Cagliari for much of the fascist period, emphasized the work's utility for examining questions of genetics, the economic condition of women in society and questions of feminism. Castaldi, the editor responsible for the *Biological Writings* series, noted the work's far-reaching application that was "not contained within the limits of pure scientific inquiry, but extend[ed] to sociological problems of importance both in vital practice and in current affairs."[25] The work's contribution to explaining the regime's biological aims was important enough to merit publication of the work despite Pieraccini's support for socialist politics and ties to antifascist intellectuals including Salvemini.

The men who held the reins of the state when Paulovich's case wound its way through the fascist bureaucracy certainly saw it as their responsibility to preserve and protect the "political, juridical, and social" as well as "biological economy" of the state.[26] Men dominated the legal professions and educational academies. Their views, embedded in the cultural and social climate of the age, upheld the gendered perspective in the law and judicial institutions. In theory under the provisions of a citizenship law passed in 1919, the professions admitted women on par with men. Women earned degrees in law, political science, social science, economics, and commerce and organized in professional groups like the Federation of Italian Women Jurists. Women lawyers could work in private practice, but the judiciary and government legal service remained closed as women were prohibited from all positions in sectors "implying public juridical powers."[27] Of those studying law and jurisprudence in Italy in 1935, 391 were women while 10,118 were men.[28] Male domination of the legal and court system went deeper than simply the gap in numbers. Socio-institutional structures reflected ideas of male's superior intellect and fitness for legal understanding and practice.[29]

Paulovich's complaint against the prefect did not call into question any of the common assumptions regarding women. It asked judges to define more clearly the scope of women's responsibilities to defend their families. Paulovich's challenge of the decree that appeared to threaten her family was consonant with the kind of legal activism that female lawyers supported under the regime. Zara Olivia Algardi, a noted Roman jurist, author of several works on women and the law, and an activist in favor of women's rights and equality, argued emphatically that women were as fit to be lawyers and jurists as men and that there was no incompatibility between "women and the [practice of] law." However, she maintained that essential differences of temperament existed and that a woman should not seek to "denature" herself from her [natural] temperament, an action "which at times seems to demonstrate a lack of good taste."[30]

Lina Furlan, who in 1929 became the first Italian woman to argue before the Court of Assizes, accepted without question the gender differentiation and inequality that characterized fascist society and pervaded the legal system and defended motherhood and women's roles in the home and family. She agreed that men were more adapted "to the role of counsel for the defense," but argued that women might derive the upper hand through their sensibilities and intuition. Like Algardi, she saw "excessive modernity" as in "bad taste."[31] Algardi and Furlan translated the gendered role assigned to them to their work in the halls of justice. They supported women's education but claimed to seek education to understand the man's world and to help women to defend traditional rights in their own realm. They did not aim to enter the man's world.[32]

Women as National "Bodies"

As fascism was to represent an innovative third way between liberalism and socialism in European politics, fascist women were to be model new women occupying a place between the conscious feminist (dismissed with scorn and ridicule), and the low and sentimental woman (unreliable, needy, and unable to contribute to society). The fascist *donna muliebre* actively supported the state but understood her role as different from that of the fascist man.[33] The fascist government placed women's value in their ability to help to strengthen Italy and remake Italians in the fascist image, not in their labor in the public sphere. In physiological terms, Pieraccini explained, "Pulling her [the woman] away from [reproductive work] to engage in superior mental work or hard physical labor goes against "the laws of physiology and sociology."[34] In other words, women best served the state as "social bodies."[35] Women's responsibilities were vested in their roles as wives and mothers. They were asked to act as reproductive agents of the state, to maintain the Italian racial stock and to embrace their reproductive, biological roles. The fascists took pains to convince women that, due to their biological capabilities, they were full participants in a thoroughly modern political enterprise. Women's biological function to "exercise a preponderant interest in determining the destiny of human societies" formed the basis for satisfying and useful citizenship.[36] Leaders of the *fasci femminili* enjoined women to remember their responsibilities "for the most delicate and sensitive part of the Patria: the purity, the linearity, the strict transmission of the stock [stirpe]."[37]

The regime instituted policies designed to safeguard women's health for the nation. The regime invested in girls' and women's exercise for its health and "hygienic" benefits.[38] Paulovich must have watched with interest tentative efforts in 1923 to introduce physical education that gave way in 1927 to Opera Nazionale Balilla (ONB) programs dedicated to the fascist education of children, including the physical education of girls. In 1932, when Paulovich's case was being settled, the regime cemented the place of physical education in women's curricula with establishment of the fascist Women's Academy of Physical Education in Orvieto.

Visions of the healthy and fit Italian woman evolved over the course of the *ventennio* as debates continued over the appropriate amount of physical exertion, the appropriate activities, and the social implications of physical activity for girls and women. Some social scientists like Ferdinando Loffredo, influenced by traditional assumptions and Catholic sentiments, adamantly opposed women's participation in sport as dangerous to reproduction, a contributing factor to emancipation that led to decadence, and a waste of energies. But, the Ministry of National Education quashed conservative arguments referring to the opinions and recommendations of medical experts who judged women's activity to be healthful rather than harmful to their reproductive capabilities and therefore beneficial to the Italian nation.[39] Ondina Valla, an Italian runner, competed and won at the Berlin Olympics, capturing hearts as an Italian heroine who demonstrated to the world the "thriving state of womanhood under Fascism."[40] By the 1940s, the regime linked exercise directly to the preparation of "vigorous and healthy mothers ready to [stand up to any challenge] to defend the sacred borders [of Italy], for any sacrifice for the strength of the Fatherland."[41] This call to defend Italian borders was already familiar to women in the borderland. Irredentists relied on women like Paulovich to defend *italianità* before Italy annexed the Adriatic provinces.

Fascist Heroines

Fascist support for the new active *donna muliebre* and the promotion of athletes like Ondina Valla did little to change public visions of the ideal Italian woman that had been formed in the Risorgimento era. Fascist women continued to find inspiration in Eugenio Comba's *Donne illustri italiane* (*Renowned Italian Women*), a book first published in the mid-nineteenth century and in its fourth edition by 1885. The book was characteristic of studies of worthy women, a genre that can be traced from Plutarch through the medieval period and the Renaissance to the nineteenth century. In the fascist version, edited and amplified for publication in 1935, editor Luisa Steiner boldly stated the book's aim to "demonstrate the virtues of old to the new generations." She lauded women included in the nineteenth-century version and those added in the fascist edition as "superior figures" that "embody good, show enthusiasm for responsibilities, offer comfort."[42]

Comba's heroines of the nation included Adelaide Cairoli, "one of the sublime figures of the Italian Risorgimento" and mother of Italian Prime Minister Benedetto Cairoli. Adelaide Cairoli worked alongside her husband, a doctor, serving Italian soldiers until his death in 1849. A young widow, she raised five sons and lost four in the wars of the Risorgimento, her sacrifice to Italy.[43] In the fascist edition, Steiner retained the sketches of such nineteenth century heroines and added additional figures reflecting the post–World War I emphasis on women as female citizens engaged in patriotic work.[44] Anna Sauro, mother of Nazario Sauro, a naval officer executed for treason by Austria and considered an Italian martyr, would have been familiar to Paulovich. Sauro's place in the women's "martyrology" stemmed from her refusal, even under torture, to identify her son to Austrian authorities after his capture, a vain attempt to save him from the hangman's noose.[45] Sauro was a model of wartime femininity, a symbol of commitment to Italy and patriotism as the noblest cause for sacrifice.[46]

Sacrificing women like Cairoli and Sauro played a key role in fascist mythology. Fascism extended the traditional hagiography of widows and mothers to include women or girls who suffered for the Italian nation. In 1927 *Il Balilla* (a supplement to *Il Popolo d'Italia* published periodically for Italian youth) called for nominations for a special edition recognizing young national heroines. The mayor of Grado, a small seaside village on the Adriatic coast between Trieste and Venice, nominated Lucia Degrassi, a girl who had received the silver medal of valor from the Italian navy. In 1916 Degrassi and her father had risked their lives, leaving the safety of their isolated fishing hut to save members of the Italian financial police. They braved the "stormy sea" in their small boat to reach the officers when waves demolished the "poorly secured hut" from which the officers tracked spies. Degrassi made a particularly poignant young "martyr" as she died of tuberculosis in 1924 at the age of 23.[47]

In their alacrity to promote sacrificing patriotic women, the fascists made heroines of symbolic women, even if the women personally fell short of fascist ideals. In the case of Lidia Bugliovaz, widow of Francesco

Rismondo, the "martyr of Spalato," the regime's desires to maintain the image of the widow's husband allowed for a deliberate blindness to the realities of his wife's life and character. Typically, widowed bourgeois women saw the state as responsible for maintaining their lifestyles in light of the trauma, abandonment, and very real possibility of deprivation that many faced on the loss of a husband. In the words of one war widow, state assistance was their entitlement to enable them to maintain their "appearance of dignity."[48]

In 1921 liberal government officials had suggested Bugliovaz as a possible candidate for special state honors and a supplemental pension in remembrance of her husband's special contributions to Italy. However, the prefect of Trieste equivocated with respect to her merit of the special award. She was a young woman who seemed to "prefer the company of officials other than her husband" even before he enlisted. On the eve of Italy's entrance into World War I against Austria, Rismondo had fled Spalato for Venice with his young wife in tow to volunteer with an Italian cycling regiment of the *bersaglieri* (special infantry). In 1915 he was awarded the medal of military valor for his actions at Monte San Michele in the Carso near Gorizia, but he never returned, purportedly having been taken prisoner and hanged (some reported burned alive). Authorities noted that in her husband's absence and even after he "met his terrible end," Bugliovaz appeared with other men at the theater, seemingly with no respect for her husband or his memory. She "did not take part in any of the public ceremonies honoring widows" nor did she "seem to understand her husband's greatness."

When fascist officials took over, they inquired further. Engaged in honoring Rismondo as an Italian symbol of Dalmatia "which suffers and waits," they sought further information on the widow. The prefect of Trieste's follow-up letter in December 1922 was blunt. Calling Bugliovaz's "moral conduct somewhat questionable," he noted that she was estranged from her in-laws and appeared to live beyond her means, noting "her elegant and expensive clothes seem incompatible with her modest resources."

Despite the prefect's assessment, the fascist government added the extraordinary sum of 6,000 lire to Bugliovaz's annual widow's pension.[49] This largesse came when the stipend set in 1921 for widows of ordinary soldiers without children was 630 lire per year. Childless widows of the highest grade senior generals received only 4,000 lire per year.[50] Nearly a decade later in 1930, cleaning women working in city government offices earned about 250 lire per month, and shipyard workers earned about 475 lire per month.[51]

In the pantheon of fascist heroines, widows held an exalted position. Middle aged or elderly widows could represent sources of local authority.[52] Widows were afforded special privileges under the laws that meant that they wielded authority, but they were expected to act only carefully and within the narrow scope of action allotted to them in the patriarchal fascist society. When the fascist government dismissed women hired before May 1915 from work for the Italian railways, they excluded war widows and orphans from the ban. Widows of war veterans were included in the limited categories of women accorded the right to vote in administrative elections in 1925.[53]

At the same time, widows were feared for their transgressive role: they were the embodiment of family and at the same time were free from constraints imposed by marriage and husband. Young widows, in particular, posed a potential threat to the community.[54] The regime held high standards for conduct relating to the biological preservation of the nation. Those flouting these standards presented a particular affront to fascist and nationalist conservative opinion. Official reaction to a novel by Mura (pen name of Maria Volpi) *Sambadù amore negro* testified to the regime's reaction to perceived threats to the nation's biological purity. The fascists censored and recalled the book, published in 1931 the same year that the Paulovich appeal wound its way through the fascist bureaucracy, that told the story of a young Italian widow who chose to marry the black African Sambadù.[55] Relationships between white European women and black men had long been taboo.[56] The novel's cover depicting miscegenation and cross-racial sensuality and desire had been enough to incite public furor.

Biological Essentialism and Nationalism

Fears of miscegenation and wanton sensuality reflected fascist acceptance of socio-biological and psychological theories that saw women's importance to strengthening the nation, not only in *numbers* but also through their role in transmitting *characteristics* and attitudes. Pieraccini found in his scientific study of genetics, anthropological character, and inherited characteristics (both physical and intellectual) that women "represented an element more stable and conservative of ethnic characteristics." They bore responsibility for the transmission of the characteristics and culture of particular societies and races.[57] Racial psychologists, including Mario Canella, a leading fascist proponent of psychological theories of race, echoed the findings of medical professionals. Canella noted "profound differences between the feminine and the masculine mentality" and tied these "radically distinct biological destinies" to "structural and physiological distinctions, based on a diverse 'endocrinological formula,'" which made women superior in "conserving the race."[58]

Nineteenth-century German Romanticism traced national characteristics to emotions and biology as well as territory. At the turn of the twentieth century, Austrian writer Otto Weininger, whose controversial book *Sex and Character* was highly influential in Italy and particularly in Habsburg Trieste, popularized ideas that linked national belonging to inherited physical and emotional characteristics.[59] Theories underlining the importance of national distinctiveness and differentiation propounded across Europe afforded women a biological role in the development of the nation. Writing in the Italian context in *Vita moderna* in August 1898, Sibilla Aleramo claimed the Italian was "less mystical than the Slav, more passionate than the Frenchwoman, less practical than the Anglo-Saxon, more intellectual than the Spaniard." These inherited characteristics allowed the Italian woman to strike a balance between "the Latin and Nordic types," deriving her distinctive "charm and fervor" from the Nordic type and her "habit of dreaming and the intensity of her emotions" from the Latin type.[60]

When European governments encouraged women's biological, reproductive patriotism in the wake of World War I, they recognized that this entailed reliance on essentialist beliefs that women were responsible for transmitting the characteristics of nationhood. In fascist Italy, women's responsibility for temperament and emotions translated to women's duty to instill in fascist citizens "the pride of the Roman *civis*."[61] In this respect, Paulovich's defense of her married surname in memory of her deceased husband and in honor of her sons and their heroic acts for Italy typified the action expected of the idolized heroic woman of Ancient Rome. Paulovich was the kind of woman "sung of by our great poets and our most ancient writers," the woman who "with all of her virtues, all of her marvelous feats, all of her admirable greatness, her epic deeds of faith, of heroism and of glory" defended the honor of Rome and whose "return after centuries" the fascist government hailed.[62]

Yet, the assumptions of western European racial hierarchies made Paulovich's attachment to her Slavic surname incomprehensible. The Latin and Germanic races stood above the Slavic or eastern races, and women in the Adriatic borderlands bore special responsibilities under fascism to guard against inferior and "uncivilized" Slavs. An unspoken assumption of the surname campaign was that Slavic sounding surnames indicated an ethnic taint. According to this logic, women like Paulovich should have been proud to bear names that better reflected their biological and racial origins and should have been eager to pass on ethnically appropriate names to future generations. Paulovich and her lawyer rejected the importance of nationalist trappings. They elevated deeds over biology in national belonging.

Working for the State

Before the March on Rome, the fascists appealed to women as progenitors of the nation, warning of the dangers posed by those who "want to kill your *stirpe* [stock] and your blood." In 1921 the *fascio* in Milan called on the "Women of Italy" to convince their husbands "to vote for the fascist candidate" to save the *patria*.[63] This call for women's involvement in their husbands' politics reflected the realities of the post–World War I political arena in Italy in which the ideal woman was an active patriot rather than a passive housewife.[64] Women's defense of Italy was a common theme of wartime and fascist propaganda. Prewar feminist of socio-Marxist bent Theresa Labriola explained, "The era of the mute woman is finished. . . . We need to make it so that the woman begins to become eloquent in speaking of the Fatherland."[65]

In the late nineteenth century, women's rights proponents had argued for political participation and suffrage on the premise that gaining the right to vote was the only way that women could protect their rights and defend their interests. After the turn of the century such outspoken women's rights advocates as socialist leader and reformer Filippo Turati proclaimed suffrage "an inherent right of citizenship," which women should enjoy equally with men.[66] Early in his career and during his rise to power Mussolini supported women's suffrage. Pressure from women's groups across the political and social spectrum in the wake of the Matteotti assassination in 1924 prompted the weakened fascist government to pass a measure into law in 1925 that allowed specific categories of women to vote.[67] However, following World War I, the rise of conservative nationalist politics in response to socialist challenges, and the withdrawal of women from the workforce to make way for men returning from military to civilian life changed the trajectory of women's politics, shifting focus away from the pursuit of equal civil rights with men.[68]

Paulovich's lawyer's emphasis in 1931 on the widow's womanly traits and defense of the surname Paulovich to honor the memory of her husband and his family tapped into expectations of women's *italianità* that became more pronounced over the course of the *ventennio*. Fascism abrogated feminist ideas of the prewar period to convince women that emancipation would be achieved through affirmation of their own rights and abilities within their "natural" sphere. Struggles for political recognition, equality, and suffrage should be abandoned in favor of transformative experience through women's work for the family and the nation.[69]

Conservatives applauded fascism's call to women to serve in philanthropic enterprises, which linked women's traditional church-based philanthropy to civic duties. In 1924 Maria Magri Zopegni, Italian journalist, writer, and founder of the Catholic-influenced women's periodical *La Donna Italiana*, called for "Christian feminism" (as opposed to "modern feminism") asking women to promote "the good Italian traditions of the Catholic spirit."[70] According to Magri Zopegni, women should struggle for equal rights, but respect "the struggle for the strengthening of family ties, to check raging immorality."[71] By 1937 fascism's concessions to women's suffrage were forgotten in the emphasis on women's complementarity and commitment to the state. Some fascist ideologues went so far as to claim that women were uninterested in the political rights and responsibilities of men and "did not want to vote."[72]

The fascist appeal to women to serve the community that resonated in traditional Italian society and echoed Catholic teachings specifically targeted middle class women. The fascists called on the *Signore* and *Signorine*, the polite Madams and Mistresses, of the salons and social clubs to mobilize as *donne fasciste*, fascist women who stood ready to fight for the nation.[73] After 1925 the ONMI, comprised of middle-class women, assisted the fascist woman seeking to "attain a suitable knowledge to carry out her mission as a mother intelligently and, at the same time, to protect the new offspring of the race."[74] The organization institutionalized middle-class norms of motherhood and child rearing. At the same time, it allowed the state to intervene in the mother / child relationship, blurring public and private domains.[75]

The fascist demographic campaign instituted in 1927 to work "in favor of the 'number' and the 'quality' of citizens" was emblematic of the transformation of women's responsibilities tied to family and home into public duty for the nation.[76] The *Almanacco* pointed out the "vast and profound repercussions" of "women's industriousness" in the demographic realm and called on women to heed the call to "participate broadly in the life of the nation" as "sanctioned by the new legislative acts for social welfare."[77] The magazine highlighted women's public role in defense of hearth and family rather than in the push for emancipation that had characterized the women's activism of the prewar decades. In 1928, Fanny Dini's "Dedicated to certain women" in *Rassegna femminile italiana* tied bourgeois women's involvement in education and social betterment through state programs to their duties to assist and elevate the poor.[78]

If women remained in the workforce, they should limit themselves to professions for which they were suited. In an article in *Almanacco della donna* Armando Michielj insisted he was not being "antifeminist" in his preference for seeing women at work as nurses, doctors, and teachers, maintaining that women in these "sympathetic" professions engaged in essential emotional and spiritual work, "curing the health of the body and curing the health of the spirit" of the Italian population. Their activities constituted the "most elevated and humane expressions of femininity," those most evident in the mother.[79] Michielj also singled out teachers for particular merit.

By the late 1930s promotion of the "femininity of the mother" gave way to more militant calls for engagement of the woman as an "untiring, efficient social worker." In 1937 Maria Luisa Astaldi noted that all careers and professions, "with the exception of the magistrate, diplomacy and the military," remained open to women and that women enjoyed "brilliant situations in the bureaucracy, in the banks, in journalism, in commercial enterprises." She praised the efforts of the Federation of Women Lawyers, which, in a conference held in Rome to celebrate the tenth anniversary of the fascist revolution, promised to undertake an "important study of the fascist legislation relative to the woman and the family."[80]

By the late 1930s it was apparent that the regime's demographic campaign was not a success. The Italian rate of marriage declined throughout the 1920s, from 94 per 10,000 inhabitants in 1923 and 85 per 10,000 in 1924 to 70 per 10,000 inhabitants in 1928 and 1929.[81] The fecundity of women continued a downward trend begun in the late nineteenth century. The median number of children for Italian women of Paulovich's age, born from 1851 to 1871, was five. For those born from 1871 to 1886, it fell to 3.55.[82] In the interwar period, from 1926 to 1930, the rate was 2.35.[83]

Contemporary periodicals illustrated the mood of women unmoved by the regime's institutional and political reforms and deaf to calls to produce children for the nation. The Milanese satirical weekly *Guerin meschino* poked fun at the campaign's aims with a depiction of two men commenting on a large family passing by, "now we say quantity to the detriment of quality."[84] For the majority of women in the interwar period, reproductive decisions were based more on personal circumstances and beliefs than on state desires. In 1931 the editors scolded *Almanacco*'s audience for failing to heed the call of the nation. They chided both men and women for failing to act in the "spirit of the people" and blamed "the egotism of men who do not want to sacrifice a carefree and comfortable life to preoccupations of family" and "the vanity and frivolousness of women who do not want to sacrifice diversions, luxuries and personal aesthetics to the birth and care of children."[85] At the same time, ideologues sought to deflect attention from the initial failures, constructing arguments to highlight instead other forms of women's activism and engagement. In an article in the same magazine discussing the achievements of ONMI, the author argued, "we cannot limit ourselves to absolute numbers." She urged women's organizations to shift their attentions and adjust their efforts to respond to new social concepts and their new mission in the fascist state.[86]

Justice and Women under the Law

Cases involving women that came before the Administrative Court in the early 1930s reflected the clashing visions of women and the dynamic nature of fascist thought regarding women's roles in Italian society. By the end of the 1920s, feminists had abandoned attempts to gain equal access in state employment, and the women's press in Italy no longer supported such causes.[87] Nonetheless, the Administrative Court continued to hear cases related to women's activities and employment in the public sector. Gender bias was rooted in Italian law, in Risorgimento legal structures and reforms, and in the process of legal professionalization.[88] Under the Italian civil code of 1865, the wife was "like a piece of furniture or an accouterment belonging to the husband." Paulovich, born and married under Habsburg laws, became an Italian citizen after she had passed her sixtieth birthday. The Habsburg laws to which she was accustomed were a bit more liberal. Austrian marriage laws had allowed the wife to retain certain rights and responsibilities of property and citizenship, and to act without her husband's consent in matters related to her own property, but women were undeniably second class citizens in both the Habsburg and Italian societies.[89]

Despite the basic legal inequities, the fascist regime remained committed to maintaining women's juridical rights, which were, as an article in the *Almanacco della donna* argued, "in all [ways] equal to those of the man."[90] Misogynist interpretations of equality and notions of complementarity influenced decisions and appeared to circumscribe women's rights, but fascist insistence on offering equal justice was not an empty rhetorical promise. As Paulovich's case showed, women enjoyed access to institutions of justice, and the courts upheld women's civil rights as far as they were understood and written in the law. Fascist legal professionals accepted the responsibility to protect women from arbitrary action that jeopardized their rights or interests. The regime worked to promote (and even force) public / private collaboration in institutions and in the practice of law to insure the care of mothers, infants, children, the disabled, the old, and other groups considered lacking in capacity and protections.[91]

The Administrative Court of the Council of State, bound to its traditional role as an arbiter of legal rights and privileges between various arms of the government and between the government and individuals, decided cases within the framework of the gendered assumptions and expectations of fascist society. But Administrative Court justices interpreted the intent and applicability of administrative laws in the same manner for women and men. The justices engaged in careful and painstaking fact-finding to inform their deliberations and interpret the laws based on their belief in individual rights.

Women's cases generally came before the Administrative Court in three types of disputes—in disagreements with the National Ministry of Education over posts, transfers, pay grades, and pensions; in complaints against localities or national entities that had seized immovable property and land by eminent domain for public projects; and in matters related to the grant, suspension, or revocation of commercial licenses or pensions.[92]

A case brought before Section Five in 1929 affirmed the Administrative Court's commitment to women's rights to hold civil service posts despite the regime's efforts to dissuade them from employment in the public sphere. The court ruled that an official could not annul the results of a public competition because a woman had won it. The magistrates affirmed local officials' right to annul the results of the competition in the face of overriding public interest, but argued that women as public workers enjoyed full juridical protection.[93]

In another case, the court upheld the mayor of Ascoli's ruling in a dispute between two women over a teaching post. The decision testified to the administrative judges' attention to requirements of the laws within the framework of fascist assumptions regarding women, work, and family. In awarding the disputed post, the mayor had considered first reasons of family. According to fascist guidelines, "married women or widows with minor children needing assistance of their mothers" had precedence over others. Second, he took into account reasons of health. Only after he had evaluated these two biological or organic states did he consider seniority and quality of service. The mayor's ranking of the considerations of family and health before seniority and quality of service conformed to the fascist statutes that placed biological and social circumstances over professional accomplishments.

In the Ascoli dispute, at issue was the relative weight given to each of several different factors used to assess familial status and standing. The judges found that the mayor's priorities conformed to the requirements of the law. Despite the regime's push to honor women with multiple children, Rosa Clary's desire to be united with her husband and to facilitate her child's schooling took precedence over the argument of her adversary who claimed precedence for the post based on the fact that she had two children, not one.[94] Another case in 1932 involving Neapolitan teachers affirmed the judges' commitment to the law and the precedence of biological over professional factors in decisions regarding women's work. Precedence for the post, in an entirely different region of the country, was decided on the same grounds.[95] Even in 1937, criteria for precedence and the tenor of the court's decisions remained the same.[96]

The Administrative Court was not the only forum open to women seeking personal justice. Special petitions to the king or to Mussolini led to exceptions to the laws delineating men's from women's working spheres. In 1930 Leopalda Snidersich, the widow Malli, appealed to Mussolini for revocation of an order dismissing her daughter from a municipal banking position in Trieste. Snidersich had lost one son to World War I and a second died in 1928. She noted that her husband had passed away after a long and paralyzing illness in 1929, leaving her destitute with one unemployed son and her only support coming from her forty-one-year-old daughter Emilia Malli. Police officials affirmed the veracity of the woman's letter. Emilia Malli returned to her post.[97]

Malli's success contrasts with the failure of Elsa Tobien, a younger woman dismissed from a banking post when local banks were consolidated in April 1932. Tobien pleaded for return to employment with which she claimed to support her elderly parents and sister. Perhaps because she was younger than Malli, because officials judged the family to have other resources, or because officials felt she should seek employment more appropriate for women, her request was denied.[98]

The magistrates claimed to base their decisions solely on requirements of the law, but fascist philosophy, political ideology, and gendered expectations affected their deliberations. For example, the court upheld fascism's conservative standards for comportment or public behavior. In 1932 a Sicilian court declared legal the suspension of a teacher who had quarreled publicly with his wife over his infidelity and used obscenities in public. The Administrative Court supported the decision of the lower court in Catania based on the plaintiff's "compromising his reputation and the prestige of educators."[99] In another case in 1935, the court supported a teacher's transfer due to "questionable conduct."[100] Fascist standards for comportment and laws were uniform across Italy, challenging local courts and officials scattered throughout the country to navigate successfully inconsistencies between national expectations and local exigencies.

Women in the Borderland

In the new territories joined to Italy after World War I, local social circumstances did not necessarily conform to national expectations. Throughout Italy women occupied the ranks of teachers at the elementary level, Michielj's praise of women's involvement in public education had less resonance in the New Provinces. Venezia Giulia boasted a high ratio of teachers per one thousand inhabitants, but had the lowest percentage of female teachers as compared to male teachers in the country. The new northern territory of Venezia Tridentina had the lowest percentage of women at the middle school level.[101] In the Habsburg monarchy, teaching had been more professionalized than in Italy, making elementary school teaching more a male preserve in the German model.

Along with the common struggles for education and equal rights, women's political advocacy in the Adriatic borderlands had included ethnic defense and nationalist patriotism. Nationalist politics and political squabbles in the Habsburg monarchy had summoned women, metaphorically at least, to man the barricades against cultural and ethnic intrusions into family life. Paulovich had supported her husband Antonio's irredentist politics and, according to court documents, had encouraged her sons to desert Habsburg Austria to fight for Italy in World War I.

Fascism recognized borderland women's unique position. Nationalism, irredentism, and Fiumianism (or support for D'Annunzio's stance in Fiume) were catalysts for Italian women's political participation from the movement's beginnings. D'Annunzio's March on Ronchi with his legionnaires in September 1919 to occupy Fiume served as a catalyst for the organization of nationalist and proto-fascist women's groups. The National Association for the Sisters of the Legionnaires of Fiume and Dalmatia was among the most popular, particularly among middle-class women in the northern cities. Marginalized by men's organizations, the association concentrated on cultural and philanthropic activities to promote the *italianità* of Fiume and Dalmatia. Although the adherents' central concern was the irredentist cause, many fascist women, particularly in Milan, participated actively in the organization. Mussolini capitalized on early adherents' involvement in nationalist women's organizations in 1919 and 1920 to assist in the formation of the *fasci femminili*.[102]

By the mid-1920s local branches of the *fasci femminili* offered upper- and middle-class women a leadership role within their own sphere. They

had the opportunity to "inculcate the official fascist credo" or, if they
were professionals, to engage in work that "enforced the idea of work as
a social mission."[103] Like most branches, the local Triestine branch appealed to women on Fiumian nationalist grounds and asked them to support anti-Bolshevik efforts. Founded in August 1920, and reestablished in
May 1921 cleansed of members considered "politically or morally" un-
healthy, Trieste's *fascio femminili* functioned among the panoply of local
women's organizations. It adopted a conservative rather than feminist
orientation and pursued traditional women's philanthropic and cultural
activities rather than militant, aggressive political strategies favored by
squadriste (women's squad members) elsewhere.[104]

Prior to World War I educated women in Trieste were often associated
with the Civico Liceo Femminile. Theoretically a training ground for
women who wanted to be elementary school teachers, it became a gathering point for young bourgeois Italian women. Founded in 1881 with thirty
students, by 1911 the school served more than one thousand. Populated by
young women from overwhelmingly nationalist Italian families, the school
fostered a link between Italian patriotism and education.[105] Pro-Italian
political sentiments served as the common ground to oppose Habsburg
authority and Slavic nationalist agendas. Shared Italian affinities and educational experiences allowed urban, middle-class women to separate
themselves from the mass of workers and peasants.[106]

The local branch of the Consiglio nazionale donne italiane (CNDI, the
Italian branch of the International Council of Women established in 1903)
in the Adriatic city worked with ONMI and workers organizations aimed
specifically at women. In 1914 the intervention question caused a crisis in
CNDI's ranks, and by 1919 the rightist faction split off to found the Unione
Nazionale Politica, a violently anti-Bolshevik organization that was the
forerunner of women's *fascio*. An alternative to the socialist and leftist
organizations supporting suffrage and other feminist aims, in the 1920s
and early 1930s CNDI continued to function as a nationalist women's organization.[107] The local branch in Trieste took advantage of the high level
of education, professional talents, and patriotic zeal of Triestine women
to support local and national projects. In 1929 Signora Jona, along with
women lawyers throughout Italy, led Triestines conducting legal research
on the issue of paternity. Triestine women's efforts formed a small part of
broad national efforts to bring attention to legal prejudices against women.
At the same time, Triestines supported the emerging social reforms and

paternity laws. Signorina Pasini led a team of women working to achieve women's suffrage, a right that even in 1929 the CNDI insisted Mussolini "recognized and promised to concede."[108]

In 1929 the Fascio worked directly to further the regime's agenda by supporting a branch of the worker's organization *Dopolavoro* aiming to help poor women. The Triestine *fascio* also assisted in fundraising efforts for a new section of the *fasci femminili* in Fiume, where the Oberdan Cell sought monies to erect a monument to the memory of its namesake the "martyred" Guglielmo Oberdan.[109] The Fiumian section's dedication to Oberdan testified to local women's commitment to the defense of Italianness against foreign threats and commitment to nationalism in the borderland.

Statistics on local participation in women's organizations of the PNF affirm the particular commitment and loyalty of Triestines. In 1930 women's participation in organizations of the PNF in Italy hovered at only 3.88 percent. Trieste and Zara boasted the third highest regional participation in the country at 5.94 percent, after Umbria (8.73 percent) and Piedmont (6.02 percent). Such commitment was not evident in Venezia Tridentina (3.15 percent), the other new territory, and Triestine women stood in stark contrast to their sisters in the nearby Veneto, which had the lowest rate of participation (2.69 percent) after Campagnia (2.37 percent).[110]

Women in the eastern provinces understood their duties to include a special role as protectors and promoters of the Italian people in the territory of the nation protected by men. Italian philosopher, sociologist and racial theorist Giulio Cogni saw woman's role as "the true central hinge of the stock [stirpe]: the conservator and preserver of all the aspirations of the blood [sangue]." This vision took on particular relevance in borderlands "most vulnerable to foreigners" who sought to undermine national strength and contaminate or subsume the Italian race.[111]

Through her support and sacrifices for irredentism and Italy, Paulovich had met and overcome the Slavic threat in the Habsburg lands to help bring the eastern borderland to the bosom of the nation. Her service to irredentism in the Habsburg frontier zone was commensurate with support for the Risorgimento on the peninsula. Fascist officials recognized irredentist activity as patriotic and even considered those engaged in irredentism and nationalist activism for Italy in the borderlands to have been forerunners or early promoters of the fascist revolutionary and expansionary spirit.

In 1934 Michele Risolo, editor of the fascist daily *Il Popolo di Trieste* and head of the Interprovincial Union of Professionals and Artists Syndicate, lauded the "exquisite nationalism of local women even before the annexation (or Redemption)" in a speech celebrating the establishment of a local branch of the National Association of Women Artists and Graduates. He contended that the "richness of fascist life" in Trieste "equalled" that of Rome and Florence, but reminded the educated, elite women and artists of the border city, that their cultural life had to be tied not only to centers in Italy, but "within the Triestine nucleus, to the environment open to world culture—prepared, cultured, polite, modern."[112] This emphasis on the women's "modern" role certainly ran counter to the image propagated by the regime and the typical perspective of a committed fascist who had participated in the March on Rome. Yet, Risolo, a native of Puglia, was firmly ensconced in the Triestine international literary orbit. He was the husband of Amalia Popper, a Jewish Italian writer and a student of James Joyce, who was generally identified as the subject of Joyce's love poem "Giacomo Joyce" and seen as a possible model for Molly Bloom, the wife of the main character Leopold Bloom in Joyce's novel *Ulysses*.[113] While Risolo saw Trieste's heart as Italian, he placed the city's special role, and therefore the unique role of its women, in the international politics of the borderland. An article in *Il Popolo di Trieste* published on October 25, 1934, reiterated Risolo's view. "Trieste standing at the eastern limit of the Patria is the access door for foreigners who from nearby countries come to know, study, and appreciate the luminous collections of Latin knowledge." Women were in the best position to do the "delicate" work of introducing guests to Italy "spiritually" through appreciation of "precious art and culture."[114]

The Contradictions of Fascism

Throughout the fascist era, women were depicted in ambiguous and contradictory ways. In the women's press, managerial and editorial autonomy survived well into the first decade of fascist rule. Teresa Labriola was one of several prewar feminists who contributed to interwar feminist and women's publications. Despite some measure of fascistization, *Almanacco della donna* maintained its support for progressive women's organizations throughout the 1920s.[115] The regime's failure to clamp down on the women's press reflected the fascist tendency to consider women's organizations, press, and public outlets as secondary to men's and outside the scope of men's society. The women's press was useful to disseminate propaganda but remained relatively unmolested as long as it did not openly oppose the regime.

"Success in the Court of Law," published in the Milanese satirical magazine *Guerin Meschino* in August 1926, lampooned fascism's conflicting messages in a caricature of a successful female attorney educated in Paris and dressed in modern style, who performed a can-can before cheering male spectators and court officers.[116] The depiction hinted at modern female decadence, while at the same time presenting the reality of the well-educated and successful woman in the courtroom performing for a male audience and society.

Another *Guerin meschino* image, published in 1930 and entitled "Handbook for recognizing the modern woman," depicted three stereotypes—the Rubenesque woman of art, the emaciated woman of fashion, and the confused woman of reality, implying that women needed a guide to navigate contemporary society.[117] The woman of art absorbed by decadent luxury was incapable of assuming her civic responsibilities. The emaciated woman of fashion succumbed to the dangers of modernism, flapper culture, emancipation, and sterility. Liberalism lured her into materialist decadence that threatened Italian fascist family life. Both the woman of art and the emaciated woman of fashion stood in contrast to the befuddled authentic woman.

Evidence of the regime's contradictory impulses and aims that appeared in the satirical press littered the mainstream press as well, albeit in a more subtle manner. The women's press of the *ventennio* introduced a variety of images of women and supported a panoply of women's voices.[118] From 1923 to 1930 *Almanacco della donna italiana* presented contradictory images. Next to a woman "lost in sentimental thoughts" appeared a woman of emancipationist sentiments engaged in feminist activism. The "woman-housewife" did not predominate. Work outside the home was not condemned. The periodical celebrated the "intellectual role" of women and invited readers to submit literary profiles.[119] In March 1930 women associated with the *Almanacco* sponsored the First Women's Exhibition of Decorative Art in Milan. Supported by a "group of women of the Milanese aristocracy," it intended to be "philanthropic and social in its scope" illustrating the "true attributes of the working woman, whether a worker or artist, whether from a humble family or noble house."[120]

Rassegna femminile italiana, more feminist in its orientation than *Almanacco*, sought to reconcile support for feminist organizations and militant activism with adherence to the regime, reassuring its readers that the "revolutionary forces of change [of fascism] could not but contribute to creation of the new woman."[121] The regime did not ban or censor works that portrayed women in powerful public roles but subtly steered literature away from attacks on the family and motherhood.[122]

The contradictory impulses and inconsistent actions of the regime with respect to women's work carried over to affect the ranks of women who might have been seen as serving the regime's biological interests. For example, authorities dismissed midwives, potential collaborators in the demographic campaign, because they appeared to work at odds with the medical establishment and the modernizing impulses of the regime. Not until the mid-1930s were midwives professionalized and welcomed as assistants in the government's demographic initiatives to increase the Italian population. Even then, although legally prescribed and defined within the bounds of the regime's pronatalist policy, midwives' activities were never brought fully into line with fascist aims.

Throughout the *ventennio*, midwives continued to serve women in two primary functions, legally providing assistance in birth and illegally providing assistance in birth control, including abortion. Their ability to act with autonomy and survive outside the law relied on the complicity of the women they served across the social and cultural spectrum. In the world the midwives inhabited, women ignored the regime's interference in matters considered private and personal.[123] The midwives' experience pointed to the significant gaps that remained between the regime's understanding of the women's world and women's quotidian experience. It reflected similar impulses to those evident in the divergence of Paulovich's understandings of women's role in promoting nationalism from the regime's perspective on women's nationalist activism that lay at the heart of her opposition to the surname measure.

Fascism continued the contradictory attitudes and treatment of widows that had characterized European society for centuries. In medieval communities, widows' marginalization made them vulnerable. Yet in many areas, the death of a husband increased women's independence and even in some cases financial power. By the eighteenth century, the contradictory images of the widow as a figure "of love, of despair, and of liberty," became the source for considerable dramatic material.[124] Among the most playful popular depictions of widowhood that Luigia Paulovich and other women in the Habsburg monarchy would have recognized was Franz Lehár's "Merry Widow" Hanna Glawari, in the operetta that premiered in Vienna in 1905. This dramatic vision of the young, moneyed widow did not apply to Paulovich's situation, but the image of widow's liberty depicted in dramas reflected the real ability of women to enjoy particular freedoms in society after the death a husband. This freedom scared officials trying to maintain social stability and public order.

While the regime took pains to laud and fete war widows or mothers of the fallen, it did not entrust them with political responsibility, even in their own organizations.[125] Fascism moved quickly to subvert the National Association of Mothers and Widows of the Fallen in War, founded in the winter of 1917/18. Under the liberal government, the association enjoyed a relatively autonomous bureaucratic structure with mothers and widows taking leadership roles. In 1925 the regime began to absorb the organization and coordinate its bureaucratic apparatus and structure. By the end of the 1920s, the organization's independent prerogative was eliminated.[126]

The government's treatment of the widow's association typified its stance toward women's organizations. While seeming to promise women's input into the development of fascist society, women's activist organizations had little influence in the fascist hierarchy. Women's activities were generally peripheral and outside the field of the fascist gaze, to be paid close attention only when they could be used to further the regime's aims or, alternatively, when they acted in a manner perceived as threatening to the regime. The fascists co-opted women's public institutional efforts and maneuvered them into roles that directly served the state and confined them to traditional family-based roles. This "co-opting" was not simply a matter of hoodwinking women through the use of smoke and mirrors. Rather, it resonated in fascist society by tapping into the expectations of men and women of Paulovich's pre–World War I generation, who were accustomed to institutionalized restrictions on access to direct public power.[127]

The fascist government brought women into public life and paraded them in public spaces in support of the regime's politics. Public accolades rested on their fulfillment of traditional expectations related to home and family, not the modern achievements for which feminists had fought. Nonetheless, women did garner public respect and attention. Public promotion of mothers and widows cast them as representatives of the regime, turning them into well-known, if unofficial, representatives of fascist life. This public attention encouraged women to see themselves as having public rights and to assert these rights to rally for policies, particularly in areas of social interest where the regime had insisted on women's vital role.[128]

A Widow Defending Her Italian Family

Court documents relating to Paulovich's surname restoration appeal demonstrate that Morpurgo played to the court's expectations for a woman of her age and position by presenting the widow as the victim of an overreaching and ambitious prefect. The lawyer looked to the law to support his client's petition. Yet, he also recognized the importance of the court officers' and the prefect's commitment to uphold the conservative social agendas in support of the state and its institutions.[129] Paulovich's lawyer shrewdly begged the court's indulgence of the elderly woman, a widow who should be treated with consideration and respect.

Studies of widowhood suggest that the loss of a husband or son in war motivates some women to become engaged in political protest outside the customary or traditional realm of the home. Free from the social constraints of marriage or no longer protected by the securities afforded by their husbands, widows historically have taken more public roles than have married women. In the interwar period, war widows or those who had lost their spouses in the national cause felt that they had accrued social and economic *credit* with the state. This credit made them somewhat more aggressive in pushing for their rights from the government for whom their families had sacrificed.[130] In the absence of her husband, Luigia Paulovich likely felt little compunction in pushing the state to recognize her personal worthiness and sacrifice over a long lifetime.

Morpurgo argued that the prefect's treatment of Paulovich violated her rights and was disrespectful to her husband's family forcing her to relinquish the name associated with the "venerated memory" of Antonio Paulovich.

Widows played a time-honored role as "custodians of the family memory" and "prolong[ing] the presence of their husbands through their bodies."[131] Further, forcing Paulovich to change the name she had adopted through marriage, a contract by extension with the nation, "not to mention with God," seemed against the intent of the fascist state.[132]

Morpurgo held up Paulovich's exemplary conduct in a long life of motherhood, sacrifice and patriotism. Paulovich was a dedicated wife and mother and an Italian patriot. Her sacrifice had not been as striking as that of Anna Sauro or other women in the fascist pantheon of heroines, but she too had dedicated her life to nationalist struggles at the side of her husband in his irredentist activities. She had encouraged and assisted her sons in irredentist and Italian nationalist activities, supporting in particular Ernesto's decision in 1915 to volunteer for the Italian army.[133]

Fascism's contradictory impulses to preserve women's traditional role dedicated to hearth and home and yet to motivate them to serve the state as patriotic citizens created the interstices in which Paulovich effectively challenged the fascist decree. Paulovich's petition to the Administrative Court relied on legal process and precepts, and reflected her faith in the principles and practice of Italian justice. The arguments made on her behalf not only respected the system but also were couched carefully in the language expected of a "woman in question." The prefect's intransigence in the "restoration" of her married surname appeared as an unthinking and unfair bureaucratic attack on an innocent and virtuous woman. Luigia Paulovich sought to affirm her worth to the state, to stand for her family, to fight an injustice perpetrated against her as a woman and as the protector and guardian of her family in the name of the nation.

7 A Matter of Law

Italian jurist Piero Calamandrei insisted, "He who seeks justice must believe in justice, who like all divinities, shows her face only to the faithful."[1] Luigia Paulovich's faith in Italian justice was rewarded. She prevailed in her bid to keep the surname Paulovich. Her case came down to a struggle among various factions of local officials and national authorities representing center and periphery, party and bureaucracy, and nation and city over the scope and boundaries of local power in the centralizing regime. Paulovich capitalized on leadership conflicts to turn differing interpretations of the meaning and intents of nationalization to her advantage.

Nationalists succeeded handily in nationalizing territories and incorporating them into new nation states in the interwar period. The process of nationalizing populations across Europe, however, was considerably more complicated.[2] Individuals, like Paulovich, welcomed politically and legally into the national fold of new nations, joined national communities on their own terms and with their own priorities. In the interwar environment, the confusion of nature and nurture, conservative and modern, and ideal and real that characterized the fascists' treatment of women enabled Paulovich to challenge the surname measure and to triumph in court.

The Administrative Ruling and Reception in Trieste

After filing the documents requested by the magistrates in April and May 1931, the prefect in Trieste heard nothing about the Paulovich case for several months. In late November, officials in his office contacted the attorney general in Rome seeking information on the case's status. They learned it would be heard on December 5. On January 9, 1932, the court registered the results of the hearing in public law. In mid-January, the Interior Ministry's Personnel Office transmitted the decision to the prefect of Trieste. "One cannot reduce to an Italian form a name that never had an Italian form," the Administrative Court justices chided the prefect. The surname provisions dealt with "one of the most delicate of personal prerogatives, the family name," an attribute "that our fundamental laws jealously protect." The language of the provision was clear. The title of the legislative decree "Restitution of Surnames to Italian Form" demonstrated the specific intent to restore names. The legislation could not be applied extensively using broad criteria.[3]

On January 26, the prefect of Trieste voided the restoration decree.[4] Luigia Paulovich was no longer required to use the form Paoli. The Administrative Court enjoyed considerable prestige, but its power extended only to interpretation of proper application of the laws and judgments relating to officials' exercise of power. The court could cite government parties for lack of authority, excessive use of power, or violation of the law.[5] Then, they could instruct the authority on the proper course of action.[6] In the Paulovich case, the Administrative Court found the prefect of Trieste guilty of "excessive use of power, violation and false application of the 1926 and 1927 decrees." The magistrates instructed the prefect to annul the decree and provide Paulovich with compensation for her costs.[7] The power to void, modify, or issue a new decree remained the purview of the prefect.

Paulovich's triumph in January 1932 likely passed unnoticed by the Triestine public. Notices regarding the details of the restoration and correction of surnames had been appearing in the local press since the legislation's enactment in 1927. After 1929 surname notices became a regular feature of the daily Il Piccolo. The list of names subject to automatic restoration accompanied information regarding the affirmation or rejection of individual petitioners' bids for surname correction. More sensational or timely news items overshadowed the name notices.

In the early 1930s Triestine public tastes continued to be driven by conservative agendas and, even after a decade of fascist rule, by social and cultural interest in the Italian and former Habsburg monarchies. Il Piccolo announced in the summer of 1930 that the three books voted most popular by its readers dealt with the traditional thematic triumvirate—king, country, and Church—respectively, Umberto di Savoia: Il principe soldato e studioso (Umberto of Savoy: The Soldier and Student Prince), Giuseppe Fanciulli's Il Duce del popolo italiano (The Duce of the Italian People), and Monsignor Del Corona's La vita di Gesù (The Life of Jesus).[8] In January 1932, when the decision in the Paulovich case was announced, the latest film, a historical romance entitled "L'Arciduca Giovanni" or the Archduke Giovanni entertained Triestine audiences with the story of a young nobleman willing to relinquish everything for his love of the daughter of a Styrian mailman, despite the machinations of Prince Metternich and his uncle, the emperor of Austria, Ferdinand.[9]

Economic worries related to the world economic crisis and competition in the post-Habsburg world among the port of Trieste, other Italian ports, and Hamburg preoccupied Triestines. They pinned their hopes on the fascist "rationalization" of local industries and the integration of Trieste-based commercial shipping lines under the United Fleet banner and on the development of the shipping sector, which dominated the economic news. They also looked forward to the tourist season and plans for the Giugno Triestino or Triestine June, a new summer festival designed to draw visitors to the Adriatic city.[10]

Undertaken in the shadow of national planning for the 1932 Exhibition of the Fascist Revolution in Rome, the local exhibition was the border-land's response to the national showcase. The fascist Dopolavoro planned a folklore parade in the city with an eye to underlining Trieste's Italian-ness. The event sponsored by the national leisure time organization was reminiscent of the national costume exhibition in Venice in 1928 that had celebrated the diversity of Italian culture with particular emphasis on the cultures of the Three Venices. A planned international tourism confer-ence and an exhibition of the Far East highlighted Trieste's links to foreign markets and shipping lines' regular service to the Orient to advertise eco-nomic opportunities in the Adriatic port city. The Triestine June also in-cluded events to entertain and dazzle the public including an international soccer tournament, national sailing competition, national fireworks com-petition, and elaborate lighting of the city's fountains.

In this atmosphere, the prefect of Trieste accepted without comment the decision of the national court in Paulovich's case. In the hierarchical authoritarian system, local officials dared not ignore the recommenda-tions of Rome. On January 26, the prefect's office voided the surname decree and "rerestored" the surname Paulovich.[11] By the end of January, the city records office had updated its ledgers.

The Magistrates and the Prefect

The magistrates' liberality toward Paulovich was not surprising in the overall context of the functioning of the regime. Members of the Council of State enjoyed particularly secure positions in the fascist structure. Although the prime minister and cabinet oversaw all appointments to the council, half of the councilors were drawn from the ranks of civil service employees with law degrees who were already serving in the court administration as referees. Although the members of the council were not truly independent, nor were they free of government influence, they were experts in administrative law and, relative to the local commissions or councils, were much freer to interpret and apply the laws without prejudice.[12]

With respect to her victory in Section Four of the Council of State, the widow was in the minority. From 1931 to 1935, Section Four considered 2,830 appeals, only 475 (17 percent) were granted. Petitioners' chances were significantly better against public entities outside of direct state administrations that were considered in Section Five. There, of 4,116 petitions considered from 1931 to 1935, 2,047 (50 percent) were granted.[13]

When Paulovich came before the Administrative Court, the scope of administrative power with regard to individual rights under fascism remained unclear. In 1928 noted jurist and former Prime Minister Vittorio Emanuele Orlando, having left political life in 1925 with Mussolini's declaration of dictatorship, published a revised edition of his *Principles of Constitutional Right* (originally published in 1889). While the book had been re-edited and amplified under fascism, it retained the general format and even the forewords to the fifth edition of 1917 and the fourth edition of 1904. Orlando, a staunch advocate of the power invested in the people, emphasized the science of law and constitutional right with respect to individuals, groups, the king, and Italian institutions with nary a nod to the fascist government.[14] Continued circulation of his ideas pointed to the incomplete and uncertain nature of the fascist legal takeover and to the continuing influence of liberal precepts and leaders on jurists serving in the public and academic spheres.[15]

In the Paulovich matter, the Council of State magistrates expressed particular displeasure with the prefect's handling of the complaint. The award of compensation, a power reserved exclusively to the discretion of the judges of the Administrative Court, signaled their intention to underline the prefect's fault.[16] The Paulovich appeal closely resembled the earlier complaint brought by Nicolich in 1930. In the Nicolich decision, the court had instructed the prefect of Trieste to provide specific proof in each and every case that the name was deformed from a Latin or Italian root. The

Paulovich appeal demonstrated that the prefect had failed to heed the magistrate's counsel in the Nicolich case. The national court was once again being asked to rule on the matter of surname restoration, and once again the prefect had failed to provide the requisite proof.

Despite their annoyance at having to deal with a second case relating to a surname restoration, the magistrates did not cite the prefect of Trieste for "abuse of power," a charge that implied acting with deliberate malice, malfeasance, or intent to do harm.[17] "Excessive use of power" differed considerably with respect to intent. A decision of 1902 had defined "violation of the law" through "excessive use of power" as "fault of motives from which arise suspicions of arbitrariness." In other words, authorities who exhibited excessive use of power generally erred on the basis of false assumptions or acted illogically or arbitrarily.[18] In the Paulovich case, the court sought to correct the prefect's error but not to punish him for a mistaken judgment. The court's decision implied that the prefect's zealousness to demonstrate the eastern borderland's cultural *italianità* led him to misinterpret or misjudge the national governments' intents in the Italianizing campaign. The prefect had overstepped the bounds of his authority and arbitrarily assigned Italian forms.

Local Authority and the Scope of Nationalization

Despite the fascists' insistence on increasing Rome's power at the expense of local administrations, under fascist rule Italy suffered ongoing problems related to regionalism and administrative fragmentation. Even within the narrow scope of cases related to the application of the surname measure, the court's findings and rulings were inconsistent due to misunderstandings or diverging interpretations. In the Paulovich case, the administrative court scolded the prefect of Trieste for failing to prove that previous authorities had deformed the Paulovich name. "While the name Paulovich could admittedly be derived from the Latin Paulus of the Roman period," article 1 of the legislation could not be applied. There was no evidence that the Roman form Paoli ever applied to this Paulovich family.[19]

In a seemingly contradictory decision, in a 1932 case involving the restoration of the surname of the Bratus family, the magistrates ruled that the burden of proof of the name rested with the family. The Bratus family sued the prefect of Gorizia on the grounds that their name could not be restored because it was Latin in origin and referred to an Asiatic cypress tree in the Friulian dialect. Guidelines for restoration specifically prohibited applying the law to dialectical or Latin names. Yet, the state (again represented by Petrilli) maintained that the connection between Bratus and Latin and Friulian terms was a chance one. He argued that the prefect had restored the name based on its Slovene root *bart* or Bartolomeo, changed over time to *Brat*. The Administrative Court recognized that obscure origins made it difficult to ascertain the name's original form. In this case, the magistrates sided with the prefect. The family failed to prove the Friulian etymology of the name, the restoration to *Bertorsi* should stand.[20]

Had the burden of proof in the Paulovich case rested on linguistic foundations of onomastic diffusion and linguistic arguments rather than on the state's need to provide proof for the individual family's name, Petrilli might have won the day. A roster listing the nobles in Zara dated 1283 included a family named de Paoli. A list of hostages from Zara taken by Venice in 1345 included Lampro de Paolo.[21] Famous figures of Zara included fourteenth century writer Paolo di Paoli.[22]

Taken together the two rulings, one for Trieste and the other for Gorizia, suggest that the court was keen to rely on hard evidence, but uncertain of the bases for determining Latin or Italian origin and unwilling to examine closely the linguistic assumptions and details that governed local processes of surname restoration and correction. The court's decisions allowed one family, the Pauloviches, to keep a Slavic surname, while forcing another, the Bratuses, to relinquish one that appeared possibly to have been derived from Friulian, considered by fascist linguists to be a dialect of Italian.

The progress of Paulovich's appeal and the outcomes of the Bratus and Paulovich cases testified to the interwar Italian justice system's inability to deal with the issues at the crux of the Pauloviches' disagreement with the prefect of Trieste—the intractable problems of the multiethnic, polyglot frontier zones. Misunderstandings between Rome and officials in the New Provinces over issues relating to nationalization, Italianization, and measures for loyalty were deeply rooted. In 1918 Triestine expectations for incorporation into Italy were based on romantic irredentist visions of "an Italy more idealized than real."[23] Throughout Italy, the fascists came to power playing on the weakness of the liberal government, but the fascist movement in different regions was tailored to local concerns.[24] In Trieste, the early fascists capitalized on local disenchantment with the liberal government's handling of the annexation. Once in power, Mussolini's government exhibited no better understanding of the contours of local politics or the complexities of local issues.

Fascist propaganda touted local diversity as a factor contributing to the strength of the nation. However, fascist emphasis on the unitary nation meant that each region's distinctive characteristics were expected to fit into the "common nation" that would then "assume the characteristics of the various regions in such a manner as to represent the [Italian] median with respect to other nations."[25] The politics and experience of the borderland with its Austrian heritage, the influence of Central European and Balkan politics, and its Adriatic culture, lay far from the norm on the Italian peninsula. Divergence from the normative Risorgimento experience was not unique to the newly annexed provinces, but the differences accentuated borderland difficulties in conforming to national fascist expectations.

From the beginnings of fascist rule with the March on Rome in 1922, relations between the capital and Trieste were strained. Political mistrust compounded Italian uneasiness regarding local ethnic loyalties. As Rino Alessi, director of the major Triestine daily *Il Piccolo*, later wrote, "The city is convinced that it is not included by the Italians."[26] Central initiatives designed to strengthen fascism's political position or enhance the government's prestige grafted poorly onto the circumstances of the borderland.

For example, the central government's 1925 campaign against Freemasonry, designed to eliminate individualist tendencies and discourage candidates outside of party ranks from seeking leadership positions, translated poorly to the political arena in Trieste. Freemasons in Adriatic cities included many who had championed the nationalist, irredentist Italian vision of the modern state over the conservative religious politics of the Habsburg monarchy. In Trieste, included among the Freemasons were prominent civil leaders who had been Italy's most loyal and staunchest supporters and who, far from being enemies to fascism, were perhaps the government's best allies in assimilation and Italian development. The fascists' reliance on conservative Church-centered political elements to combat Masonic individualism, a strategy that had proven useful on the

peninsula, meant promotion of less respected, less educated, and less politically reliable elements in the local population including the unruly
squadristi that the central government sought to bring under control.[27]

Local Squabbles

The local struggle for power exploded in violence in Trieste in 1925 when
a local celebration of Mussolini's escape in the Zaniboni 1925 assassination
attempt devolved into attacks on the offices of the Slovene paper *Edinost*
and other institutions associated with the city's Slavic population. Zaniboni was tied to the socialist opposition, but local *squadristi* unleashed
their wrath on the Masonic Lodge and the property of various Freemasons.
Prefect Moroni attributed the violence to "rogue squads" composed of rash
"hooligans," who only became part of the fascist movement to "further
their gestures of unconsidered violence."[28] However, his sympathies were
clear.[29] He identified *La Sera*, a newspaper targeted in the attacks, as a
periodical "of Aventine and masonic character hostile to fascism," and
denounced its director, Colonel Cesare Pettorelli-Finzi, as "a Freemason
with a poor reputation in the city." Moroni glossed over the fact that local
party leader or *federale* Carlo Lupetina, a former *squadrista* with a reputation for violence and dishonesty, had a hand in escalating the violence.
The prefect downplayed the importance of testimony of an eyewitness
who saw Lupetina enter the Masonic Lodge and reported that after his
arrival furniture began "being thrown out of the windows." Moroni also
ignored a police officer's report that implicated Lupetina in looting. The
policeman reported the he had detained the *federale* Lupetina attempting
to leave the scene carrying off a candelabra "as a trophy."[30]

Lupetina's involvement in the attacks and blatant disregard for the law
and public order revealed fissures in the local fascist hierarchy and between fascist government officials and local leaders that mirrored national competition in 1925 between fascist hard-liner and Secretary of
the Fascist Party Roberto Farinacci, and the more legalistic Minister of the
Interior Luigi Federzoni. Encouraged by the violent, *squadrista* approach
adopted by Farinacci, Lupetina, and other hard-liners resorted to violent
tactics to challenge and wrest local power from the traditional nationalists who had joined the party with more moderate aims and who maintained predominant influence in the Adriatic city.[31]

The 1925 attacks served as the catalyst for moderate party leadership to coalesce to rebuff the hard-liners. In the wake of the incidents, Moroni, who had recommended Lupetina to his post, expressed his regrets to prominent local lawyer and commercial leader Camillo Ara, whose office had been sacked and villa set afire. Ara responded, "Too late." A verbal exchange ensued in which the prefect proclaimed himself to be "bestially insulted." Moroni notified his superiors, suggesting that Ara's comments constituted one of the "many indications of the disrespect that certain circles here [in Trieste] have for the Italian government." Eventually, a "cordial conversation" resolved the matter.[32] However, the prefect's interpretation of the incident highlighted the mistrust between officials representing the fascist government, the party, the prefect, and local interests and demonstrated his lack of ability to deal with local tensions.

Moroni's hard-line stance also elicited disfavor on the national level. In 1925 Giovanni Gentile ordered Italian prefects presiding over former Habsburg territories to allow populations still being educated in *italianità* to use German or Slavic languages, mitigating the difficulties caused by an earlier ban on the use of languages other than Italian in court and other public capacities. Moroni responded curtly to the directive, assuring Gentile that the situation in the Province of Trieste had been "resolved." Ignoring the very real obstacles the ban posed even for individuals wishing to be loyal to the Italian government, he dismissed the linguistic problem in the province as "nothing more than an invention of the Slovene lawyers."[33] The fascist government recalled Moroni. His replacement Giovanni Gasti, known for his experience in policing and for his moderation, transferred from Ferrara. Gasti calmed local tempers but served for just a year before being replaced by Bruno Fornaciari, a prefect committed to legal reforms, but more sympathetic to fascist methods.

In 1927 another public uproar erupted, this time over the appointment of the new mayor or *podestà*. Triestines accepted that the prefect, as primary representative of the national government in the area, would be appointed by Rome. However, local leaders saw government appointment of a new mayor as unwarranted and unwelcome interference in local matters. Ostensibly to regularize the hierarchy of administration throughout the country, to eliminate locally entrenched bias in the municipal administration, and to further the interests of the entire community, the fascists had changed the mayoral post from an elected to an appointed one.[34]

Although the mayor was subservient officially to the prefect, in Trieste the *podestà* traditionally occupied a position associated with the city's autonomy. He had functioned under the Habsburgs and the subsequent Italian administration as a mediator between local elements and national officials. In this light, the government's "surprise gift" of new mayor General Giorgio Nobili appeared to impinge on local prerogative. "The city declared itself to be humiliated by the choice" of someone not from Trieste. Nobili showing "good sense" refused the post. Local nominations of Fulvio Suvich and Camillo Ara for the mayoral post testified to provincial myopia and disregard for the city's real position in the Italian state. Neither Suvich, a native Triestine and former Nationalist Party representative serving in Rome as Mussolini's undersecretary for finance, nor Ara, the lawyer so recently targeted in attacks and engaged in the dispute with Prefect Moroni, was appropriate for or particularly interested in the mayoral post.[35]

Throughout Italy, the fascist administrative reforms of the late 1920s, particularly the mayoral and provincial reforms of 1928, altered the balance of power developed over the seventy years since unification.[36] But, in Trieste, concurrent integration of the new Adriatic territories into the Italian provincial system and the harmonization of their legal system with that of the peninsula magnified the reforms' effect. By 1927 Rome exercised preponderant power, but the spat over the mayoral post indicated that local elements still held considerable influence. The laws of Italy and the Italian system were not firmly established, and the memory of provincial autonomy developed under Habsburg domination remained strong.

In the wake of the Nobili debacle, the absence of another suitable candidate forced the government to recall local leader Giorgio Pitacco to the mayoral post. The tendency to compromise and resort to old leaders to help fashion the new fascist man was characteristic of fascist appropriation of leadership throughout Italy. New recruits rising through the ranks of fascist organizations often were too inexperienced or incompetent to deal with the challenges and complexities of local leadership.[37] Local leaders, recruited from the ranks, had accrued valuable bureaucratic experience serving the Italian liberal government in the decades since the Risorgimento. In the newly annexed borderlands, this pool of dependable, local talent was not available. Local leaders may have long exhibited pro-Italian sympathies, but their experience was in the Habsburg not the

Italian system. Born in Pirano in Habsburg Istria, Giorgio Pitacco had served as a deputy from the Adriatic region to the Vienna parliament prior to and during World War I. From 1922 to 1926, he was Trieste's mayor. In the power transfer from locally elected officials to nationally appointed representatives, Rome had sought unsuccessfully to replace him. After his recall in 1928, he remained *podestà* until October 1933.[38]

Further complicating the political situation in Trieste was civil servants' and professionals' traditional alliance with local elites in Venezia Giulia, including members of the nobility and commercial leaders.[39] Allegations that local elites failed to support fascism continued into the 1930s. Officials' response to a complaint from an Italian immigrant living in Brooklyn, New York regarding Commander Aristide Cosulich, a member of the family of shipping magnates and commander of the new steamship *Vulcania*, indicated fascist authorities' awareness and resignation to the status quo. The immigrant denounced Commander Cosulich for antifascism. Allowing that the ministry had investigated Cosulich the previous year, the responding official noted in a cynical tone that Cosulich came from an old Giulian maritime family, and "such elements save a few, have in their intimate circles not been animated by sincere Italian sentiments. Among these [elements], we should note, that the Cosuliches cannot be considered worse than the others."[40]

National representatives' distrust of local elites' continued influence and suspicions regarding local officials' loyalties spilled over to affect their opinion of local policing in the borderland. Under the supervision of the prefect, the local police enjoyed extensive powers. Provincial commissions could issue official warnings or inflict severe punishments including "internal exile" or "restriction of liberty" without resort to the courts.[41] In 1929, in a confidential memo to head of the MSVN (black-shirt militia) Attilio Teruzzi, a member of the local Triestine militia complained of the lackadaisical attitude of the police in the Province of Trieste. He claimed that local forces failed to silence Slavic irredentist groups because the head of the police (*questore*) was "incompetent" and "chose agents poorly adapted to carry out investigations."[42]

While the writer could have been motivated by personal animus, his perception reflected differences in policing priorities between the fascist militia and career police who, like civil servants, were not beholden to the

Fascist Party. Local police employed their broadened powers as they saw fit to maintain order and control.[43] Their efforts to infiltrate local Slavic irredentist groups aimed to forestall local violence and maintain the fragile local peace, while the militia members pursued aggressive ideological aims.

National agents and hard-line fascists had no patience to sort through the local varieties of Slavic, Slovene, or Croat nationalism and their relationship to terrorism and violence in the borderlands. Increased oversight and pressure from central authorities in the late 1920s and early 1930s escalated tensions and widened the gap between local understandings and national perceptions of the border situation and the ethnic relations in Venezia Giulia. Incidents of political violence and public disturbances became more frequent in early 1930 just as Paulovich launched her complaint against the Italianization of her surname.

Repression in the Provinces

In the late 1920s discontent simmered in small cities and in rural areas throughout the eastern borderlands, and officials in Trieste received frequent reports of disturbances in frontier zones, particularly near the village of Planina in the area of Postumia. In 1929 five peasants from Pisino in Istria went before the Special Tribunal charged with attempts to undermine the security of the state. The court held them responsible for the death of a man killed in the disruption of a public plebiscite that the defendants had allegedly provoked. One received the death penalty, the other four got thirty years of incarceration each.[44] In early 1930 the violence crossed an invisible boundary, and brought rural disturbance to the heart of the city. Terrorist acts, before then frequent in the countryside, targeted the population of Trieste.

The February 1930 bombing of *Il Popolo*, the newspaper presenting the views of hard-line fascists in Trieste, was clearly an antifascist attack. Traditionally minded conservatives (labeled fellow travelers in fascism by some) looked to the daily *Il Piccolo*—the bombing of *Il Popolo* targeted fascists and fascist ideas. In the explosion's wake, the police arrested several suspects. Some were released for lack of evidence, but prosecutors charged eighteen with committing terrorist acts in Trieste and Istria, including the bombing of the newspaper, Trieste's Victory lighthouse, and several fascist meeting sites. Some were also charged as spies acting as part of a conspiracy to subvert Italy and incorporate Venezia Giulia into Yugoslavia. Several were charged with *strage* (multiple homicides) related to the newspaper bombing incident. As their offenses were deemed crimes against the state, the case was referred to the Special Tribunal. In early September 1930, in a trial moved specifically to the Adriatic city to make a show of the national government's might and success in finding the culprits, the Special Tribunal sentenced four to death. The next day, a firing squad executed them in the nearby Slovene enclave of Basovizza.[45]

During the trial and in the wake of the execution, the Prefect reported that the "air of Trieste was saturated with electricity," and local authorities feared "grave incidents." The prefect did not attribute the tensions to the threat posed by disgruntled ethnic minorities or members of local populations. Nor did he suspect Yugoslav provocateurs. Instead, he blamed the provocations on fascist elements including "more than 1,400 *carabinieri*" and on "the fascist militias" called in from other parts of the country to help maintain order. These troops that "should have offered reassurance," did not instill confidence or bring comfort or safety.[46] The executions passed without an outbreak of violence.

Government repression and use of the death penalty had little effect on the general unrest and rising resistance in the Giulian countryside. The *Il Popolo* trial and executions sparked international protests from Paris to Maribor (Slovenia) and Croatia, and international leaders lodged official protests against the fascist government.[47] In the month following the verdict, MSVN Chief Attilio Teruzzi made a personal inspection tour of the rural borderlands of the Carso. Prompted by the heightened tensions and unrest and spurred directly by the murder of party informant Goffredo Blasina in the small village of Cruscevie (on the road between Trieste and Postumia), Teruzzi's presence heightened the sense that the fascists kept the frontier under close surveillance and underlined their willingness to apply force to exercise the government's will.[48]

In January 1931 the first issue of *La Porta Orientale*, Trieste's new cultural periodical published by the Association for Giulian and Dalmatian Volunteers, included a feature on border guards placed prominently in the section on "Life and Problems of the Region." In the article, Triestine journalist Livio Ragusin Righi separated "pacific Carsic-Isontine populations" from agitators from across the border "without faith and without ideals" who served the Yugoslav irredentist and terrorist organization Orjuna. He blamed these agitators for unrest in Venezia Giulia. Righi contrasted Orjuna's attacks on Italian civilization to the indigenous population's cooperation in higher aims of "noble and heroic" irredentism against the Austrian Habsburgs. While he called on government forces to repress foreign elements, he claimed that the population inside Italian borders "exhibited no trace of [Yugoslav] irredentism" or disloyalty and had no desire to lose their rights of citizenship which offered "success, security, and superiority."[49]

Righi exaggerated the complacence and contentedness of the autochthonous population, but his reference to citizenship was not a casual one. Those born in Italian territories of the former Habsburg Adriatic Littoral automatically gained citizenship and full rights by the terms of the treaties of World War I. However, the status of those born in lands assigned to Yugoslavia or from other Habsburg lands or from abroad was less certain. The treaties of St. Germain and Rapallo allowed many to elect or opt for Italian citizenship depending on their particular circumstances of birth, residence, property ownership, or declared national sentiments. For many in the frontier zone, Italian citizenship was not a foregone conclusion but a conscious choice.[50] With respect to the surname legislation, this allowed an official, as late as 1940, to recommend name correction for a petitioner who was not a member of the Fascist Party, but in his opinion, "nourished Italian sentiments favorable to the regime."[51] During the interwar period, some two thousand Yugoslav citizens chose residence in Trieste. Most were members of families that had long been resident in the territory.[52] Citizenship and legal resident status was likely not something they wished to place at risk, and they also had a stake in promoting good relations between the bordering states.

However, local interests' insistence that members of autochthonous ethnically non-Italian populations were not foreign provocateurs was lost on national officials. They saw unrest and violence as symptomatic of an internal Slavic threat to the fascist state, danger from a "fifth column" (as it would come to be termed after the internal subversion in Spain in 1936). This disjuncture between local descriptions of the border population as peace-loving and quiescent and national interpretation of the borderland as the home of indigenous enemies was characteristic of the portrayal of multiethnic, polyglot frontier zones of central Europe prior to and after World War I.[53]

Reports of borderland unrest permeated the fascist press lending the New Provinces an air of dangerousness. The press played on national fears that hostile border elements were colluding to undermine the Italian nation and depicted the borderland regions as dangerous and akin to a war zone. In the press, violence appeared to rule the day in Venezia Giulia. In 1932 an article in *La Porta Orientale*, reporting on an altercation between a Triestine fascist patrol and a group from Livorno that had visited the Adriatic city, complained of the truculent tone in the national press. In 1931 on the way to a military celebration in honor of Dalmatian volunteers, the Livornesi had clashed with Triestines in a fight that left one Triestine dead and one Livornese in jail. Writer Federico Pagnacco blamed the visitors for the tragedy. "Evidently Trieste and Gorizia are suspect areas, they are not [considered] Italian like the other cities of Italy." With resentment he noted, anyone attending "a national convention in Mantua or even in Tripoli would not take precautions to arm himself as did those coming to Trieste and Gorizia."[54]

National fears that Triestines did not feel allegiance to Italy were largely unfounded. The history of support for Italian causes and conservative nationalist sympathies that had led the city to early support for fascism continued, and many came forward to support Italian agendas and nationalizing campaigns. The handbook for Italianization praised the example of the noble Thurn und Taxis family in the town of Duino (nearby Trieste) that had volunteered for a correction to Torre e Tasso. It underlined the nobility of the family's action and compared it to the British royal family's adoption of the name Windsor during World War I.[55]

Pizzagalli suggested that "modest commercial agents and humble workers" were among the first to ask for name corrections. He attributed their alacrity to their being "less tied to their names than the elevated classes."[56] But their eagerness was likely, instead, a mark of their economic and social vulnerability and a testament to their pragmatism or opportunism. Name correction could be a means to avoid being branded, or seeing one's children branded, as foreign, unworthy, or inferior members of society. In turn-of-the-century Germany economic mobility and the desire for social advancement had motivated Jews to change their names.[57] Certainly

in the eastern borderland of interwar Italy, the case was similar for some
with Slavic names who saw the option to adopt an Italian sounding name
as a means to accelerate assimilation.

Justice in the Prefecture

Although the prefect and naming officials maintained that surname Italianization was a scientific process, and officials claimed to adhere to the
laws and to respect members of the local population's rights, their justice
was not blind. The handbook for Italianization lauded nationalizing impulses and encouraged Italianization at all social ranks, but, in practice,
officials steered clear of restoring the names of well-known and influential
families. They simply failed to identify an Italian or Latin root for the surnames of prominent families. The names of shipping magnates, including
the Cosuliches and Tripcoviches, despite the *ich* or *vich* suffix that had
served as a characteristic marker for restoration, did not appear on the
commission's list. Nor did the families come forward to have their names
corrected. If functionaries restored the name of an influential family
against the family's desires, generally a phone call or conversation with the
prefect was enough to have the restoration voided and the original name
returned.

Viewed in this light, Paulovich may have interpreted Triestine officials'
refusal to accede to her request for a stay of the decree issued to her family
as a personal affront. Despite demonstrated irredentist commitment, the
support of the prefect of Sondrio, and the family's good standing, the Pauloviches did not merit the prefect's special consideration. Certainly the Paulovich family was aware, by rumor if not through first-hand knowledge, that
officials afforded special treatment to a select few and tended to apply
standards inconsistently. In the text of the widow's appeal, Paulovich's lawyer, in fact, raised objection to the inattention shown by the prefect in his
treatment of loyal citizens of Italy. In the more neutral and disengaged
atmosphere in Rome, this complaint coupled with the court's opinion that
the prefect had applied the law arbitrarily led the justices to affirm that the
family's choice to challenge the restoration did not call into question the
purity of their Italian sentiments.

Evidence that the committee acted on the basis of a selective list compiled by different experts in each affected province further undermined

the prefect in the eyes of Rome. Corrections granted or denied on a case-by-case basis affirmed the arbitrary nature of the surname process. Neither the modification to Paoli nor the court's decision to allow Luigia and Ines to maintain the name Paulovich standardized the family's surname in a manner consistent with the government's expectations for familial and patrilineal transmission of surnames. The correction of Enrico's name to Paolucci created an anomaly and violated legal principles that held that all members of a family should maintain the same name. The handbook for Italianization had underlined this commitment to maintaining familial consistency, affirming the *as before, so after* principle with respect to maintaining name concordances for family members after correction or restoration.

Yet, Pizzagalli had to admit, the "reduction of a surname remained a private initiative." Triestine authorities faced numerous cases like the Pauloviches where questions of consistency of the family name, individual preferences, and nuclear families' aspirations clashed with aims for Italianization. Requested changes affected the immediate family, but they could not be applied to the extended family.[58] In essence then, in the borderland, rather than affirm ties to the family and the broader state, surname alteration erased markers of family networks and familial ties. In some measure, it affirmed the importance of the nuclear family unit prized by the fascists as a building block of the nation.

Authorities also faced questions in cases where the prefect in another province affected by the legislation had acted on a name in a way that officials in Trieste interpreted to be inappropriate. Many immigrants shared the experience of the Pauloviches and came to Trieste, either before or after World War I, from small villages along the Adriatic coast in Istria or Dalmatia or from inland mountain hamlets near Gorizia. Many families, therefore, had members scattered across the frontier prefectures. The files include several petitions asking for rectification of the spelling or revision of a correction or restoration to match the form given to an uncle, brother, or other family member.[59] The handbook cited, for example, the case of a man named Pachor whose brother had been given the name Pace in another province. Officials in Trieste pointed out that the correction of Pachor to Pace did not conform to linguistic guidelines for reductions, but argued that the Triestine should be appeased and allowed to maintain the same name as his brother.[60]

Not only were the specific names and alterations inconsistent across various prefectures, but the various prefects' zeal and interpretations of the measure's scope and the importance of the surname campaign varied as well. Prefect Porro elected to move forward with the restoration for Ernesto Paulovich, despite his residence in Sondrio and against the counsel of Prefect Vaccari of Zara, who was a special favorite of the leadership in Rome. Triestine officials also entertained requests for Italianization from citizens living abroad, against the counsel of Vaccari and others who suggested that the legislation was limited to residents. Some emigrants to the United States who claimed their Italian residence as Trieste succeeded in having their names Italianized.[61]

Further contributing to inconsistencies in the surname measure's application was provincial officials' hesitance or reluctance to disturb the fragile ethnic terrain to pursue the cases of those who failed to comply with restoration orders. Officially, the persistent use of the old form of a surname or noble predicate after restoration was punishable by a fine of five hundred to five thousand lire.[62] In 1931 the mayor of a small village north of Posthumia, in an area populated primarily by ethnic Slovenes, denounced a local resident who "resolutely refused" to use the new Italian form of his name when signing the birth registry for his new baby.[63] A political appointee and a civil servant reliant on fascist favor to keep his position, the mayor in the Slovene enclave may have felt compelled to forward the information to the prefect out of a sense of loyalty, duty, or commitment to the nationalizing legislation. He may have filed the report to draw superiors' attention to his diligence or for fear that someone might denounce him for failing to report the infraction. Or, the denunciation could have been his way of settling a personal score or getting the upper hand in a feud in the small town. No matter what the motivation, the filing of the report implies that the mayor expected some response from the prefect in Trieste.

Provincial officials disappointed him. The mayor's report reached Pizzagalli's desk, but it appears that he simply initialed it and placed it in the files. A linguist and Italian nationalist academic, Pizzagalli certainly saw the process of surname nationalization—tracing the etymology of names, identifying those to be restored or corrected, and constructing what he judged to be *elegant* new Italian forms—as an engaging intellectual project. Intimately involved in the elaboration of the administrative process, the head of the Triestine committee appeared to have little interest or motivation to pursue individual cases of noncompliance. Acts of defiance by disgruntled individuals in isolated environments would have little effect on the integrity of the process and no impact on the triumph of Italy and Italian civilization in the borderland.

Paulovich's refusal to comply could not be filed away and ignored. She did not simply flout the legislation. She engaged the Italian justice system in her struggle against it. Accepting the mantle of responsibility Paulovich offered them to maintain the integrity of Italian justice, the magistrates in Rome scolded Triestine officials for their careless application of the surname restoration measure. "The law of 1926 represented an exceptional provision with the prescribed political aim to repair works of Germanization and Slavicization, conducted by any method, under the Habsburgs, among the populations of the Italian lands, now re-conquered and rejoined to the Mother Country."[64]

Morpurgo had proven that the family bore the surname Paulovich in Dalmatia prior to Habsburg domination. He also called into question the presupposition that Paulovich derived from Paulus, a Roman root. Morpurgo suggested that the suffix *ich* was common in Istria and Dalmatia prior to the Habsburg takeover and that it was no indication that a name had been "deformed under the Habsburg yoke."[65] The assumption that the addition of the suffix *ich* had been the result of deliberate Slavicization had served as the justification for many of the alterations. In one case, a petitioner took the emphasis on Western civilization further back than ancient Rome, requesting correction of his name to its Greek root by removing the final *vich*. Despite the unorthodox nature of the request that did not conform to the requirement to revert to an Italian or Latin root, authorities had acceded to the request.[66] Fascist sympathies for classical civilization no doubt guided authorities' decisions. The case made evident the fact that authorities had lost sight of the nationalizing intent of surname restoration decree. De-Slavicization trumped Italianization in clear violation of the measure.

Early in the surname campaign, despite his stated commitment to maintain the law and enforce the surname legislation without bias, Pizzagalli revealed his inclination to interpret the measure as a means to erase evidence of Slavic influence or presence. In response to a fascist official's complaint that his Genovese surname appeared on the committee's list as the restored form for a Hungarian name, "probably of Slovene origin," and this "tainted" his pure Italian name, Pizzagalli responded, "in a generation or two the memory of the Slavic origin will be entirely lost."[67] He apparently forgot that names of Slavic origin were not subject to the legislation. It covered only names Italian or Latin in origin.

The court's ruling in the Paulovich case that required the prefect to prove a name was deformed reined in authorities in the borderland. It was intended to remind them that the legislation's intent was to welcome and educate to promote Italian culture and belonging. It called into question the prefect and commission's handling of the entire surname restoration process. Italian law required the prefect to take action to comply with the court's decision. But, it did not require the prefect to apply the decision to others who shared in the complainants' circumstances.[68] Effectively, this meant that restorations already granted stood as they were, and that local officials in Trieste remained free to interpret and enforce the legislation as they saw fit and appropriate. The varieties of interpretations of the surname measure and the inconsistencies in its application reflected the ways in which the fascist administration (particularly through the prefects' offices) acted neither as an "opaque nor a reflecting glass," but rather like a "prism, receiving and refracting light" from the environment to redirect it back and change the look of the environment itself.[69] As Orestano noted, legal professionals recognized their role in ruling on the legality of variations as the result of the "extreme complexity of the phenomena of law [that] requires a series of approximations and progressive definitions."[70]

Interpreting the Court's Decision

The prefect did make some changes to the surname restoration process to avoid clashing with Rome over similar issues in the future. No law had required that widows continue to use a deceased husbands' surname, although in common practice most did. In the name handbook, Pizzagalli had contended that it would be inopportune to hold two surnames in diverse languages and had signaled his intention to restore both.[71] Paulovich's maiden name seemed to have escaped his scrutiny, but the result of the hearing meant that the linguistic consonance of her two names was restored. The magistrates had affirmed in their ruling that a dead man's name was sacrosanct and could not be altered. Prefect Porro and Pizzagalli interpreted this to mean that widows' married surnames could not be restored or corrected. After 1932, several widows' petitions bore a note, written and signed by Pizzagalli, "no, because she is a widow." This did not, however, have an impact on their maiden names, which were still subject to the restoration and correction legislation. No mention was made of the fact that these names were inherited from fathers, who, like spouses, might be living or dead when the surname was corrected or restored.

Obviously the shift in policy and inconsistencies in dealing with women's names led to confusion among petitioners. Functionaries referred several cases to Pizzagalli and the linguistic experts for their opinions, and here too, official action was inconsistent, with officials making exceptions to their own rules based on their interpretations of the law and social norms. In enforcing the standards for nationalization or name change, the desires of male relatives and the strength of the family and traditions of family law sometimes proved stronger than officials' commitments to force consistency in the application of legal standards. A young widow successfully petitioned for a correction of her married name in 1934, seeking to make the name consistent with that of her father-in-law and to allow the grandchildren to carry on the Italianized form of the family's name. The paternal grandfather's rights and wishes paired with desires to maintain consistency in the family obviously swayed officials in favor of granting the widow's request.

The general adjustment made with respect to widows aside, the prefect's approach to corrections and restorations remained essentially the same after the Paulovich verdict. Formal appeals to Rome remained few, but Giulio Morpurgo continued to bring cases before the Administrative Court, and the court became increasingly curt in subsequent rulings. In 1937, the tone of the Advocate General's memo to the prefect of Trieste in response to a surname restoration appeal reflected annoyance. The case once again referred to a family of Dalmatian origin, one that had immigrated to Trieste from Ragusa in 1850. Again the case referred to the restoration of a widow's married surname. Morpurgo reiterated the family's objections and reminded the court that the name would not have been deformed in independent Ragusa in the years prior to the Napoleonic occupation. The magistrates responded, "It is impossible to forget that in this argument the Council of State has repeatedly affirmed its point of view in the sense that purely etymological investigation is insufficient to authorize restoration of surnames to an Italian form." They cited the prefect for "excessive use of power" and affirmed the decision in the Nicolich case, the Paulovich case, and two additional cases decided in 1934. They admitted that prefectural officials might be "inspired by high and important political aims," but they acted in error and were once again required to pay the court costs.[72]

In reality, Rome was concerned with the overall picture of Italianization and with the provincial authorities' obedience to central initiatives and actions to uphold the fascist law, but they were not particularly preoccupied with the mechanics of restorations or with the finer linguistic points of name transformation that engaged Pizzagalli and his commission. Officials in Rome wrote to Trieste begging for a swift name correction to be issued to a captain receiving a medal in a formal public ceremony. Authorities in the prefect's office in Trieste promised to expedite the correction, but insisted that the form suggested by Rome was "illegal," lacking "an Italian resonance" and could not be approved. The Triestine committee suggested a different Italianization, which was granted forthwith and in time for the national ceremony.[73]

As time passed, more anomalies surfaced that compelled officials to deal with complicated situations arising from the legal inconsistencies and contradictions embedded in the renaming process. Regulations became more stringent, and more rules were applied. Particularly after 1940, petitioners found it difficult to receive permission to correct names or take on preferred name forms. Not only were requests made after 1938 scrutinized carefully to ensure that the petitioner met the regime's racial standards (i.e. was not considered Jewish) but, after Italy's entry into World War II, individuals with Slavic names were viewed with more suspicion. Before the onset of the racial legislation, the Axis Alliance, and the beginning of war, there was little direct prejudice aimed against those who bore exotic names. Many simply had not felt the need or perhaps had not bothered to pursue name correction. Italianization had been an option open to them, but was not compulsory.

Once fascist standards tightened and prejudice compelled individuals to seek Italianization, it was often too late. Failure to show alacrity for nationalization had rendered them suspect. This was true equally of those bearing names of Slavic and German etymology. Slavic names aroused suspicion as a result of Yugoslav-Italian politics and hostilities between the two states. They also raised the specter of socialism and communism. German names, while they might be expected to be more easily accepted in the borderland once the alignment with Germany became clear in 1939, were often associated with Jewishness and hence, even when not indicative of Jewish origin, became a liability after the passage of the racial laws. The wholesale drive to rename the borderland trampled on the rights of those bearing foreign names regardless of their political affiliations or national associations. Magistrates serving on the Administrative Court in Rome recognized the threat of blind nationalization to Italian justice and central power. Their view contrasted with that of Italian nationalists, party supporters, and administrators in the borderland who justified Italianization in the name of strengthening Italy, asserting control over territories, or countering the threat posed by those considered to be foreigners living in frontier lands. The fascist government intended the surname restoration measures as part of a campaign to incorporate the borderland populations seamlessly into the national fold.

The eastern borderland populations received the policies in a climate in which many were already convinced of their innate *italianità* and were insulted that Rome failed to understand local circumstances or to appreciate local devotion to Italy. Italian legislative actions and justice appeared inconsistent and idiosyncratic, and fascist officials appeared uninterested in remedying local problems. The justices of the Administrative Court interpreted the measure and ruled on Paulovich's case in light of their commitment to uphold Italian standards and traditions of justice. Paulovich benefited from misunderstandings between the Adriatic provinces and the fascist capital and from inconsistencies in the state's expectations for nationalization and *italianità*.

Conclusion

"To capture the truth of Trieste, one is tempted to speak only the names, all of the names of the people buried here in Sant'Anna. I don't do it because I don't have the courage. . . . ,"[1] wrote Mauro Covacich in his 2006 collection of essays examining the dark side of Trieste. The names of the people buried in the Sant'Anna cemetery, Calandruccio, Koushza, Valente, Korenčan, Pissek, Baucer, Navratil, Wilhelmi, and Arnerrytsch changed to the "family's new name" Arneri allude to generations of inhabitants of the city who came to settle from all parts of Europe and the Mediterranean to live out their lives in the Adriatic port city.[2] Many who lie in the cemetery, like the renowned writer Ettore Schmitz, whose pen name Italo Svevo (Italian Swabian) captured the national-ethnic-linguistic dilemma of Trieste, were known by a variety of names in their lives and assumed a variety of identities in the complicated culture of the city.[3]

Commenting in 1948, after the convulsions of World War II and while Trieste remained in the international limbo of Zone A of the Free Territory of Trieste under Anglo-American control, poet Umberto Saba condemned racial hatred particularly that between Italians and Slavs as not only harmful but stupid. Saba, who in 1928 had changed his surname from that of his Friuli-Veneto father Ugo Edoardo Poli, described Trieste's "conglomerate of individuals . . . with twelve different strains of blood in their veins . . . held together by the Italian language and by Italian culture, which imposed itself spontaneously" in the cosmopolitan city on the shores of the Adriatic.[4] This impression of "spontaneous imposition" of the Italian language and notions of the city's "natural inclinations" toward Italy lie at the heart of Italian nationalists' incomprehension of resistance to Italianizing legislation.

However, those who insist on the city's cosmopolitan air and diversity and argue that Trieste's *italianità* arose as a result of persecution and repression of non-Italian ethnic elements face a dilemma as well. The broad acceptance and enduring effects of cultural Italianization, including the surname campaign, cannot be denied. Since the end of World War II, Anglo-American authorities and the Italian government have offered legal means to recover cultural patrimony, including surnames, taken by the fascists. Yet, few have come forward to take advantage of de-Italianization opportunities. Individual responses to the broad processes of nationalization remain shrouded in mystery and obscured by complicated personal motivations and agendas.

In 1936, *Life-and-Death Struggle*, a booklet intended to alert an English-speaking audience to fascist abuses and to recount the detrimental effects of fascist measures of nationalist oppression, published the details of Paulovich's case. The author Lavo Čermelj, a Triestine by birth working for the Minorities Institute in Ljubljana in the early 1930s, used the widow's appeal to demonstrate that persecutory cultural policies offended *Italian* (referring to the Paulovich family) sentiments as well as *Slavic* interests. Čermelj, an Italian citizen of Slovene ethnic origins and educated in German, had escaped across the Italian border to Yugoslavia in the late 1920s to avoid prosecution for antifascist activities. He emphasized the arbitrary nature of the surname alteration process and argued that the Administrative Court's decision in the Paulovich case declared the prefects' actions with respect to surnames in the eastern borderlands "null and void."[5]

Cultural reforms like the surname measure intended to assimilate or Italianize populations of "foreign extraction" might have been interpreted simply as part of fascism's maturation process and as evidence of the "passage of the violence of the piazza to the violence of the institutions." However, the fascist progression from violence to legal repression was not linear.[6] Rather, the fascists' use of violence was opportunistic, pragmatic, and episodic. Steps taken "to expand the state as the sphere of law" were halting, but deliberate and lasting.[7] The change in the fascist political climate, the pursuit of more aggressive dictatorship after 1925, and increasing centralization promoted the transformation of nationalist policies from measures for inclusion to instruments of compulsive acculturation into the Italian nationalist environment. Still, the reforms were not merely a cover for Mussolini's attempts to unleash unbridled power. Acculturation was understood as the alternative to the internationalist, Slavic, communist advance in the borderland. It provided not just a tool for exerting fascist control, but the means for insuring the security of the Italian state.[8]

Čermelj's work did undermine fascist claims to tolerance and fair treatment of minorities. Published in a number of European languages, it contributed to eroding international confidence in fascist claims to uphold justice in a unified and centralized system that afforded fair treatment of all Italian citizens. However, it did not alter the reality that by 1936 as many as one hundred thousand individuals bore Italian-sounding surnames that they had not borne a decade earlier. Restorations issued on the basis of Pizzagalli's list were completed in the early 1930s. Authorities continued to process corrections under the terms of article 2 of the legislation, but the frequency of requests declined considerably, to peter off and finally end with the fall of Mussolini and the Nazi takeover of Trieste in 1943.

Surnames after Fascism

After World War II, the Allied Military Government (AMG) in charge of Trieste from 1945 to 1954 passed measures that allowed for the reversion of names. Fascist Italy was unable to "nationally saturate" the eastern borderland or to render it indisputably Italian.[9] While interwar repression, fascist violence against Slavs and forcible denationalization through cultural policies like the surname restoration campaign took a tremendous toll on local populations, few whose names were Italianized came forward to reclaim prefascist name forms. Most often Jews of Central European origin took advantage of the AMG measures to recover the Italian or Italianized forms of their exotic surnames, forms granted under the 1927 surname measure that they were forced to relinquish in 1939 by the racial laws.

The Paulovich appeal offers a striking example power of surnames captured in the oft-quoted comment by John Berger: "All nationalisms are at heart deeply concerned with names . . . Those who dismiss names as a detail have never been displaced; but the peoples on the peripheries are always being displaced. That is why they insist upon their continuity—their links with their dead and the unborn."[10]

Yet, in the frontier zone on the eastern border of Italy, individuals failed to come forward to insist on the continuity of their names. Their reticence hints at the existence of an alternative perspective on the relationship of names to identity. It testifies to a distinctive understanding of Adriatic ethnicity and nationalist associations in wartime, postwar politics, and on the fringes of the iron curtain in the Cold War where understandings of ethnic oppression and attitudes towards denationalization were relational and time dependent. It also attests to an alternative vision of displacement. Many were not physically displaced, but rather remained rooted to contested territory that changed hands and administrations frequently. The German takeover of the Ljubljana province with the Axis dissolution of the Yugoslav state and the fall of the fascist state in Rome in 1943 altered the relationship among the various ethnic groups in the upper Adriatic. From 1943 to 1945, Nazi oppression proceeded at a quicker pace and was more brutal than Italian infiltration and nationalization. The common fight against Nazism brought various groups together in an uneasy alliance, if not cooperation, in the lands of the Adriatisches Küstenland, or Adriatic Littoral, under German control.[11]

After World War II, Italy stood in sharp contrast to Yugoslavia, which adhered to Tito's brand of communism and eventually, after 1948, to a neutral nonaligned international stance. Yugoslavia offered few of the commercial and economic advantages to which Triestines in the port society were accustomed. In Zone A of the Free Territory of Trieste, under Anglo-American occupation from 1945 to 1954, Italian surnames implied association with Western Europe and seemed to offer social and political advantages. Italian nationalists and irredentists emerged as local leaders in the postwar period, and they remained powerful enough to dissuade anyone wishing to come forward to relinquish an Italianized name.[12] Critics charged that fascist Italy intended to "liquidate Slovenedom." Yet, Slovene partisan activity and wartime resurgence of Slovene and Yugoslav nationalism in the Adriatic played a major role in the fascists' downfall. In the postwar world, those of Slovene, Croat, Serb, or other Slavic origins living in the Free Territory hesitated to revert to surnames that associated them with the Soviet world of eastern European socialism and communism. Many families had borne Italianized names for two decades. A generation had been raised with Italian names. Name reversion may have been a low priority or even undesirable.

In 1954, when Zone A of the Free Territory of Trieste returned to Italian control, the alignments of the Cold War were clearly drawn. Tito's Yugoslavia had been expelled from the Comintern, but Yugoslavia remained part of the socialist world and therefore east of the iron curtain. Until the late 1980s Slavs appeared generically to the West as enemies in the communist Soviet camp, regardless of Tito's political stance and Yugoslav alignments. The Osimo Accords of 1975 officially affirmed the territorial division between Yugoslavia and Italy, but the ethnic and political tensions in the region did not dissipate. The frontier zone remained a territory of international friction.[13]

Memories of ethnic atrocities in the region, particularly the murder of partisans during World War II in the *foibe*, or Carsic limestone sink holes (the stories of which grew to mythic proportions) kept ethnic conflicts alive.[14] Grievances over lost or seized property kept Istrian and Dalmatian exile (or refugee) claims and questions of minority rights in the news and in memory.[15] The fate of the Paulovich family after reverting to the name Paulovich in January 1932 is unclear. Of Luigia Paulovich, there is no trace. A mention at the Free Dalmatia website names Ernesto Paulovich, born in Supetar in 1891, as vice prefect and civil commissioner of Italian Šibenik and charges him with involvement in war crimes associated with the region and at the Italian prison camp on the island of Molat in northern Dalmatia.[16] The brief mention places him in an administrative position in Sebenico (Dalmatia) (a natural progression from his position in Sondrio as a career civil servant). He was not officially charged with war crimes, and his name is associated only with an administrative position in the war-torn region. He does not appear on the Croatian informational site discussing Italian camps in Croatia.[17] However, the camp on Molat was notorious as "a graveyard of the living," and, as an Italian and not an occupied territory, Molat was administered by civil authorities, like Paulovich, reporting to the Ministry of the Interior rather than the military.[18] Ernesto Paulovich's role in overseeing the camp and his duties remain unclear, and his personal stance and attitudes impossible to ascertain. Lines of collaboration and resistance were muddied by internecine conflicts in Dalmatia, and the Italian civil authorities clearly concentrated on determining allegiances, dealing with the effects of war, and on bringing stability to the region.[19] The mention of Paulovich and accusations against him highlight the continuing impact of his Dalmatian origins on his life as an Italian citizen and on the particular challenges facing those from the borderlands. It points to the polemical appropriation of Adriatic identities that survived the fascist and postwar periods to the contemporary era.

Despite the history of violence and ethnic conflict and the propensity to ethnic polemic, after World War II local populations in the frontier zones did recognize the ethnic distinctions elided in internationally accepted visions of the Yugoslav versus Italian conflict, and did accommodate a local brand of *convivenza* or cohabitation. Special border arrangements encouraged interaction among local Italians, Slovenes, and Croats. Surname alterations remained in the back of the minds of some, and periodically gave rise to stories in the press regarding the history or peculiarities of local names or the effect of name changes on local families like the brothers Mr. Starec and Mr. Vecchi, separated from one another by name and the international border.[20] Little energy was devoted to putting aside political agendas to undertake a systematic examination of the specifics of the surname campaign, the processes adopted by the fascist government, and the autochthonous responses to fascist Italianization campaign.

The opening up of Eastern Europe and the collapse of the Soviet Union after 1989 precipitated a reconsideration of European alignments and a reawakening of Central Europe. The explosion of conflict in the Adriatic and the disintegration of Yugoslavia prompted nuanced attention to the specificities of ethnic identities such as Croat and Slovene, but also initiated a new era of ethnic political polemics. In 1991 an Italian measure allowed for reversion to surnames held prior to fascist machinations, and a few did come forward to return their names to prefascist forms. But, after more than fifty years, reversion to the earlier form effectively meant changing the name to a form the petitioner, and often the petitioner's parents, had never held. In some cases, changes of sovereignty in the region and migration clouded family memory. Descendants remained uncertain of the original form of their surnames, and, like the Paulovich family's documents that reflected both Paulovich and Paulovič, records for many families indicated a variety of surnames used in various contexts or at different times in the Habsburg monarchy.[21] In the eastern borderlands, torn by war and foreign occupation, distinctive understandings of Adriatic ethnicity and nationalist associations lay buried in wartime, postwar politics, and the political alignments of the Cold War. Perhaps, as Covacich suggests, many were simply afraid to scrutinize their names and uncover their pasts.

The Memory of Names and Nationalism

Individuals' trepidations with respect to uncovering the past through resurrection of prefascist surnames resonates in the worldwide climate of nationalist and ethnic tension today, a climate in which choices made by national authorities for political exigency may not correspond to ethnic or nationalist ideals or local perceptions. Memories of the aggression and militarism that marked fascism and the violent oppression and repression of the Adriatic populations in the war years supplant the vision of an interwar city still coming to terms with inclusion in Italy. Study of the particulars of the surname campaign and the Paulovich case bring into sharp relief the insecurities of the Italian state and the varieties of Italian patriotism articulated in border identities.[22] The uncertainties of the interwar period, buried by post–World War II events and conflicts related to the bifurcation of identities in the Cold War, resurfaced for Italy in the eastern Adriatic in the early 1990s with the end of the Cold War and the emergence of the new independent states of Slovenia and Croatia.

Triestine poet Umberto Saba's aggravation at the "absence of any valid cultural signposts" is lost in modern hypersensitivity to the multiplicity of conflicting signposts.[23] The competition to parse out the constituent elements of Adriatic identity and the politically motivated drive to be sensitive to reified categories of Slovene, Croat, Serb, and Italian, based in contemporary statal associations ignores the flexibility, malleability, and inconstancy of overlapping and competing associations that composed (and continue to compose) individuals' identities. Discourses on Adriatic hybridity offer conceptual roadmaps useful for assessing the nuances of political alignments in the frontier region.[24] Yet, by their very nature, they rely on assumptions of the mixture of essentialized categories or reified identities. Analysis of Paulovich's experience reflects as much on the nature of fascist totalitarian society in the interwar period as it does on the response of individuals to nationalist politics and policies today in its attempt to plumb the depths of individual associations and the ever changing and relational contexts for understandings of ethnic and cultural positions.

The manner in which Triestine authorities chose to enforce nationalist provisions paved the way for the widow's protest. The ambiguities and systemic inconsistencies of fascist governance, the push and tug of reform as the fascist government sought to centralize and define the boundaries of state power in the first decade of rule, and the survival of liberal juridical institutions and ideals allowed for her triumph. To cast the widow Paulovich simply as a heroic elderly woman who refused to allow herself to be the victim of an overly aggressive state ignores the complex nature of power, the influence of status and gender, the prevailing notions of the law and justice, and the realities of quiescence and dissent under the fascist regime. Unlike the Nazis who tended to ignore ethical questions in the formulation of justice or obscured breaches of commonly accepted ethical precepts by "reformulating them as questions of administrative technique," the fascists accepted that the articulation and execution of justice was not an objective "science" based on blind adherence to the precepts and practice of law. The Paulovich case makes evident their reliance on interpretations rooted in political assumptions and climate. Prefascist ethical precepts and socio-cultural values were not abandoned nor were they rendered meaningless and used to disguise unpalatable government administrative action.[25] Paulovich's lawyer's ability to win the magistrates' support and to secure the widow's victory demonstrates the interconnectedness of notions of judicial independence and standards of legality with fundamental ideas regarding ethics and morality. In this respect, the analysis suggests a need to explore the impact of contemporary politics and interpretations of morality on judicial independence and its role in shaping a just society based on the rule of the law.

Certainly, fascist bureaucrats participated in the purge of political opponents and repression of opposition. In most cases, they attempted to justify political repression using the legal system. The Paulovich case demonstrates that fascist officials differentiated between those who challenged fascist laws and those who challenged or opposed the regime. Even under the strictures of fascist dictatorship, government officials recognized that not all protest was antifascist. They used the various means at their disposal to mete out justice that did not always reflect repressive aspects of fascist governance. The success of Paulovich's appeal pointed to the multiplicity of interpretations of law in Italy and impact of the social philosophies of fascism that favored education and gradual reform over repression, revolution, and violence.

The Rule of Law in the Provinces

In the 1930s the provincialism that the fascist government sought to eliminate with its centralizing policies remained a hallmark of local fascist administration. Members of the local populations saw the same local leaders occupying positions of power they had enjoyed for decades. In Trieste, this meant that many functionaries that Paulovich faced had served the Austro-Hungarian, Italian liberal, and fascist governments, while local leaders like the prefect were nonnative fascist appointees.

Paulovich's challenge may have been a manifestation of the cynicism some Triestines felt in light of Rome's failure to meet the needs of the borderland populations and understand their concerns after a decade of fascist rule.[26] Paulovich's disaffection was, perhaps, merely a precursor to the broader disappointment, discontent, and later resistance the fascist government faced in the borderland. Her appeal suggested the workings of "two parallel processes" identified by scholars—the one in which "the formal structures of fascism were being extended and reinforced in order to increase the possibilities of fascist control of society" and at the same time, the other in which "the actual impact of fascism on society—the way in which fascism was experienced on a day-to-day basis—pushed people away from any commitment to the regime," particularly in the provinces.[27]

Nonetheless, the case does not support the conclusion that, in the battle between the center and the periphery, the periphery won. While the persistence of clientism, localism, and provincialism did ultimately have "disastrous results for the regime,"[28] the distinctions between the party and government were maintained. In the Paulovich case, the administrative disagreement and the court's verdict did not signal a defeat for the Italian government or traditional elements within the bureaucratic hierarchy on either the national or local levels. The prefect merely lost the case; he was not censured. The justice system had checked local power exercised by its own representative, but the system continued to function and the processes for recourse to justice and the law remained intact. The losers were fascists associated with the party and overzealous nationalists who sought stricter adherence to what they perceived to be Italian cultural standards and stronger allegiance to fascist priorities.

Perhaps Pieter Judson's question with respect to the populations of the linguistic frontiers of the Habsburg lands—the question of "why or even whether the inhabitants of such language frontiers ever became national"[29]—bears further scrutiny in the case of Italians and in particular Triestines. Despite the borderlands' reputation for avid irredentist and

Italian nationalist policies of the Right, the Paulovich case suggests that the nationalizing project of the interwar period, even under the fascist dictatorship, remained incomplete. The state exerted its power in the political and economic realms and incorporated the Adriatic territory into the fabric of the state but proved unable to transcend deep historical cultural and social currents that defied statal organization and institutionalization. The fascist state and those acting on its behalf could not understand the areas of the border or frontier to be anything but aberrant in their embrace of various languages and cultures. Cultural myopia contributed to the fascists' failure to construct a universally accepted vision of Italian nationalism and nationhood.

For authorities in Trieste, the surname restoration campaign seemed a high priority to affirm the borderland's obedience and inclusion in the nation. In the context of broader Italian priorities, restoration of Italian-sounding surnames in the eastern borderland represented mere window-dressing. By 1931 the fascist government was in the process of abandoning the surname campaign in the Brenner provinces where there had been significant opposition. To assure the population's complicity in the fascist experiment, the government needed to maintain the respect of the people. In the late 1920s and early 1930s, this included maintaining Italian legal traditions and practices and protecting individual rights and interests to which the Italian population was accustomed and which other European and western states expected.

While in some sectors the seeming contradictions or inconsistencies of fascist enforcement of cultural policies may have amounted to little more than "hypocritical displays of tolerance that characterized the system," in this case of nationalizing legislation they revealed significant divergences of cultural and nationalist visions at the various levels of government. They resulted in the erratic and incomplete process of fascist nationalization and allowed for the survival of competing notions of *italianità*. Local and central officials may not have been "as eager as militant fascists . . . to implement [cultural or censorship] policies that had a clear political agenda."[30] But, as the Paulovich case reveals, in some areas representatives of the central government (like the prefect) remained confused and uncertain as to the contours of acceptable or expected acculturation and nationalization of fascist society.

Women and the State

The Paulovich case also points to the need to examine further women's interactions with institutions and officials of the fascist government. In 1976 Alexander De Grand doubted "the success of the regime in accomplishing its aims regarding women." In particular, he suggested that fascism "contributed to strengthening conservative trends but it failed to carry out any of the drastic totalitarian measures which it proposed."[31] Victoria De Grazia emphasized the fascist state's struggle for modernity while attempting to maintain traditional power structures and lifestyles.[32] The examination of Paulovich's case illustrates this deep conflict and fits well with this observation made more than thirty years ago regarding the general failure of the regime to achieve its revolutionary ends. Yet, it demonstrates that propaganda and rhetoric to discourage women's ambitions and independent political consciousness was not matched by a zealous abnegation of women's legal rights. Legal protections and equality continued to be protected and even promoted, at least for women who conformed to societal expectations and trusted in the justice of the system. Nor were women necessarily deterred by the state's conservative agenda. Paulovich's petition for annulment of the decree did not challenge fundamental beliefs with regard to women and their place in society. It did not push the limits of increasingly rigid fascist social controls. Luigia Paulovich used the state's biases as a basis for her appeal. She actively embraced the role the fascist state assigned to women and used it to assert her individual rights, embedded in liberal traditions, to cast the protection of her interests as in the interests of the state, promoted by the fascists.

Fascism sought to *nationalize* women, but the regime's conception of nationalization for women differed significantly from its perspective on the nationalization of men.[33] Observers and scholars recognize Italian regionalism but assume that ethnic homogeneity made internal cleavages along ethnic or cultural nationalist lines invisible. Yet, periodically, debates on irredentism, Italian culture, and nationhood consumed Mussolini's government. These debates were not unimportant to women, but rather the laws under which they were essentially devoid of individual associations or affiliations rendered them mute with respect to questions of nationhood and legal citizenship. Women derived their legal identities and citizenship from their fathers, then from their husbands. Paulovich's

struggle to maintain her husband's surname reflected her own acceptance of her status as essentially a family being as opposed to a citizen or
state being. Hers was a gendered demonstration of patriotism and devotion to Italy.

Fascism touted the development of a mass society in which all Italians
played on a level field, but also paid homage to the traditional ideas of
social order at the Italian state's foundations. Neither Paulovich nor her
lawyer Morpurgo did anything to challenge the assumptions on which
fascist expectations of women rested. The appeal played to broad understandings and expectations related to the specific place the widow was
assigned on the fascist social scale and in the misogynist fascist order.[34]
Paulovich's ability to throw down the gauntlet resulted from her acceptance of her social and cultural status. She used the legal order and her
own resources to achieve her ends.

Legal Opposition

Paulovich's appeal, pursued through bureaucratic channels and with full
knowledge of officials at all levels of the process, could hardly be seen as
subversive. In her lawyer's hands, Paulovich's opposition became a mark
of her desire to be complicit in maintaining the traditional social, gender,
and legal order. Her unwillingness to accept an Italianized version of the
married surname was not disobedience. She sought compliance with the
law, careful attention to procedure, and action through legal channels.
Hers was simply an objection to an administrative error. The prefect's
supporters intimated that a woman as loyal as Paulovich purported to
be should not mind the correction of what they saw as the anomalous
foreignness of her name. However, they did not seriously challenge the
picture presented of her as a loyal and patriotic Italian who had striven
throughout her life to further Italian interests and to support the Italian
nation. They failed to recognize that her support for Italy was not consonant with support for the fascist state.

In its examination of patriarchy's affect on institutional protection of
legal rights and interests, the Paulovich case reflects not only on the experience of women of the interwar period in Europe, but speaks to visions
of womanhood, women's roles, and women's identity today. Debates continue regarding the legality, morality, and propriety of women's adoption

of and use of married names. The variety of perspectives testifies to the broad spectrum of political positions and cultural beliefs that affect women's political status, legal rights, and access to justice.

The case raises questions relating to the boundaries of state power and individual rights that extend beyond the realm of women's rights. In essence, Paulovich tested how far the fascist state could or should impinge on individual rights and prerogatives to enforce cultural and social ideals for nationalism related to patriotic concerns. Paulovich's case, like the Nicolich case brought before hers to the Administrative Court by a man, begged the question of whether or not the state had the right to intervene in private matters in the name of vaguely defined ideas about national security and national belonging. As a legal theorist, Orestano maintained that the practice of law was connected to "the constant certainty of socially-determined efficient practice" exercised on basis of the "typical definition of human relations and actions, collective and personal, necessary or elective."[35] The Paulovich appeal tested the limits of the government's certainty. It forced the fascist state to define publicly its expectations with respect to nationalization in the borderland and to make clear the limits of its willingness to impinge on individual rights in the name of the Italian community or in the interests of the nation.

Analysis of the Administrative Court's willingness to protect citizen's rights offers an avenue for comparison and contrast to the approaches taken by other totalitarian regimes of the interwar period. Totalitarian impulses, given impetus by the expansion of state powers during World War I, emerged in a variety of forms in the interwar period. The proceedings of the Paulovich case illustrate the differences among the Italian fascist approach, which adapted and incrementally revised the legal system and structures, the German Nazi "double state" that subsumed or displaced existing institutions, and the Russian Stalinist revolution that abnegated the existing legal structure and institutions.[36] Fascism's links to traditional state conservatism and commitment to conservative social agendas made institutional innovation difficult. Various reforms enhanced the prefect's power carrying the state's authority into the provinces, but conservatism at the top and adherence to embedded cultural understandings meant that individuals experienced only subtle changes in their relations with the state and government authorities.[37] As Orestano had explained, "Each experience is a contest and construction of relationships, stable and unstable."[38] The importance of consociational relationships and understandings to the practice of law and in the development of the Italian system allowed individual members of fascist society to negotiate the bounds of legality inside as well as outside legal and institutional channels.

Questions of the ephemeral nature of understandings of nationalism and national character and the presentist perspective of nationalizing policies highlighted in the Paulovich case mirror questions that plague Europe today. On November 12, 2009, Nicolas Sarkozy called for open debate on French identity. "Becoming French is adhering to a form of civilization, values and morals. . . . Being French is an honor. It behooves us all to deserve it."[39] Italian officials in the interwar period struggling to define Italianness and to ascertain who merited membership in the Italian nation faced dilemmas similar to those confronting Sarkozy. Only some in the new borderlands "deserved" to be Italian. How were Italian civilization, values, and morals to be defined? Who conformed to Italian expectations? Such decisions could not be made solely on the basis of national priorities but had to be rendered with sensitivity to the international climate, to the problems caused by transnationalism, migration, population dislocation, and international assumptions regarding humanitarianism and human rights.

Such concerns continue to haunt Italian lawmakers attempting to define nationality in Italy's eastern borderland today. In 2000 and 2006 the Italian parliament passed statutes recognizing the Italianness of some citizens of the border territories of former Yugoslavia and allowed for Istrians, Fiumians, and Dalmatians to apply for Italian citizenship. As in the Habsburg period, language became the determining factor in assessing claims to Italian nationality.[40]

The political construction and use of names remains relevant today as it was during Paulovich's time. In 1951 Italian language teacher Guido Posar published an article entitled "Are names ending in *ich* really Slav?" decrying name politics in Istria and arguing that the Slavic *ich* or *ič* actually derived from the Latin *icus*.[41] Despite the argument's obviously prejudicial political intent, given the article's publication in the Free Territory of Trieste by the Association for Istrian Studies and the History of the Patria located in Pola, a city at the southern tip of the Istrian peninsula and part of Yugoslavia under the postwar agreements, name politics clearly continued to resonate.

The conflict over names imposed by Mussolini's Italy continues to seethe today. In 1985 calls for the elimination of some eight thousand Italianized place names introduced in South Tyrol during the fascist period and the request for their replacement with organic German names "grown historically" spurred an international academic conference in Bozen / Bolzano. There, discussions of place names and politics revolved around considerations of the complexities of place name issues and the scholarly attempt to find a "mediating middle ground."[42] The European Community's support for the development of autonomous regions and the protection of the rights of their populations has enshrined rights to the maintenance of multilingual place names as part of the protection of minority rights.

The latest installment in the surname debate in Italy's Adriatic provinces relates to the legislation of 1991 that allowed for resumption of names changed in the fascist era. Radical political changes in the region with the collapse of Yugoslavia, the recasting of states, and the reemergence of discrete national identities that had been discouraged in Yugoslavia, has altered the "traffic-habits" or "flow of subject populations through various cultural, educational, and political institutions."[43] Cultural reawakenings have spurred discussion and debate regarding ethnic roots and cultural identities. Yet, local populations recognize the interconnectedness of frontier lands and the impossibilities of defining, let alone segregating, ethnic groups. As Raoul Pupo has suggested, the situation in Italy's eastern borderland might be better described as one of national *contrasts* than *conflicts*.[44] No clear lines of conflict or separation exist.

With respect to the name Paulovich in the city of Trieste, the state's fantasies of *restoring* Italianness and eliminating exotic name forms became the reality. A 2001 study of Triestine surnames does not list the names Paulovich or Paolucci among the 197 most popular family names in the city. Paulovich can be found only under the name Pàolí (ranked 122nd in the city), the Italianized version given by fascist authorities. It appears as a name associated with Croatian Istria (not Dalmatia), where the census of 1945 registered 42 families bearing the name Pavlović. Twelve of these families were traced directly to the Grimalda zone of Pinguente (Buzet, Croatia) with ties to lands owned by Pietro Paulovich in the late eighteenth century.[45] Of eleven listings for Paulovich in the 2009 Italian white pages, only one is in Trieste. There are 5247 listings for Paoli, including 50 in Trieste.[46]

Modern states rely on names as "mutually exclusive and exhaustive designations."[47] The Paulovich case demonstrates that the state's expectations for administrative standardization of names diverged from the reality of the individuals' naming situation and from their desires for recognition. At some level, naming is an issue over which the state is forced to compromise—to accept individual notions of identity and individual rights to the maintenance of identity, even if they conflict with state intentions to regularize or homogenize for reasons of cultural aesthetics or security. The case also suggests that ultimately the state is incapable of erasing name pluralism. Alternative and unofficial names survive alongside official identities and testify to the limits of the reach of the state and to the power of individuals to navigate and interpret cultural frameworks to test the bounds of nationalism and patriotism.

Notes

Introduction

1. Archivio di Stato, Prefettura della Provincia di Trieste, Divisione I (hereafter cited as TS, AdS-PPT/DI): Riduzione Cognomi, No. 11419 (1926–1943).

2. Adrian Lyttelton, *The Seizure of Power: Fascism in Italy, 1919–1929* (Princeton: Princeton University Press, 1988) and Renzo De Felice, *Mussolini il duce: gli anni del consenso* (Turin: Einaudi, 1974).

3. Benedict Anderson, *Imagined Communities: Reflections on the Origin and Spread of Nationalism* (London: Verso, 1991) and Anthony Giddens, *The Nation-State and Violence* (Berkeley: University of California Press, 1987).

4. The father of Italian Unification Giuseppe Mazzini articulated this vision of the Italian nation in 1848. Giuseppe Mazzini, "To the Young Men of Italy," William Jennings Bryan, ed., *The World's Famous Orations, vol. 2: Continental Europe* (1906), http://www.bartleby.com/268/7/43.html.

5. Julius Stone, "Theories of Law and Justice of Fascist Italy," *The Modern Law Review* 1, no. 3 (1937): 192.

6. In the German national context, Alon Confino, *The Nation as a Local Metaphor: Württemberg, Imperial Germany, and National Memory, 1871–1918* (Chapel Hill: University of North Carolina Press, 1997), xii, 3.

7. Dennison Rusinow's, *Italy's Austrian Heritage, 1919–46* (Oxford: Oxford University Press, 1969) is a notable exception. James Sadkovich, *Italian Support for Croatian Separatism 1927–1937* (New York: Garland, 1987), offers an international account from the diplomatic and military perspective. Recent works, particularly migration studies, take a more nuanced approach to the study of the history of minority populations in Italy. See for example, Donna Gabaccia, *Italy's Many Diasporas* (Seattle: University of Washington Press, 2000).

8. On fascism and geopolitical integration, see Marina Cattaruzza, *L'Italia e il confine orientale* (Bologna: Il Mulino, 2007), 165–206.

9. See Alexander J. De Grand, *The Italian Nationalist Association and the Rise of Fascism in Italy* (Lincoln: University of Nebraska Press, 1978).

10. In the text, the term *italianità*, commonly used in historical as well as contemporary Italian works, refers to "Italianness" as an array of characteristics,

traits, and associations that can be used to identify with cultural sympathies and connections, political or territorial affiliations, or a vaguer sense of nationhood and national preference depending on the context.

11. On legitimating choices, see Simona Cerruti, "Microhistory: Social Relations Versus Cultural Models?" in *Between Sociology and History: Essays on Microhistory, Collective Action, and Nation-Building*, ed. Anna-Maija Castrén, Markku Lonkila, and Matti Peltonen, 17–40 (Helsinki: SKS Finnish Literature Society, 2004), 27.

12. Edward Berenson, *The Trial of Madame Caillaux* (Berkeley: University of California Press, 1992) and Helmut Walser Smith, *The Butcher's Tale: Murder and Anti-Semitism in a German Town* (New York: W. W. Norton, 2002). Berenson's *Madame Caillaux* offers a contrast in its examination of a public trial of a well-known woman.

13. Carlo Ginzburg, *The Cheese and the Worms: The Cosmos of a Sixteenth-Century Miller* (Baltimore: Johns Hopkins University Press, 1980); David Kertzer, *The Kidnapping of Edgardo Mortara* (New York: Knopf, 1997), and David Kertzer, *Amalia's Tale: An Impoverished Peasant Woman, and Ambitious Attorney and a Fight for Justice* (Boston: Houghton Mifflin, 2008).

14. Members of the legal profession needed government issued licenses to practice, and members of the judiciary were government appointees.

15. Alberto Febbrajo, "Higher Legal Education and Models of Legal Culture in Italy," in *Higher Legal Culture and Postgraduate Legal Education in Europe*, ed. Vittorio Olgiati, 93–110 (Naples: Edizioni Scientifiche Italiane, 2007), discusses *external* and *internal* legal cultures in Italy.

16. Emphasis on institutional arrangements and the fascist legal system answers some critics who charge that microhistory often displays "a lack of appreciation of the formative role of legal rules and procedures" that govern texts and affect "the acts they purport to disclose." Thomas Kuehn, "Review: Reading Microhistory: The Example of Giovanni and Lusanna," *The Journal of Modern History* 61, no. 3 (1989): 516.

17. Kuehn, "Review: Reading Microhistory," 519, discusses the *plurivocality* of documents.

18. Aldo Pizzagalli, *Per l'italianità dei cognomi nella provincia di Trieste* (Trieste: Treves-Zanichelli, 1929).

19. Unless otherwise noted, references to the case come directly from documents held in collections in TS, AdS-PPT/DI 11419 or in Rome, Archivio Centrale dello Stato, Consiglio di Stato Sezione IV: Giurisdizionale (hereafter Rome, ACS, CdS-Sez. IV).

20. Lavo Čermelj, *Life-and-Death Struggle of a National Minority (The Jugoslavs in Italy)* (Ljubljana: Jugoslav Union of the League of Nations Societies, 1936), discusses the case and the implications of the Administrative Court's decision,

114–15, as part of a chapter on the "Italianisation of Personal and Place Names," 103–15.

21. Febbrajo, "Higher Legal Education," 93.

22. Adrian Lyttelton, *Seizure of Power*. See Vittorio Olgiati, "Law as an Instrument of 'Organizational Totalitarianism': Fascist Rule over Italian Lawyers," in *Totalitarian and Post-Totalitarian Law*, ed. Adam Podgorecki and Vittorio Olgiati, 123–67 (Aldershot: Onati International Institute for the Sociology of Law [Dartmouth], 1996), 128–29.

23. Olgiati, "Law as an Instrument of Organizational Totalitarianism," 124.

24. Robert C. Fried, *Italian Prefects. A Study in Administrative Politics* (New Haven, CT: Yale University Press, 1963) is an exception.

25. See, for example, Diemut Majer, *"Non-Germans" under the Third Reich: the Nazi Judicial and Administrative System in Germany and Occupied Eastern Europe With Special Regard to Occupied Poland, 1939–1945* (Baltimore: Johns Hopkins University Press, 2003), 1–79, and Michael Stolleis, *The Law Under the Swastika: Studies on Legal History in Nazi Germany* (Chicago: University of Chicago Press, 1998), 127–64.

26. Paul Corner, "Italian Fascism: Whatever Happened to Dictatorship?" *Journal of Modern History* 74, no. 2 (2002): 327.

27. R. J. B. Bosworth, *Mussolini's Italy: Life under the Fascist Dictatorship, 1915–1945* (New York: The Penguin Press, 2006).

28. Letters were sent to all eleven listed. The author would like to thank Santina Paulovich, David Di Paolo Paulovich, Franco Paulovich, Attilio Paulovich, and Silvana Campione for Dolores Calviani Paulovich for their kind responses and encouragement.

29. The phrase *donna in oggetto* is borrowed from Giovanni De Luna, *Donne in oggetto: l'antifascismo nella società italiana, 1922–1939* (Turin: Bollati Boringhieri, 1995).

30. Alf Lüdtke, "Introduction: What is the History of Everyday Life and Who Are Its Practitioners?" in *The History of Everyday Life: Reconstructing Historical Experiences and Ways of Life*, ed. Alf Lüdtke, 3–40 (Princeton: Princeton University Press, 1995), 14–15, points to the importance of the "historical form of individuality."

31. For a sampling of this debate on the Nazi judiciary see Anthony McElligott, "Dangerous Communities and Conservative Authority: the Judiciary, Nazis and Rough People, 1932–1933" in *Opposing Fascism: Community, Authority and Resistance in Europe*, ed. Tom Kirk and Anthony McElligott, 33–47 (Cambridge: Cambridge University Press, 1999), 34–35.

32. Adriano Dal Pont, *L'Italia dissidente e antifascista: le ordinanze, le sentenze istruttorie e le sentenze in camera di consiglio emesse dal tribunale speciale fascista contro gli imputati di antifascismo dall'anno 1927 al 1943* (Milan: La Pietra, 1980)

and Zara Olivia Algardi, *Processi ai fascisti* (Florence: Vallecchi, 1992). The Tribunal is also referred to as the Special Tribunal for the Security of the State (to differentiate it from the Italian Social Republic's tribunal from 1943 to 1945) and as the Special Fascist Tribunal. Special Tribunal for the Defense of the State (Tribunale speciale per la difesa dello stato) appears most often in the literature of the period.

33. Tom Kirk and Anthony McElligott, "Introduction: Community, Authority and Resistance to Fascism" in *Opposing Fascism: Community, Authority and Resistance in Europe*, ed. Tom Kirk and Anthony McElligott, 1–11 (Cambridge: Cambridge University Press, 1999), 11.

34. See Jacques Semelin, *Unarmed against Hitler: Civilian Resistance in Europe, 1939–1943* (Westport, CT: Praeger, 1993).

35. Examples include Stanislao Pugliese, *Fascism, Anti-Fascism and the Resistance in Italy, 1919 to the Present* (Lanham, MD: Rowman and Littlefield, 2004) and Tom Behan, *The Italian Resistance: Fascists, Guerillas, and the Allies* (New York: Pluto, 2009).

36. See, for example, Morgan, "'The Years of Consent'? Popular Attitudes and Forms of Resistance to Fascism in Italy, 1925–1940" in *Opposing Fascism: Community, Authority and Resistance in Europe*, ed. Tom Kirk and Anthony McElligott, 163–79 (Cambridge: Cambridge University Press, 1999), 163–65. Questions of the nature of fascist dictatorship have fascinated scholars for decades. Debates spurred by DeFelice's emphasis on the role of the Italian population and "consensus" have been followed by discussions of acquiescence, passivity, and collaboration on a variety of levels. Counter arguments tend to focus on the role of violence, intimidation, and persuasion through official and unofficial channels and legal and extra-legal means. On the debate, see Paul Corner, "Italian Fascism," 325–51.

37. Morgan, "Years of Consent," 169.

38. Enzo Collotti, "Sul razzismo antislavo" in *Nel nome della razza: il razzismo nella storia d'Italia, 1870–1945*, ed. Alberto Burgio, 33–62 (Bologna: Il Mulino, 1999), 57–58, examines ideas and studies of cultural genocide, concluding that accusations against the fascists "appear adequate in synthesizing the characteristics of fascist politics."

39. Paolo Parovel, *L'identità cancellata: l'italianizzazione forzata dei cognomi, nomi e toponimi nella "Venezia Giulia" dal 1919 al 1945, con gli elenchi delle province di Trieste, Gorizia, Istria ed i dati dei primi 5300 decreti* (Trieste: Eugenio Parovel, 1985) and Miro Tasso, *Un onomasticidio di stato* (Trieste: Mladika, 2010).

40. For a recent discussion of hybridity in the Italian Adriatic context, see Pamela Ballinger, "'Authentic Hybrids' in the Balkan Borderlands," *Current Anthropology* 45, no. 1 (2004): 31–49.

41. Although in the Adriatic families remained rooted to the same physical territory and government sovereignty changed, the Adriatic experience might,

in some cases, have been analogous to that of immigrants who shed ethnic surnames as a matter of convenience or to speed assimilation. Waves of emigration in the second half of the nineteenth century would certainly have familiarized Italian migrants with this experience. On the Italian experience abroad, see Mark Choate, *Emigrant Nation: The Making of Italy Abroad* (Cambridge, MA: Harvard University Press, 2009).

42. James C. Scott, John Tehranian, and Jeremy Mathias, "The Production of Legal Identities Proper to States: The Case of the Permanent Family Surname" *Comparative Studies in Society and History* 44, no. 1 (2002): 4–6.

43. David Horn, *Social Bodies: Science, Reproduction, and Italian Modernity* (Princeton: Princeton University Press, 1994), Ruth Ben-Ghiat, *Fascist Modernities, Italy 1922–1945* (Berkeley: University of California Press, 2001), Carl Ipsen, *Dictating Demography: The Problem of Population in Fascist Italy* (Cambridge: Cambridge University Press, 1996), and Roger Griffin, *Modernism and Fascism: The Sense of a Beginning under Mussolini and Hitler* (New York: Palgrave Macmillan, 2007).

44. Giovanna Fiume, "Women's History and Gender History: The Italian Experience," *Modern Italy* 10, no. 2 (2005): 209.

45. Natalie Zemon Davis, "'Women's History' in Transition: The European Case," *Feminist Studies* 3, nos. 3/4 (1976): 85–86.

46. Alexander De Grand, "Women under Italian Fascism," *The Historical Journal* 19, no. 4 (1976): 947–68. Works that laid the groundwork appearing in Italian included, Piero Meldini, *Sposa e madre esemplare* (Rimini: Guaraldi, 1975), a document and source collection with an extended introductory essay.

47. Victoria De Grazia, *How Fascism Ruled Women, 1922–1945* (Berkeley: University of California Press, 1992), and Michela De Giorgio, *Le italiane dall'unità all'oggi: modelli culturali e comportamenti sociali* (Bari: Laterza, 1993).

48. Angela Kershaw and Angela Kimyongür, "Women in Europe Between the Wars: a Culture of Contradictions," in *Women in Europe Between the Wars: Politics, Culture, and Society,* ed. Angela Kershaw and Angela Kimyongür, 1–22 (Aldershot: Ashgate, 2007), 4–6, and Robin Pickering-Iazzi, "Introduction," in *Mothers of Invention: Women, Italian Fascism, and Culture of the Twenties and Thirties,* ed. Robin Pickering-Iazzi, ix–xxxii (Minneapolis: University of Minnesota Press, 1995), xi.

49. See, for example, Horn, *Social Bodies.*

50. Luisa Passerini, *Torino operaia e fascismo: una storia orale* (Rome: Laterza, 1984); Perry Willson, *The Clockwork Factory: Women and Work in Fascist Italy* (Oxford: Clarendon Press, 1993); and Perry Willson, *Peasant Women and Politics in Fascist Italy: the Massaie Rurali* (London: Routledge, 2002).

51. See, for example, De Luna, *Donne in oggetto* and Patrizia Gabrielli, *Tempio di virilità: l'antifascismo, il genere, la storia* (Milan: Franco Angeli, 2008).

52. Major studies in English include: Claudia Koonz, *Mothers in the Fatherland: Women, the Family, and Nazi Politics* (New York: St. Martin's Press, 1987);

Jill Stephenson, *Women in Nazi Germany* (New York: Longman, 2001); Anna Maria Sigmund, *Women of the Third Reich* (Richmond Hill: NDE, 2000); Matthew Stibbe, *Women in the Third Reich* (London: Arnold, 2003); Alison Owings, *Frauen: German Women Recall the Third Reich* (New Brunswick: Rutgers University Press, 1993).

53. On the recent interest of historians in onomastics, see Joel T. Rosenthal, "Onomastics and Its Uses," *Journal of Interdisciplinary History* 36, no. 1 (2005): 57–62, and Guy Brunet and Alain Bideau, "Surnames: History of the Family and History of Populations," *History of the Family* 5, no. 2 (2000): 153–60.

54. On the "civilizing intent" of the development of permanent surnames (patronyms), see Scott, Tehranian, and Mathias, "The Production of Legal Identities," 23.

55. Meron Benvenisti, *Sacred Landscape: The Buried History of the Holy Land Since 1948* (Berkeley: University of California Press, 2002) focuses on Hebrew place names assigned by the Israeli government after the 1948 creation of the state of Israel.

56. See, for example, Meltam Türköz, "Surname narratives and the State-Society Boundary: Memories of Turkey's Family Name Law of 1934," *Middle Eastern Studies* 43, no. 6 (2007): 893–908.

57. Controversy over the names continues today. The reprint of Ettore Tolomei's, *Elenco dei cognomi dell'Alto Adige: la restituzione del cognome atesino* (1936) in *Die gewaltsame Italianisierung der Familiennamen in Südtirol: wie wären heute mein Familienname?* (Meran: Südtiroler Heimatbund, 2003) sparked debate over the science of names, history, and memory in Italy's northern provinces.

1. Inculcating *Italianità*

1. Pizzagalli, *Per l'italianità dei cognomi*, 33–34.

2. Attilio Tamaro, *La Vénétie Julienne et la Dalmatie: histoire de la nation italienne sur ses frontières orientales*, vol. 1 (Rome: Imprimerie du sénat, 1918), 904.

3. Ernst Renan, "What is a Nation?" in *Becoming National: A Reader*, ed. Geoff Eley and Ronald Grigo Suny, 42–55 (Houndsmills: Palgrave Macmillan, 2004), 45, 52–55. A lecture by Renan in 1882 at the Sorbonne.

4. Dominique Reill, "From Bond to Border: The Position of the Adriatic in the Mid-nineteenth Century" (PhD dissertation, Columbia University, 2007), 58–67.

5. Anthony Giddens, *The Nation-State and Violence: Volume 2 of A Contemporary Critique of Historical Materialism* (Berkeley: University of California Press, 1987), 118, explores the importance of symbolic nationalism emanating from a historic capital in the formulation of the "national" perspective of modern nation-states.

6. Luciano Monzali, *The Italians of Dalmatia: From Italian Unification to World War I* (Toronto: University of Toronto Press, 2009), 74–75, 79.

7. See Monzali, *Italians of Dalmatia*.

8. For the text of Smodlaka's speech, see Robert William Seton-Watson, *The Southern Slav Question and the Habsburg Monarchy* (New York: Howard Fertig, 1969), 406–16.

9. Some Italian residents of Brazza looked further abroad. In 1902 two families named Barbarovich left Brač and headed to the United States to land in California. "Barbarovich, John," http://tinyurl.com/croatian-bio.

10. She evidently maintained contact with family members in Brazza as evidence suggests that her son Ernesto was born on the island. See a mention in the political periodical *Free Dalmatia* identifying him as one of the officials involved in Italian war crimes in the Molat concentration camp during World War II in Josip Grbelja, "Molat- Najstraštrašniji fašisticki konclogor na svijetu," *Slobodna Dalmacija*, January 10, 2002, http://arhiv.slobodnadalmacija.hr/20020110/feljton.htm.

For information on the Molat camp in Jaza Bay, see "Italian concentration camp in Jaza bay on the island Molat," http://tinyurl.com/molat-jb.

11. Angelo Nani, *Notizie storiche della città di Zara* (Zara: G. Woditzka, 1883), 120.

12. Carlo Maranelli, ed. *Dizionario geografico: Alto Adige-Trentino-Venezia Giulia-Dalmazia* (Bari: Giuseppe Laterza & Figli, 1915), 212–13; Thomas Graham Jackson, *Dalmatia: The Quarnero and Istria with Cettigne in Montenegro and the Island of Grado* (Oxford: Oxford University Press, 1887), 232, 238–39.

13. Douglas Goldring, *Dream Cities: Notes of an Autumn Tour in Italy and Dalmatia* (London: T. Fisher Unwin, 1913), 162.

14. T. D. M., *Italy and the Jugo-Slavs in Istria and Dalmatia* (Philadelphia: Joseph Bruno, 1919), 9.

15. Ernest Peixotto, *By Italian Seas* (New York: Charles Scribner's Sons, 1907), 68, 72, 75.

16. Louis Voinovitch, *Dalmatia and the Jugoslav Movement* (London: George Allen & Unwin, 1920), 277–81.

17. TS, AdS, PPT/DI-11419.

18. Leo Valiani, *The End of Austria-Hungary* (New York: Knopf, 1973), 21–22.

19. Text of the "Resolution of Fiume (October 4, 1905)" reprinted in Seton-Watson, *Southern Slav Question*, 393–94.

20. Text of the "Resolution of Zara (October 17, 1905)" reprinted in Seton-Watson, *Southern Slav Question*, 395–96.

21. See the text of the declaration to the Diet in Zara read on November 18, 1905, reprinted in Seton-Watson, *Southern Slav Question*, 396–97.

22. Goldring, *Dream Cities*, 148.

23. Ibid., 128–29.

24. Anna Millo, "La società triestina agli inizi del novecento" in *Friuli e Venezia Giulia: Storia del '900*, ed. Istituto regionale per la storia del movimento di liberazione nel Friuli-Venezia Giulia, 43–53 (Gorizia: Libreria Editrice Goriziana, 1997), 44.

25. Giorgio Negrelli, "In tema di irredentismo e di nazionalismo" in *Intellectuali di frontiera: triestini a Firenze (1900–1950)*, ed. Roberto Pertici, 251–92 (Florence: Olschki, 1985), 258.

26. Reill, "From Bond to Border," 109–20, discusses the reputation of Trieste in the mid-nineteenth century.

27. Millo, "La società triestina," 47.

28. Maranelli, *Dizionario geografico*, 161. The Habsburg census relied on attestations of linguistic preference to determine loyalties or nationalist affiliations. On the implications of using "language of daily use" as a determinant of ethnic affiliation and national consciousness in the Adriatic see Marina Cattaruzza, "Slovenes and Italians in Trieste, 1850–1914" in *Ethnic Identity in Urban Europe*, ed. Max Engman, 189–219 (New York: New York University Press, 1992). For the impact on Slovene, German, and Czech speaking areas, see Pieter Judson, *Guardians of the Nation: Activists on the Language Frontiers of Imperial Austria* (Cambridge, MA: Harvard University Press, 2006).

29. See table "Immigrazione ed emigrazione interne (1910)," in Giotto Dainelli, *La Dalmazia: cenni geografici e statistici* (Novara: Istituto geografico de Agostini, 1918), 59.

30. Camillo Boito, "Gite di un artista," in 1884 quoted in Lina Gasparini, ed. *Impressioni su Trieste 1793–1887* (Trieste: Zibaldone, 1951), 101.

31. Attilio Tamaro, *Trieste* (Rome: S.A. "Edizioni Tiber", 1930), 200.

32. According to figures published in Dainelli, *La Dalmazia*, table "Immigrazione ed emigrazione interne (1910)," 58 (broken down according to region), some 763 from Trieste were in Dalmatia while 5,110 Dalmatians were in Trieste. An additional 4,982 were listed in Istria, as opposed to 1,207 Istrians in Dalmatia. This far outweighed internal migration to other parts of the monarchy, with the second highest number of Dalmatians at 1,290 in Lower Austria.

33. Valiani, *End of Austria-Hungary*, 5.

34. Tamaro, *Trieste*, 219.

35. Attilio Tamaro, *L'Adriatico—Golfo d'Italia: l'italianità di Trieste* (Milan: Fratelli Treves, 1915), 137–284.

36. Peter Vodopivec, "Slovene Intellectuals' Response to Political and Social Modernization in the Nineteenth and at the Beginning of the Twentieth Centuries," *Slovene Studies* 23, no. 1–2 (2001): 3–13, discusses assimilation and integration into Austro-German cultural, social, and political networks prior to World War I.

37. Vivante, *Irredentismo adriatico* (Trieste: Edizioni "Italo Svevo", 1984 [reprint 1912]), 253.

38. Virgilio Gayda, *Gli slavi della Venezia Giulia* (Milan: Ravà & Co, 1915), especially 14–17. Of note is the alternative spelling of Gayda's first name that appears either as Virginio (related to Virginia and *virgin*) and Virgilio (related to the Latin Virgil). Virginio appears more often, but Virgilio is listed on the frontispiece in this cited source. In the interwar period, Gayda would become famous as the fascist regimes' official spokesman and the editor of *Il Giornale d'Italia*,

39. Virginio Gayda, *L'Italia d'oltre confine* (Turin: Fratelli Bocca, 1914), 83.

40. On Gayda's career see, Edoardo Savino, *La nazione operante: albo d'oro del fascismo: profile e figure* (Novara: Istituto Geografico de Agostini, 1937), 579.

41. Attilio Tamaro, *Italiani e slavi nell'adriatico* (Rome: Athenaeum, 1915), 39.

42. On the Slavs as German agents or tools of Germans, see Collotti, "Sul razzismo antislavo," 47–49.

43. Amedeo Nasalli Rocca, *Memorie di un prefetto* (Rome: Casa Editrice Mediterranea, 1946), 232–37, discusses the impact of extremist irredentism in Venice.

44. Vivante, *Irredentismo adriatico*, 190–220. Reflecting the language of the politics of the period, Vivante referred to Slavs rather than Slovenes or Croats.

45. Raoul Pupo, "Guerra civile e conflitto etnico: italiani, sloveni, e croati," *Clio: Rivista Trimestrale di Studi Storici* 36, no. 3 (2000): 498–99.

46. For this interpretation of the origins of the name, see Oscarre Ravisini, *Toponomastica stradale: Compendio di notizie sulla nomenclatura di località e strade di Trieste* (Trieste: La Editoriale Libraria, 1929), 45.

47. Fabio Zubini, *Scorcola e Cologna: amene colline di periferia, sin dal secolo scorso residenza di cittadini laboriosi e benestanti di differenti provenienze e religioni, che nascondono ancora angoli tranquilli in mezzo al verde* (Trieste: Edizioni Italo Svevo, 1997), 135–37.

48. Antonio Trampus, *Vie e piazze di Trieste moderna: toponomastica stradale e topografia storica* (Trieste: Edizioni "Italo Svevo", 1989), 672.

49. Ravasini, *Vie e piazze*, 72. (From whose name the word *galvanize* derives.)

50. Ibid., 206. (From whose name come the terms *volt* and *voltage*.)

51. On Cologna, see, Zubini, *Scorcola e Cologna*.

52. Zubini, *Scorcola e Cologna*, 200.

53. On the history of the Trieste-Opicina tram, see Walter Fontanot and Fabiana Romanutti, *Tramway: Trieste-Opicina* (Trieste: Danubio, 1992).

54. Maximilian I of Mexico, born Austrian Archduke Ferdinand Maximilian, served as commander in chief of the Austrian Navy headquartered in Trieste and Pola.

55. Santi Nepitello, *The History of Trieste* (Trieste: Zigiotti, 1951), 113.

56. Ibid., 118.

57. Tamaro, *Vénétie Julienne*, 1:961.

58. Tamaro, *Italiani e slavi*, 303.

59. Monzali, *Italians of Dalmatia*, 265.

60. TS, AdS, PPT/DI-11419.

61. A member of the nationalist Dante Alighieri Society from the 1890s, in 1906 Tolomei founded *L'Archivio per l'Alto Adige*, a periodical dedicated to "unearthing" and promoting the Italian heritage of the South Tyrol. At the end of World War I, as Italian commissioner for Italian Language and Culture in the South Tyrol, Tolomei was consulted by negotiators of the Paris Peace as an expert on the Tyrol region. *Chi è?: Dizionario degli italiani d'oggi* (Rome: A. F. Formiggini Editore, 1936), 903.

62. Ettore Tolomei, *Memorie di vita* (Rome: Garzanti, 1948), 80–81.

63. Roberto Pertici, "Irredentismo e questione adriatica," in *Intellectuali di frontiera: triestini a Firenze (1900–1950)*, ed. Roberto Pertici, 635–59, (Florence: Olschki, 1985), 635–36.

64. Cited in Ferdinando Pasini, "Ufficio della letteratura in terra di confine," *La porta orientale* 2, no. 12 (1932): 883.

65. René Albrecht-Carrié, *Italy at the Paris Peace Conference* (Hamden, CT: Archon Books, 1996), 336.

66. Ibid., 370–71, 378–86.

67. Ibid., 306.

68. On Italian claims and disappointments see James Burgywn, *The Legend of the Mutilated Victory: Italy, the Great War, and the Paris Peace Conference, 1915–1919* (Westport, CT: Greenwood Press, 1993).

69. On the D'Annunzio affair, see Michael Ledeen, *The First Duce: D'Annunzio at Fiume* (Baltimore: Johns Hopkins University Press, 1977).

70. Trieste, Biblioteca Civica, Raccolta patria (hereafter cited as TS, BC, Racc. Pat.) Attilio Tamaro papers (correspondence received) from Silvio Benco, 12 November 1920, on the local mood.

71. The term *minority* must be used with care. From the Italian government's perspective non-Italians were members of ethnic minority groups. In much of the Alto Adige (Südtirol), ethnic Germans were not a minority. The same held true for Slovenes and Croatians in some Adriatic territories assigned to Italy.

72. For a brief discussion of this situation, see Almerigo Apollonio, *Venezia Giulia e il fascismo 1922–1935* (Gorizia: Libreria Editrice Goriziana, 2004), 187.

73. Antonio Marcello Annoni, "Le lingue straniere e gli stranieri in Italia," *Vita Internazionale* 25 (1922): 312.

74. Pupo, "Guerra civile e conflitto etnico," 503–5.

75. Annoni, "Le lingue straniere," 312–13.

76. Alessandro Volk, "Sloveni e croati tra le due guerre" in *Friuli e Venezia Giulia: Storia Del '900*, ed. Istituto Regionale per la storia del movimento di liberazione nel Friuli-Venezia Giulia, 297–308 (Gorizia: Libreria Editrice Goriziana, 1997), 297–98.

77. Rome, Archivio centrale dello stato, Presidenza consiglio dei ministri, Ufficio centrale per le nuove provincie (hereafter, Rome, ACS, PCM, UCNP), b. 139, "Istria - Tutela pubblica sicurezza."

78. Maura Hametz, "The carabineri stood by: The Italian State and the 'Slavic Threat' in Trieste, 1919–1922," *Nationalities Papers* 29, no. 4 (2001): 559–74.

79. Giovanni Gentile, "The Philosophic Basis of Fascism," *Foreign Affairs* 6, no. 2 (1928): 302.

80. Mazzini's thoughts on education appear in Joseph Mazzini, *An Essay On the Duties of Man Addressed to Workingmen* (New York: Funk & Wagnalls, 1898), http://tinyurl.com/mazzini-essay.

81. M. E. Moss, *Mussolini's Fascist Philosopher* (New York: Peter Lang, 2004), 19.

82. A. James Gregor, *Giovanni Gentile: Philosopher of Fascism* (New Brunswick: Transaction Publishers, 2001), 52, 54, 58.

83. Moss, *Mussolini's Fascist Philosopher*, 37.

84. Marino Raicich, "La scuola triestina tra 'La Voce' e Gentile 1910–1925," in *Intellettuali di frontiera: Triestini a Firenze (1900–1950)*, ed. Roberto Pertici, 320–44 (Florence: Olschki, 1985), 303–4.

85. Philip V. Cannistraro, ed. *Historical Dictionary of Fascist Italy* (Westport, CT: Greenwood Press, 1982), 274–75.

86. Moss, *Mussolini's Fascist Philosopher*, 73.

87. Gentile, "The Philosophic Basis of Fascism," 299.

88. Pasini, "Ufficio della letteratura," 880.

89. Adriano Andri, "La scuola e il regime fascista," in *Friuli e Venezia Giulia: Storia del '900*, ed. Istituto regionale per la storia del movimento di liberazione nel Friuli-Venezia Giulia, 325–43 (Gorizia: Libreria Editrice Goriziana, 1997), 325.

90. Gaetano Salvemini, *Racial Minorities under Fascism in Italy* (Chicago: Women's International League for Peace and Freedom, 1934), 5.

91. Gabriella Klein, *La politica linguistica del fascismo* (Bologna: Il Mulino, 1986), 59.

92. Figures from Klein, *La politica linguistica del fascismo*, table on p. 34.

93. Judson, *Guardians of the Nation*, 24.

94. Quoted in Salvemini, *Racial Minorities*, 16.

95. Mario Todeschini, "La scuola primaria della Venezia Giulia," *La porta orientale* 3, no. 5 (1933): 335.

96. Andri, "La scuola e il regime fascista," 329.

97. Boris Furlan, *Fighting Jugoslavia: The Struggle of the Slovenes* (New York: Yugoslav Information Center, 1942), 7.

98. Apollonio, *Venezia Giulia e fascismo*, 59, 111.

99. Ibid., 143, 176.

100. Trieste, Archivio di Stato, Prefettura di Trieste, Gabinetto (1923–1952) (hereafter cited as TS, AdS, Pref. Gab.), b. 173 (1929). The property was sold to the city in 1929, and the building was turned over to the fascist youth organization Balilla.

101. In South Tyrol, where German schools were not simply a vestige of Austrian Habsburg control but a reflection of native German-speakers' preference and vibrant German cultural life, the Italian government faced resistance to the closure of German schools, comparable to that launched by Slovenes and Croats in response to closure of schools in the Adriatic borderlands.

102. TS, AdS, Pref. Gab., b. 80 (1925).

103. Apollonio, *Venezia Giulia e fascismo*, 197.

104. Ibid., 203–4.

105. On contradictions in fascist messages regarding Italian character, see Silvana Patriarca, *Italian Vices: Nation and Character From the Risorgimento to the Republic* (Cambridge, EN: Cambridge University Press, 2010), 134–46.

106. Apollonio, *Venezia Giulia e fascismo*, 192.

107. Judson, *Guardians of the Nation*, 53–63.

108. Pizzagalli, *Per l'italianità dei cognomi*, 8.

109. Ibid., 43.

110. Haskel Sonnabend, *L'espansion degli slavi* (Rome: Tipografia Failli, 1930), 104. Information on Sonnabend's collaboration with Gini is available in Corrado Gini, "Enrico Haskel Sonnabend," *Revue de l'Institut International de Statistique / Review of the International Statistical Institute* 24, no. 1/3 (1956): 162–64. Gini served as the head of ISTAT from 1926 to 1932. He resigned in protest of fascist interference in his research.

111. Sonnabend, *L'espansion degli slavi*, 135.

112. TS, AdS, Pref. Gab. (1923–1952), b. 52 (1924), "Incidente al Teatro Verdi," 25 February 1924.

113. On the history of Trieste's Teatro Verdi, http://tinyurl.com/ttverdi.

114. Duino holds a place in German literature. The Thurn und Taxis (turned Della Torre e Tasso) castle inspired German Poet Rainer Maria Rilke's "Duino Elegies."

115. TS, AdS, Pref. Gab., b. 81 (1925).

116. This perspective was a vestige of Habsburg politics and alignments. On the separation of Czech and Bohemian from German identities, see Nancy

Wingfield, *Flag Wars and Stone Saints: How the Bohemian Lands Became Czech* (Cambridge, MA: Harvard University Press, 2007).

117. TS, AdS, Pref. Gab., b. 81 (1925).

118. TS, AdS, Pref. Gab., b. 154 (1925).

119. TS, AdS, Pref. Gab., Commissione Consultiva, b. 333, Pratica generale. The commission, while officially disbanded, continued to consult on requests until 1936.

120. TS, AdS, Pref. Gab., Commissione Consultiva, b. 333, Commissione Consultiva Pola to Commissariato generale civile Trieste, March 23, 1922.

121. Pizzagalli, *Per l'italianità dei cognomi*, 15–19.

122. On ultra-nationalism in fascism see, among others, Roger Griffin, *The Nature of Fascism* (New York: St. Martin's Press, 1991).

123. Collotti, "Sul razzismo antislavo," 53.

124. TS, AdS, Pref. Gab. (1923–1952), b. 252 (1933), "Naturalizzazione di israelitici," May 7, 1930. The distinction between *ebrei* and *israelitici* was commonly understood to differentiate "Hebrews," eastern and central European Jews perceived as primitive, backward, religious, and segregated, and "Israelites," western European Jews viewed as enlightened, modern, secular, and acculturated.

2. Power and Justice

1. Alfredo Rocco, "The Transformation of the State," in *What is Fascism and Why?*, ed. Tomaso Sillani, 15–29 (London: Ernest Benn Limited, 1931), 15–16.

2. Rocco, "The Transformation of the State," 25.

3. Pizzagalli, *Per l'italianità dei cognomi*, 109–10.

4. The critique was common across the political spectrum. On the Right, it was at the basis of fascism. On the Left, it formed the foundations for socialist and communist critiques of Italian and fascist society. Perhaps most notable were Antonio Gramsci's philosophies based on his belief, voiced in 1921, that fascism was responsible for "unleashing elemental forces within the bourgeois system" that caused the "profound decomposition" of Italian society and the Italian state. Quoted in Walter Adamson, "Gramsci's Interpretation of Fascism," *Journal of the History of Ideas* 41, no. 4 (1980): 618.

5. Herbert Wallace Schneider, "Italy's New Syndicalist Constitution," *Political Science Quarterly* 42, no. 2 (1927): 164.

6. Cannistraro, *Historical Dictionary*, 460–61.

7. Stone, "Theories of Law and Justice," 182–88. According to Stone, Rocco's "Transformation of the State" was inspired by reading of Duguit's books on "the transformation of public and private law."

8. Stone, "Theories of Law and Justice," 186.

9. Rocco, "The Transformation of the State," 18.

10. Horn, *Social Bodies*, 24–25.

11. Francesco Orestano, *Opera omnia: volume terzo: opere giuridico-politiche* (Padua, Cedam, 1961), 143. This work was published posthumously. Orestano wrote the preface in 1940.

12. Domenico Caruso Inghilleri, "Politica, amministrazione, e giurisdizione amministrative" in *Il Consiglio di stato nel quinquennio 1931–1935: relazione del presidente a s.e. il capo del governo*, ed. Consiglio di stato, 323–59 (Rome: Istituto poligrafico dello stato, 1937), 328–30.

13. Emilio Gentile, "The Fascist Anthropological Revolution" in *Culture, Censorship and the State in Twentieth-Century Italy*, eds. Guido Bonsaver and Robert S. C. Gordon, 22–33 (London: Legenda, 2005), 29. Gentile quotes Giuseppe Bottai, "Appelli all' uomo," *Critica fascista*, 1 January 1934. An early adherent to fascism, Bottai was a lawyer, journalist, and founder of the periodical *Critica fascista* who held a variety of ministerial posts.

14. Orestano, *Opera omnia: opere giuridico-politiche*, 38.

15. Inghilleri, "Politica, amministrazione, e giurisdizione amministrative," 326–27.

16. See Majer, *Non-Germans in the Third Reich*, 11.

17. The Matteotti crisis was precipitated by the kidnapping and suspected murder of Giacomo Matteotti on June 10, 1924 that was linked to agents working for Mussolini. A reformist socialist, Matteotti had denounced fascist violence and exposed corruption in the recent election in a speech before the Chamber of Deputies on May 30. Matteotti's disappearance caused a political crisis and, over the next several months, outspoken opponents of fascism nearly forced Mussolini from power. On the political and legal implications of the Matteotti crisis, see Lyttelton, *The Seizure of Power*, 237–68.

18. Schneider, "Italy's New Syndicalist Constitution," 168.

19. For the full membership of the commission, see Giorgio Candeloro, *Storia dell'Italia moderna: il fascismo e le sue guerre (1922–1939)*, vol. 9 (Milan: Feltrinelli, 1981), 136n54.

20. Gentile, "The Philosophic Basis of Fascism," 303–4.

21. Alberto Aquarone, *L'organizzazione dello stato totalitario* (Turin: Einaudi, 1965), 254–58.

22. Adriano Dal Pont, Alfonso Leonetti, Pasquale Maiello, and Lino Zocchi, *Aula IV: tutti i processi del Tribunale Speciale fascista* (Milan: La Pietra, 1980), 23–24.

23. On Violet Gibson, see Frances Stonor Saunders, *The Woman Who Shot Mussolini* (London: Faber and Faber, 2010).

24. The 1889 Zanardelli Codes abolished the death penalty in Italy. Reinstated by the fascists in 1926 for the Special Tribunal for crimes against the state

and in the Rocco codes of 1930 for civil cases, it remained a judicial option until its abolition in the Italian Constitution of 1947.

25. Horn, *Social Bodies*, 26–27.

26. Rocco, "The Transformation of the State," 16.

27. Pizzagalli, *Per l'italianità dei cognomi*, 31–32, 45.

28. Giulio Battaglini, "The Fascist Reform of the Penal Law," *Journal of Criminal Law and Criminology* 24, no. 1 (1933): 278.

29. Rocco is quoted in Battaglini, "Fascist Reform of the Penal Law," 285–86.

30. In the Italian Republic of Salò, an analogous body was introduced that worked from 1943 to 1945 on similar premises but with heightened wartime vigilance and violence.

31. Mimmo Franzinelli, *I tentacoli dell'Ovra: agenti, collaboratori, e vittime della polizia politica fascista* (Turin: Bollati Boringhieri, 1999), 25.

32. Friends of Italian Freedom, "The Provisions of the Special Tribunal," *Italy To-Day* (1931): 2–3.

33. McElligott, "Dangerous communities and conservative authority," 44.

34. Dal Pont et. al., *Aula IV*, 23.

35. Franzinelli, *I tentacoli dell'Ovra*, 61.

36. Ibid., 39.

37. Ibid., 67.

38. Ibid., 106, 128, 134, 142.

39. Dal Pont et al., *Aula IV*, 149.

40. Dal Pont et al., *Aula IV*, 151.

41. Nasalli Rocca, *Memorie di un prefetto*, 289.

42. Guido Melis, *Storia dell'amministrazione italiana, 1861–1993* (Bologna: Il Mulino, 1996), 312.

43. Giovanna Tosatti, "Il prefetto e l'esercizio del potere durante il periodo fascista," *Studi Storici* 42, no. 4 (2001): 1021.

44. Fried, *Italian Prefects*, 192–93.

45. Santi Romano, *Corso di diritto amministrativo: principii generali* (Padua: CEDAM, 1937), 299.

46. Reprinted in Ugo Marchetti, *Mussolini, i prefetti e i podestà: lo stile e l'opera di un prefetto fascista* (Mantova: "Mussolinia" Edizione Paladino, 1927), 15.

47. Rocco, "The Transformation of the State," 17.

48. Horn, *Social Bodies*, 33.

49. For the dates of service of Italian prefects in each province from the Risorgimento to the founding of the Republic after World War II, see "Provincia di Trieste," 615–16, and "Provincia di Zara," 630–31, http://tinyurl.com/provincia-alessandria.

50. Pizzagalli, *Per l'italianità dei cognomi*, 42.

51. Fried, *Italian Prefects*, 126.

52. On Ettore Porro, see "I senatori d'Italia," http://tinyurl.com/porro-info, and *Chi è?*, 746. From Trieste, he was transferred to Palermo where he served until his retirement.

53. Consiglio di stato, ed., *Il Consiglio di stato, studi in occasione del centenario*, vol. 1 (Rome: Istituto poligrafico dello stato, 1932), iii.

54. On the demolitions and excavations related to the Fascists' "master plan" for Rome, and specifically for Capitoline Hill, see Italo Insolera, *Roma fascista nelle fotografie dell'Istituto Luce* (Rome: Editori Riuniti, 2001), 89–121. Paul Baxa, *Roads and Ruins: The Symbolic Landscape of Fascist Rome* (Toronto: Toronto University Press, 2010); Borden Painter, *Mussolini's Rome: Rebuilding the Eternal City* (London: Palgrave Macmillan, 2005); and Emilio Gentile, *Fascismo di pietra* (Bari: Laterza, 2007) offer perspectives on fascism's manipulation of the Roman cityscape.

55. Consiglio di stato, ed., *Il Consiglio di stato*, iii.

56. Fried, *Italian Prefects*, 120.

57. Melis, *Storia dell'amministrazione italiana*, 345–50.

58. On competition between party bosses and prefects, see Fried, *Italian Prefects*, 178–79.

59. Tosatti, "Il prefetto e l'esercizio del potere," 1027. In 1928 only twenty-four were "political" prefects.

60. Marchetti, *Mussolini, i prefetti e i podestà*, 15.

61. Paul Corner, "Everyday Fascism in the 1930s: Centre and Periphery in the Decline of Mussolini's Dictatorship," *Contemporary European History* 15, no. 2 (2006): 205–6.

62. Apollonio, *Venezia Giulia e fascismo*, 316–18. On Perusino, see Savino, *Nazione operante*, 240.

63. The regime recognized his managerial and technical talents. In 1932 he returned to public life as vice mayor of Trieste. In 1935 he was appointed undersecretary in the Ministry of Public Works, and in 1937 became minister of public works with the responsibility to oversee road building in Italy's African colonies. Savino, *Nazione operante*, 55, and Tasso, *Un onomasticidio*, 83–86 disagree on some details but trace the same general trajectory for his career.

64. Paolo Grossi, *Scienza giuridica italiana: un profilo storico 1860–1950* (Milan: Giuffrè, 2000), 134–38.

65. Pizzagalli, *Per l'italianità dei cognomi*, 36–40.

66. TS, AdS, PPT/DI-11419.

67. On this debate, see Grossi, *Scienza giuridica italiana*, 155–63. Best known as Italy's prime minister from 1917 to 1919 and representative at the Paris Peace Talks, Vitttorio Emanuele Orlando was left-leaning politician and a lawyer specializing in constitutional rights. He served on the fascist commission that examined the controversial Acerbo election law, but had a rocky relationship with

the fascist government after 1924. He occupied a chair in law at the University of Rome from 1901 to 1931, when he resigned his over refusal to take the fascist oath of loyalty required of academics. He continued to write on law throughout the fascist period and returned to political life after World War II. Sergio Panunzio, with degrees in law and philosophy, occupied a chair in political science at the University of Rome from 1927 until his death in 1944. A supporter of revolutionary syndicalism, he was a major fascist theorist of the corporative state. Cannistraro, *Historical Dictionary*, 379–80 and 390–91, offers biographical sketches of Orlando and Panunzio.

68. Petrone, *Il nuovo diritto costituzionale amministrativo* (Rome: Attilio Sampaolesi, 1927), 69.

69. Paul B. Rava, "Italian Administrative Courts under Fascism," *Michigan Law Review* 40, no. 5 (1942): 660.

70. For a discussion of the struggle between the courts see Leopoldo Mazzarolli, "La protezione del cittadino," http://tinyurl.com/mazzarolli.

71. Consiglio di Stato, *Studi in occasione del centenario*, 1:iii. The court's origins are traced to the Piedmontese legislative system inherited by the Italian Kingdom.

72. Rava, "Italian Administrative Courts," 656–57.

73. Romano, *Corso di diritto amministrativo*, 2.

74. Rava, "Italian Administrative Courts," 670, and Consiglio di Stato, *Studi in occasione del centenario*, 1:vi.

75. Schneider, "Italy's New Syndicalist Constitution," 184–85, reproduces relevant sections of the charter.

76. Sabino Cassese, *Cultura e politica del diritto amministrativo* (Bologna: Il Mulino, 1971), 49.

77. On the role of the Council of State and constitutional arrangements involving the Administrative Court, see Oreste Ranelletti, *Istituzioni di diritto pubblico: il nuovo diritto pubblico italiano* (Padua: CEDAM, 1935), 538–40.

78. Consiglio di Stato, *Studi in occasione del centenario*, 1:vi.

79. Rava, "Italian Administrative Courts," 654–56.

80. Battente, *Alfredo Rocco*, 343. On this point, Battente cites C. Guarneri, *L'ordine pubblico e la giustizia penale*, in R. Romanelli, ed. *Storia dello stato italiano dall'unità ad oggi* (Rome: Donzelli, 1995).

81. Rava, "Italian Administrative Courts," 670.

82. On the debate over public law, see Fulco Lanchester, *Pensare lo stato: i giuspubblicisti nell'Italia unitaria* (Rome: Laterza, 2004), 6–11.

83. Maria Luisa Astaldi, "La posizione della donna nel regime fascista," *Almanacco della donna* 18 (1937): 96.

84. Rava, "Italian Administrative Courts," 660, discusses the competences of Sections Four and Five.

85. Consiglio di stato, *Il consiglio di stato nel quinquennio 1931–1935*, vol. 2, appendix 2, Table 7 and Table 8.

86. Ibid, Table 7 and Table 9.

87. Mazzarolli, "La protezione del cittadino," 4. Mazzarolli sees this as evident in Romano's *Corso di diritto costituzionale* from the first edition (1926) to the sixth (1943).

88. Petrone, *Il nuovo diritto*, 41–43.

89. Mazzarolli, "La protezione del cittadino," 5–6.

90. Melis, *Storia dell'amministrazione italiana*, 344.

91. Guido Bonsaver, *Censorship and Literature in Fascist Italy* (Toronto: Toronto University Press, 2007), 5. On cultural production, see Ben-Ghiat, *Fascist Modernities* and Marla Stone, *The Patron State: Culture and Politics in Fascist Italy* (Princeton: Princeton University Press, 1998).

92. Romano, *Corso di diritto amministrativo*, 299–313, discusses the responsibilities of public administrators with respect to individuals' rights. Bonsaver, *Censorship and Literature*, 26, describes censorship of "cultural producers."

93. Rava, "Italian Administrative Courts," 669–73, judged the administrative courts to be "ineffectual in all but minor administrative squabbles." But, the impact, particularly in local contexts can be hard to assess.

94. Rome, ACS, CdS, Sez. IV 1932, vol. 5, decisioni 327 and 328.

95. TS, AdS, PPT/DI-11419, Prefettura - Riduzione cognomi, Ministro (A.) Rocco to Prefect of Trieste, "Estensione alla Venezia Giulia," April 20, 1927.

96. Romano, *Corso di diritto amministrativo*, 300.

3. Legislating *Italianità*

1. Franco Stravisi, *Considerazioni statistiche sui valori medi mensili di cinque elementi meteorologici - Trieste 1841–1975* (Trieste: Istituto Sperimentale Talassografico "Francesci Vercelli", 1976), 15 (Table 3-1).

2. Corrado Belci, *Il libro della bora* (Trieste: Lint, 2002), 48 (as measured at the S. Andrea recording station).

3. Stone, "Theories of Law and Justice," 180. Born in Britain, Julius Stone served as the Challis Professor of Jurisprudence and International Law at the University of Sydney, Australia, from 1942 to 1972.

4. Ibid.

5. Population figures for Venezia Giulia can be found in Sator (Pietro Battara, pseudonym), *La popolazione della Venezia Giulia* (Rome: Darsena, 1945), 27, 40, 42, 44, and Carlo Schiffrer, *Venezia Giulia: Study of a Map of the Italo-Yugoslav National Borders* (Rome: C. Colombo, 1946), 45. The estimate of 100,000 name alterations derives from Parovel, *L'identità cancellata*, 28; and Čermelj, *Life-and-Death Struggle*, 113–14. Boris Pahor's introduction in Tasso, *Un onomasticidio*, 9,

suggests 50,000 total linked to the alteration of 2,141 surnames. Extrapolation from the numbers of restorations and corrections in selected files in TS, AdS-PPT/DI-11419 suggests that the number of restorations was considerably greater and that 100,000 is a closer approximation.

6. Stefano Pivato, *Il nome e la storia: onomastica e religioni politiche nell'Italia contemporanea* (Bologa: Il Mulino, 1999), 206.

7. Pietro Savini, *Le origini e le evoluzioni storiche della civiltà latina e della nomenclatura locale nella Venezia Giulia* (Venice: R. Deputazione veneta di storia patria, 1918), 142.

8. Gayda, *L'Italia d'oltre confine*, 129.

9. Monzali, *Italians of Dalmatia*, 154.

10. Giampaolo Valdevit, *Chiesa e lotte nazionali: il caso di Trieste (1850–1919)* (Udine: Aries Edizioni, 1979), 221–23.

11. On Strossmayer and Croatian culture see, Seton-Watson, *The Southern Slav Question*, 118–28.

12. Pizzagalli, *Per l'italianità dei cognomi*, 26–27.

13. Nicole Lapierre, *Changer de nom* (Paris: Gallimard, 2006), 33, attributes this categorization to French linguist and onomastician Albert Dauzat.

14. Scott, Tehranian, and Mathias, "The Production of Legal Identities," 12.

15. Gianetta Murru-Corriga, "The patronymic and the matronymic in Sardinia: A Long-Standing Competition," *The History of the Family* 5, no. 2 (2000): 162, 177.

16. Scott, Tehranian, and Mathias, "The Production of Legal Identities," 11–12.

17. Tamaro, *Vénétie Julienne*, 2:261–62.

18. Francesco Semi and Vanni Tacconi, "Italiani e slavi in Dalmazia: aspetti e problemi di una convivenza secolare," in *Istria e Dalmazia: uomini e tempi, Dalmazia, le figure più rappresentative della civiltà dalmata nei diversi momenti della storia*, vol. 2, ed. Francesco Semi and Vanni Tacconi, 603–22 (Udine: Del Bianco, 1991), 613.

19. Scott, Tehranian, and Mathias, "The Production of Legal Identities," 13–14.

20. TS, AdS, CGCVG, Atti generali, b. 128, Antonio Baiz to CGCVG, April 20, 1922.

21. TS, AdS, PPT/DI-11419.

22. TS, AdS, CGCVG, Atti generali, b. 82, from Engineer Carlo Marinig to Governatorato della Venezia Giulia, June 5, 1919, and from Giorgio Amodeo (lawyer representing the Lussich family) to Governatorato della Venezia Giulia, July 17, 1919.

23. Tolomei, *Memorie di vita*, 333.

24. Savini, *Le origini e le evoluzioni storiche*, 193.

25. Savino, *La nazione operante*, 345.

26. Reale Società Geografica Italiana, *Prontuario dei nomi locali dell'Alto Adige* (Rome: La Reale Società Geografica, 1916).

27. Reale Società Geografica Italiana, *Prontuario dei nomi locali della Venezia Giulia* (Rome: La Reale Società Geografica, 1917).

28. Rusinow, *Italy's Austrian Heritage*, 57.

29. On Tolomei's nationalist renaming, Giulia Mastrelli Anzilotti, "Restituire, sostituire, creare: il metodo toponomastico di Ettore Tolomei nell 'Prontuario dei nomi locali dell'Alto Adige,'" *Ettore Tolomei (1865–1952): una nazionalista di confine. Die Grenzen Des Nationalismus*, ed. Sergio Benvenuti and Christoph H. von Hartungen, 319–23 (Trent: Museo Storico Trento, 1998) and Johannes Kramer, "Ettore Tolomeis Italianisierung der Südtiroler Ortsnamen im Europäischen Kontext," in *Ettore Tolomei*, ed., Benvenuti and von Hartungen, 295–313.

30. For a nationalist justification of the name's use in the era of the World War I, see Tamaro, *Vénétie Julienne*, 1:2–3.

31. Parovel, *L'identità cancellata*, 23.

32. Ravasini, *Toponomastica stradale*, 3.

33. Apollonio, *Venezia Giulia e fascismo*, 179.

34. Andrea Benedetti, "Postumia," *La porta orientale* 1, no. 2 (1931): 114–15. This number declined in 1930 to 171,941 (112, 368 Italians), perhaps as a result of the international economic crisis. Sperato Zanetti, "Il movimento turistico nelle stazioni balneari della Venezia Giulia," *La porta orientale* 3, no. 1 (1933): 72.

35. Angelo Scocchi, "Toponomastica italiana," *La porta orientale* 1, no. 3 (1931): 311.

36. Nicolò Cobolli, "Le alterazioni dei toponomi nella Venezia Giulia," *La porta orientale* 2, no. 5 (1932): 462–71, 575–83, 921–38.

37. Scocchi, "Toponomastica italiana," 310.

38. Ibid., 308–10. The Isonzo (Soča) River runs from the Julian Alps in western Slovenia through Friuli to the Adriatic Sea near Monfalcone, Italy. The Carso (Kras) is the interior limestone plateau shared by Italy and Slovenia. The Timavo (Timav) River flows from the Carso into the Gulf of Trieste. A mountain river, it has several underground sources in the limestone cliffs.

39. Angelo Scocchi, "I nomi pagani slavi e l'onomastica italiana," *La porta orientale* 2, no. 3–4 (1932): 275–83, and Angelo Scocchi, "Onomastica romana onomastica slava meridionale," *La porta orientale* 2, no. 5 (1932): 390–401.

40. Stanley Lieberson, *A Matter of Taste: How Names, Fashions, and Culture Change* (New Haven: Yale University Press), 8–16.

41. Marc Bloch, "Noms de personne et histoire sociale," *Annales d'Histoire Économique et Sociale* 4, no. 13 (1932): 67.

42. Pivato, *Il nome e la storia*, 224–25.

43. R.D. L. 8 marzo 1928 n. 383 "Norme per disciplinare dei nomi nelle denunzie delle nascite," http://tinyurl.com/legge383. Originally the law had included only "national sentiment." "Religious sentiment" was added at Rocco's insistence while the law was in process, perhaps in a nod to the Holy See or as a reflection of Rocco's conservative and traditional bias.

44. Pivato, *Il nome e la storia*, 239.

45. Ibid., 230–36, 243, 319.

46. Ibid., 246–47, 323.

47. Scocchi, "I nomi pagani slavi," 281–82, and "Onomastica romana," 391.

48. Scocchi, "Toponomastica italiana," 310.

49. Ettore Tolomei, "Il discorso di Bolzano," teatro di Bolzano, 15 luglio 1923 (Trent: Tipografia Cooperativa Trentina, 1923), 30–32.

50. TS, AdS, PPT/DI-11419.

51. On the impact of the Turkish surname law, see Türköz, "Surname narratives and the State-Society Boundary."

52. TS, AdS, CGCVG, Atti generali, b. 97, CGCVG to Ufficio centrale per le nuove provincie, Council of Ministers, August 13, 1919.

53. On the surname changes from 1918 to 1922, see Maura Hametz, "The Nefarious Former Authorities: Name Change in Trieste, 1918–1922," *Austrian History Yearbook* 35 (2004): 233–52.

54. TS, AdS, Pref., Atti generali, b. 26, Conte Salvatore Segrè to Prefettura di Trieste, September 27, 1923.

55. Part of the territory of Venezia Giulia at the time, Kaštelir, western Istria, now in Croatia.

56. The father of five children sought in 1919 to have his surname changed to *Susanna*, in memory of his wife and the children's mother. Having been told verbally this was not possible, in 1921, his son, working as a school inspector in Postumia, wrote on behalf of his father and siblings asking for Coceani or Cossani. TS, AdS, PPT/DI-11419, Prefettura - Riduzione cognomi, busta 26, "Cociancich in Cossani," 22 March 1921, 23 December 1921, and 19 July 1923.

57. See Parovel, *L'identità cancellata*, 39, for this list of correspondences.

58. Pizzagalli, *Per l'italianità dei cognomi*, 30–31.

59. Salvemini, *Racial Minorities*, 9.

60. Eduard Reut-Nicolussi, *Tyrol Under the Axe of Italian Fascism* (London: George Allen & Unwin, 1930), 158. An elected delegate from Bolzano to the Italian Parliament on South Tyrol's annexation in 1921, Reut-Nicolussi offered these observations from exile in Austria in 1930.

61. Tolomei, "Elenco dei cognomi." On the "religion" of Italian politics, Emilio Gentile, *Sacralization of Politics* (Cambridge: Harvard University Press, 1996).

62. Tolomei, *Memorie di vita*, 393–95.

63. Pizzagalli, *Per l'italianità dei cognomi*, 46–48. Other Advisory Committee members appointed May 6, 1927, included Prof. Ferruccio Borri, Cav. Uff. Prof. Nicolò Cobol (later Cobolli), Comm. Dott. Bruno Coceancig (Coceani), Cav. Camillo De Franceschi, Dott. Leone Fels (Della Rocca), Cav. Dott. Antonio Kabler (Cableri), Prof. Ugo Pellis, Cav. Avv. Aurelio Polacco, Cav. Uff. Prof. Giovanni Quarantotto, Prof. Piero Sticotti, Dott. Alberto Ribechi (Secretary, Secretariat of the Prefecture). Prof. Umberto Urbanaz was added on June 21.

64. Tasso, *Un onomasticidio*, 28, 64.

65. Pizzagalli, *Per l'italianità dei cognomi*, 8–9.

66. Ibid., 115, 128.

67. Ibid., 119, 136. In English the name would translate as *Dove* or *Doves*.

68. Ibid., 50–53.

69. TS, AdS, PPT/DI-11419.

70. Pizzagalli, *Per l'italianità dei cognomi*, 50.

71. Ibid., 33, 36. Corrections had to be noted in the Magistrate's tables and forwarded to areas in which the supplicant owned property. Unlike the Italian *catasto* that provided a basis for tax information, the Habsburg magisterial tables established legal ownership or title to property. Ibid., 82.

72. Ibid., 54–55.

73. See for example, "La riduzione dei cognomi," *Il Piccolo*, June 7, 1928, 5, which lists "requests not approved by the Commission."

74. Pizzagalli, *Per l'italianità dei cognomi*, 62–64.

75. Ibid., 93–94.

76. Adriano Andri, "I cambiamenti di cognome nel 1928 e la scuola triestina," *Qualestoria* (new series a) 11, no. 1 (1983): 11–13.

77. See Stone, *Patron State*.

78. Pizzagalli, *Per l'italianità dei cognomi*, 108.

79. Ibid., 97.

80. Orestano, *Opera Omnia: Opere giuridico-politiche*, 38.

81. Maria Castellani, *Donne italiane di ieri e di oggi* (Florence: Bemporad, 1937), 15–16.

82. Angelo Bongioanni, *Nomi e cognomi: saggio di ricerche etimologiche e storiche* (Turin: Fratelli Bocca, 1928), 38.

83. Scocchi, "Onomastica romana," 397.

84. TS, AdS, PPT/DI-11419. Costanzo Ciano was a close friend of Mussolini and an ardent supporter of fascism who participated in the March on Rome and continued to serve the regime in a variety of capacities. His son Galeazzo Ciano married Mussolini's daughter Edda in 1930.

85. TS, AdS, PPT/DI-11419.

86. Ibid.

87. Pizzagalli, *Per l'italianità dei cognomi*, 75–77. Linguists debate Friulian's association with Italian. Many consider it a distinct language. Fascist officials considered it a dialect of Italian.

88. On attitudes towards literature written in dialect see Bonsaver, *Censorship and Literature in Fascist Italy*, 63–65.

89. Fried, *Italian Prefects*, 204.

90. Scott, Tehranian, and Mathias, "The Production of Legal Identities," 5–6, discusses the privilege of local knowledge.

91. On the duties of the Interior Ministry as well as other fascist ministries, see Petrone, *Il nuovo diritto*, 94–98.

92. Franzinelli, *I tentacoli dell'Ovra*, 67–73.

4. The Family in Question

1. Matilde Serao, *Parla una donna: diario femminile di guerra, maggio 1915–marzo 1916* (Milan: Treves, 1916), 142. The book was published one year before Serao was widowed on the death of her husband, Edoardo Scarfaglia, in October 1917.

2. Domenico Rizzo, "Marriage on Trial: Adultery in Nineteenth-Century Rome," in *Gender, Family, and Sexuality: The Private Sphere in Italy, 1860–1945*, ed. Perry Willson, 20–36 (Houndsmills, UK: Palgrave MacMillan, 2004), 27.

3. Paolo Ungari, *Il diritto di famiglia in Italia dalla costituzioni "giacobine"al codice civile del 1942* (Bologna: Il Mulino, 1970), 179.

4. Pasini, "Ufficio della letteratura," 877.

5. Paulovich's husband and her father shared the first name Antonio.

6. Ines was born November 17, 1885, Ernesto was born August 1, 1891.

7. Pizzagalli, *Per l'italianità dei cognomi*, 62–63.

8. Morris Ploscowe, "Jury Reform in Italy," *Journal of Criminal Law and Criminology* 25, no. 4 (November–December 1934): 585.

9. "Provincia di Alessandria," http://tinyurl.com/provincia-alessandria. Pirretti was the first prefect of Aosta, nominated in 1926 when the province was separated from Turin. See "Provincia di Aosta," 402, and "Provincia di Sondrio," 596–97.

10. Savino, *La nazione operante*, 204.

11. Pirretti moved on to serve as prefect of Matera in 1934, *Chi è?*, 736.

12. TS, AdS, PPT/DI-11419.

13. Ibid.

14. TS, AdS, PPT/DI-11419, March 26, 1930. Marcello Vaccari, born in 1897 in Florence, began his fascist career serving as under-secretary of the party and squad leader in Livorno. He served as prefect for Zara from February 1, 1929, to December 1, 1932. He occupied a number of prefectural posts from 1927 to 1943,

serving most notably as prefect of Venice from 1939 to 1943. Tosatti, "Il prefetto e l'esercizio del potere," 1027.

15. Pizzagalli, *Per l'italianità dei cognomi*, 46.

16. TS, AdS, PPT/DI-11419.

17. Parovel, *L'identità cancellata*, 50.

18. TS, AdS, PPT/DI-11419.

19. Ibid.

20. "La donna madre nel Fascismo," *Critica Fascista* (1931) no. 11, reprinted in Meldini, *Sposa e madre*, 193.

21. Orestano, *Opera omnia: opere giuridico-politiche*, 152.

22. Antonio Cicu, *Scritti minori: volume primo: scritti di teoria generale del diritto, diritto di famiglia* (Milan: Giuffrè, 1965), 160–63, 229.

23. Ungari, *Il diritto di famiglia*, 191.

24. Horn, *Social Bodies*, 67.

25. Cicu, *Scritti minori*, 229–30.

26. On the Nazi perspective on the family and "authoritarian leadership," see Majer, *Non-Germans under the Third Reich*, 11.

27. William G. Welk, *Fascist Economic Policy: An Analysis of Italy's Economic Experiment* (Cambridge, MA: Harvard University Press, 1938), 46.

28. Manlio Pompei, "La crisi della famiglia," *Critica Fascista* (1933) no. 9, reprinted in Meldini, *Sposa e madre*, 202.

29. Tito Staderini, *Legislazione per la difesa della razza* (Rome: Carlo Colombo, 1940), 7.

30. Ipsen, *Dictating Demography*, 6–7.

31. *Civil* relates to the laws, professional practices, and administration of rights; *social* relates to economic and cultural practices that shape and govern everyday existence. Horn, *Social Bodies*, 10–12, offers a history of the distinction and its evolution under fascism.

32. Ferdinando Loffredo, *Politica della famiglia* (Verona: Bompiani, 1938), 1.

33. Loffredo, *Politica della famiglia*, 293–96.

34. On Loffredo, see Brienza, "1908–2008: riflessioni nel centenario della nascita di Ferdinando Loffredo: 'In memorium' di un intellettuale italiano controcorrente," http://tinyurl.com/loffredo.

35. On the Ascension Day Speech, see Meldini, *Sposa e madre*, 11–19.

36. On the family as a key structure in the militarization of Italian society see Tracy Koon, *Believe, Obey, Fight: Political Socialization of Youth in Fascist Italy, 1922–1943* (Chapel Hill: University of North Carolina Press, 1985).

37. Mariolina Graziosi, "Gender Struggle and the Social Manipulation and Ideological Use of Gender Identity in the Interwar Years," in *Mothers of Invention*, ed. Pickering-Iazzi, 39.

38. Castellani, *Donne italiane*, 7.

39. Loffredo, *Politica della famiglia*, 69.

40. Orestano, *Opera Omnia: Opere giuridico-politiche*, 38.

41. *Casti connubii*, December 31, 1930, article 76, http://tinyurl.com /casticonnubii.

42. *Casti connubii*, December 31, 1930, article 43, http://tinyurl.com /casticonnubii.

43. Loffredo, *Politica della famiglia*, 66–67.

44. Lateran Pacts of 1929, Conciliation Treaty, article 34, http://uniset.ca /nold/lateran.htm.

45. Giulio Cogni, *I valori della stirpe italiana* (Milan: Fratelli Bocca, 1937), 150.

46. Carlotta Grilli, "L'opera nazionale per la protezione della maternità e dell'infanzia," *Almanacco della donna* 12 (1931): 157.

47. Meldini, *Sposa e madre esemplare*, 226, reprint of Wanda Gorjux, "La festa del popolo che si eterna," *Augustea* 23 (1933): 651–53.

48. De Luna, *Donne in oggetto*, 179.

49. Loffredo, *Politica della famiglia*, 455.

50. On the relationship of fascist demographic policies to Catholic Church beliefs, see Ipsen, *Dictating Demography*, 75–79.

51. *Casti connubii*, 31 December 1930, articles 26, 27, and 29, http://tinyurl .com/cc-piusxi.

52. Orestano, *Opera Omnia: Opere giuridico-politiche*, 140.

53. Ipsen, *Dictating Demography*, 75–76.

54. Judson, *Guardians of the Nation*, 119.

55. Olivera Burić, "The Zadruga and the Contemporary Family in Yugoslavia," in *Communal Families in the Balkans: The Zadruga: Essays by Philip E. Mosely and Essays in His Honor*, ed. Robert F. Byrnes, 117–38 (Notre Dame: University of Notre Dame Press, 1976), 133–34, contrasts the bases of urban and *zadruga* family structures.

56. Philip E. Mosely, "The Peasant Family: The Zadruga, or Communal Joint-Family in the Balkans, and Its Recent Evolution," in *Communal Families*, ed. Byrnes, 19–30, 22.

57. Sonnabend, *L'espansione degli Slavi*, 131–32.

58. Mosely, "The Peasant Family," 19, defines the *zadruga* and these relationships.

59. On surname changes and the social restructuring of families see Scott, Tehranian, and Mathias, "The Production of Legal Identities," 24.

60. For those living in western Slovenia, the memory or myth of association with the *zadruga* system continued to play an important role in village life and in the lives of those who emigrated well into the post–World War II period. Irene Portis Winner, "The Question of the Zadruga in Slovenia: Myth and Reality in Žerovnica," *Anthropological Quarterly* 50, no. 3 (1977): 129–32.

61. Vucinich, "A Zadruga in Bileća Rudine," in *Communal Families*, ed. Byrnes, 172.

62. Ante Kadić, " 'Democratic Spirit' of the Poljica Commune," in *Communal Families*, ed. Byrnes, 210–12.

63. Türköz, "Surname narratives and the State-Society Boundary," 896.

64. TS, AdS, PPT/DI-11419. The policy legalized the extra-marital relationship.

65. Pizzagalli, *Per l'italianità dei cognomi*, 79.

66. TS, AdS, PPT/DI-11419.

67. Castellani, *Donne italiane*, 24.

68. Pizzagalli, *Per l'italianità dei cognomi*, 66–67.

69. On Lombroso and his impact, see Mary Gibson, *Born to Crime: Cesare Lombroso and the Origins of Biological Criminology* (Westport, Connecticut: Praeger, 2002).

70. TS, AdS, PPT/DI-11419.

71. Ibid.

72. Corner, "Italian Fascism," 337–38.

73. De Luna, *Donne in oggetto*, 180.

5. A Citizen Seeking Justice

1. TS, AdS, PPT/DI-11419.

2. Calamandrei, *Eulogy of Judges*, 69–70.
An antifascist associated with Salvemini's cultural circle and the Rosselli brothers in Florence, Calamandrei criticized the violence surrounding Matteotti's assassination. He never became a member of the Fascist Party but did sign the fascist oath in 1931 to maintain his university post. One of the jurists responsible for writing the Italian Civil Code of the early 1940s, after the war he emerged as a leading legal scholar and politician of the Republic. Cannnistraro, *Historical Dictionary*, 96–97.

3. Calamandrei, *Eulogy of Judges*, 70.

4. Rava, "Italian Administrative Courts," 659–60. Section Five considered matters related to conflicts with public entities outside the state's direct administrative structure.

5. Consiglio di stato, *Il consiglio di stato nel quinquennio 1931–1935*, vol. 2, 930 (by year of decisions' registration: 1931-1 case, 1932-4 cases, 1933-6 cases, 1934-0 cases, 1935-0 cases).

6. Fried, *Italian Prefects*, 208.

7. Francesca Tacchi, "Un professionista della classe dirigente: l'avvocato degli anni '20," in *Libere professioni e fascismo*, ed. Gabriele Turi, 49–86 (Milan: Franco Angeli, 1994), 49.

8. Olgiati, "Law as an Instrument of 'Organizational Totalitarianism,'" 125.

9. Luigi E. Gianturco, *Gli avvocati colonne del regime* (Naples: Edizioni del giornale "La Toga", 1937), 61.

10. Orestano, *Opera omnia: opere giuridico-politiche*, 136.

11. Aldo Mazzacane, "A Jurist for United Italy: the Training and Culture of Neapolitan Lawyers in the Nineteenth Century," in *Society and Professions in Italy, 1860–1914*, ed. Maria Malatesta, 80–110 (Cambridge: Cambridge University Press, 1995), 81.

12. Gianturco, *Gli avvocati colonne*, 144.

13. Tacchi, "Un professionista della classe dirigente," 55.

14. Tosatti, "Il prefetto e l'esercizio del potere," 1028.

15. Tacchi, "Un professionista della classe dirigente," 62–63.

16. Cannistraro, *Historical Dictionary*, 250.

17. Mazzarolli, "La protezione del cittadino," 2–4.

18. Tacchi, "Un professionista della classe dirigente," 49, 64–65, 82.

19. Cassese, *Cultura e politica*, 50–51.

20. Quoted in Lyttleton, *Seizure of Power*, 374. On Prezzolini, see Cannistraro, *Historical Dictionary*, 441–42.

21. Alfredo Rocco quoted in Guido Melis, *Due modelli di amministrazione tra liberalismo e fascismo* (Rome: Ministero per i beni culturali e ambientali, 1988), 275.

22. Rocco, "The Transformation of the State," 20, 29.

23. Lanchester, *Pensare lo stato*, 31–32.

24. Stolleis, *Law under the Swastika*, 117–19.

25. Dal Pont and Carolini, *L'Italia dissidente e antifascista*, 1:5.

26. Ibid., 1:307. Judges found insufficient proof of wrong doing in 1928. In 1930, he was charged again, convicted and sent to prison for five years.

27. Berardo Taddei, *Donne processate dal Tribunale Speciale 1927–1943* (Verona: G. Grazia, 1969), 24, 75–76.

28. Mazzarolli, "La protezione del cittadino," 4–5.

29. Rava, "Italian Administrative Courts," 667n.

30. Nino Pappalardo, "L'eccesso di potere 'amministrativo' secondo la giurisprudenza del Consiglio di Stato," in *Il Consiglio di Stato nel quinquennio*, ed. Consiglio di Stato, vol. 2 (Rome: Istituto poligrafico dello stato, 1937), 429–95.

31. TS, AdS, PPT/DI-11419.

32. Ibid.

33. The term "typical professional legal elites" is deliberately vague and hints at a rich array of avenues for further study and analysis that fall beyond the scope of this book. Use of the term in this context draws inspiration from ideas of cultural hegemony and the influence of the political and professional elite often expressed in Gramscian terms. See, for example, Adamson, "Gramsci's interpretation of Fascism," 626–29, and T. J. Jackson Lears, "The Concept of Cultural

238 NOTES TO PAGES 126–32

Hegemony: Problems and Possibilities," *American Historical Review* 90, no. 3 (June 1985): 568–72.

34. Ploscowe, "Jury Reform," 580–84.

35. Pizzagalli, *Per l'italianità dei cognomi*, 25.

36. Rome, ACS, CdS Sez. IV, 1932, vol. 1, decisione 2.

37. TS, AdS, PPT/DI-11419.

38. Ibid.

39. Ibid.

40. On Enlightenment perceptions of the Adriatic, see Larry Wolff, *Inventing Eastern Europe: The Map of Civilization on the Mind of the Enlightenment* (Stanford: Stanford University Press, 1994). In travel writing see, for example, A. L. Frothingham, *Roman Cities in Italy and Dalmatia* (New York: Sturgis & Walton Company, 1910), 264–324.

41. TS, AdS, PPT/DI-11419.

42. Lateran Pacts of 1929, Conciliation Treaty, Article 16, http://uniset.ca /nold/lateran.htm.

43. Italian claims to the Adriatic provinces later affected Italian fascist as opposed to Nazi German areas of occupation during World War II. On Italy in Croatia and Dalmatia in World War II, see Davide Rodogno, *Fascism's European Empire: Italian Occupation During the Second World War* (Cambridge: Cambridge University Press, 2006), 243–48, 307–21.

44. "I leoncini:—Passa via! Non stancare papà!," *Guerin meschino* 47, no. 48 (1928): 5.

45. TS, BC, Racc. Pat., Attilio Tamaro papers (correspondence sent), to Tomaso Sillani, April 28, 1931. Tamaro complained that this section served as "an optimal work to support Slavic claims."

46. Pasini, "Ufficio della letteratura," 881.

47. On Nicolò Tommaseo and the nineteenth century vision of the Adriatic, see Reill, "From Bond to Border."

48. Quoted in Federico Pagnacco, "Italiani di Dalmazia," *La porta orientale* 1, no. 2 (1931): 164.

49. TS, AdS, PPT/DI-11419.

50. See, for example, Tamaro, *Vénétie Julienne*, 2:261–80.

51. Pagnacco, "Italiani di Dalmazia," 165.

52. Scocchi, Toponomastica italiana," 307.

53. TS, AdS, PPT/DI-11419.

54. Curiously, his reference here is to Istria, not to the Pauloviches home Dalmatia or the Adriatic littoral in general or Trieste.

55. TS, AdS, PPT/DI-11419.

56. Ibid.

57. Ibid.

58. Ibid.

59. On Gentile and sacrifice for the *patria*, see Moss, *Mussolini's Fascist Philosopher*, 64.

60. Cattaruzza, *L'Italia e il confine orientale*, 77–79, 111, discusses the Giulian volunteers. Many adopted pseudonyms adopted for Italian enlistment, and after the war, Italian law permitted hyphenating these wartime nicknames to surnames. In the Paulovich case, no mention is made of Ernesto's adoption of a wartime pseudonym. On veterans' ability to add the name see Pizzagalli, *Per l'italianità dei cognomi*, 78–81.

61. TS, AdS, PPT/DI-11419. This assertion mirrors one made in the handbook for Italianization in anticipation of complaints. See Pizzagalli, *Per l'italianità dei cognomi*, 111–12.

62. Rocco, "The Transformation of the State," 27.

63. For a detailed discussion of the sinking and Paolucci's role see, "The Sinking of *Viribus Unitis*," in Ante Sucur, *Austro-Hungarian Tegetthoff Class Dreadnoughts*, http://croatian-treasure.com/viribus.html.

64. For the incident's diplomatic impact, see Albrecht-Carrié, *Italy at the Paris Peace Conference*, 52.

65. De Grand, *Italian Nationalist Association*, 124, 159, 168.

66. Paolucci did continue in the field of medicine as a chest and abdomen surgeon and surgery professor. He directed a surgical unit of the ambulance corps for the Italian Red Cross in the Ethiopian conflict in 1935. In World War II he served in the Navy's Department of Health until the Nazi occupation of Rome, and after the city's liberation in 1944, he returned briefly to active duty. After World War II he was elected to the Italian Chamber of Deputies as a National Monarchist and served as a member of the Parliamentary Assembly of the Council of Europe from 1954 to his death in 1958. "Raffaele Paolucci di Valmaggiore," *Annali italiani di chirurgia*, 63, no. 6 (1992): 835–39, http://tinyurl.com/63rpdv; and "M. Raffaele Paolucci," http://tinyurl.com/MRPaolucci.

67. Monzali, *Italians of Dalmatia*, 190.

68. Ibid., 109, 161, 188.

69. Ibid., 163, 193–94.

70. Under fascism, Federzoni and Corradini worked to further these Nationalist aims. See Cannistraro, *Historical Dictionary*, 140–41 and 220–22.

71. Monzali, *Italians of Dalmatia*, 330–31, 343.

72. Giovanni Giuriati, *Con D'Annunzio e Millo in difesa dell'Adriatico* (Florence: G. C. Sansoni, 1954), 154–57, 164n.

73. On Luigi Ziliotto see the work by his grandson, Luigi Ziliotto, *Lettera ad Enzo Bettiza: la risposta di un dalmata di Zara all'esilio* (Rome: La Società Dalmata,

2004), 7–12; and Giancarlo Soppelsa, "Luigi Ziliotto," in *Istria e Dalmazia*, ed. Semi and Tacconi, 479–81.

74. On Giunta and the early role of the squads in Trieste, see Mimmo Franzinelli, *Squadristi: protagonisti e techniche della violenza fascista 1919–1922* (Milan: Mondadori, 2003), 32–34.

75. Ziliotto, *Lettera ad Enzo Bettiza*, 37–40, 43.

76. Ravasini, *Toponomastica stradale*, 76–77, 161–62. The statue remains at the entrance to the public garden today.

77. On the impact of notions of place, and particularly on statues as "sites of cultural confrontation" that can be "imbued with political significance," see Wingfield, *Flag Wars and Stone Saints*, 39.

78. Salvemini, *Racial Minorities*, 6.

79. Galliano Fogar, *Trieste in guerra, 1940–1945: società e resistenza* (Trieste: Istituto regionale per la storia del movimento di liberazione nel Friuli-Venezia Giulia, 1999), 73–76. The Justice and Freedom movement, founded in Paris in 1929 and traditionally associated with antifascism in Turin, had branches throughout Italy by 1930. Foschiatti later emerged as leader of the antifascist Action Party in Trieste from September to November 1943, when he was captured and deported to Dachau.

80. Salvemini, *Racial Minorities*, 6.

6. A Fascist Woman?

1. Gina Lombroso, *The Soul of a Woman* (New York: E. P. Dutton & Company, 1923), 231. The first Italian edition was published in 1920.

2. Lombroso, *The Soul of a Woman*, 177.

3. Berenson, *The Trial*, 100, identifies women as "creatures of emotion."

4. Lombroso, *The Soul of a Woman*, 25.

5. Enrico Veronesi, *Un viaggio al femminile lungo quarant'anni: dai congressi femministi italiani del 1908 all caduta del fascismo* (Milan: M&B Publishing, 2004), 37–38, and Cesare Lombroso and Guglielmo Ferrero, *The Criminal Woman, the Prostitute, and the Normal Woman*, ed. Nicole Hahn Rafter and Mary Gibson (Durham, NC: Duke University Press, 2004), 82–85.

6. Pizzagalli, *Per l'italianità dei cognomi*, 102.

7. Robin Pickering-Iazzi, "Unseduced mothers: The Resisting Female Subject in Italian Culture of the Twenties and Thirties," University of Wisconsin-Milwaukee, Center for Twentieth Century Studies, Working Paper, no. 1 (1990): 1–2.

8. Horn, *Social Bodies*, 18, discusses "risks" individuals posed to the health of the state organism.

9. *Fascist War on Women. Facts from Italian Gaols* (London: Martin Lawrence, n.d.), 22.

10. De Luna, *Donne in oggetto*, 10, 17.

11. Taddei, *Donne processate*, 12.

12. From December 1941 to July 1943, the Special Tribunal tried twenty-eight "Giulian" women. Taddei, *Donne processate*, 91–97, lists them as "martyrs" to the Julian people.

13. Meldini, *Sposa e madre esemplare*, 225, reprint of Wanda Gorjux, "La festa del popolo che si eterna," *Augustea* 23 (1933): 651–53.

14. Ellen Nerenberg, *Prison Terms: Representing Confinement During and After Italian Fascism* (Toronto: University of Toronto Press, 2001), 15.

15. Veronesi, *Un viaggio al femminile*, 37–38.

16. Helga Dittrich-Johansen, *Le "militi dell'idea": storia delle organizzazioni femminili del partito nazionale fascista* (Città di Castello: Leo S. Olschki, 2002), 27.

17. Rome, ACS, SPDCR, b. 100, "De Seta, Maria."

18. Lombroso, *The Soul of a Woman*, 111 (italics in original) and 179.

19. Ibid., 5.

20. Gina Lombroso Ferrero, *Nuove vite di donna* (Bologna: Zanichelli, 1929), viii–ix.

21. Meldini, *Sposa e madre esemplare*, 229, reprint of Margherita Sarfatti, "L'Italia d'oggi," *Augustea* (1933).

22. Lucia Re, "Fascist Theories of 'Woman' and the Construction of Gender," in *Mothers of Invention*, ed. Pickering-Iazzi, 86.

23. Mariolina Graziosi, *La donna e la storia: identità di genere e identità collettiva nell'Italia liberale e fascista* (Naples: Liguori, 2000), 42.

24. Gaetano Pieraccini, *La donna nella conservazione e nel perfezionamento della specie* (Siena: S. Bernardino, 1931), 454–56.

25. Sabino Castaldi, "Prefazione," in Pieraccini, *La donna nella conservazione*, v–vi.

26. Orestano, *Opera Omnia: Opere giuridico-politiche*, 137–38.

27. Vittorio Olgiati, "Professional Body and Gender Difference in Court: the Case of the First (Failed) Woman Lawyer In Modern Italy," in *Women in the World's Legal Professions*, ed. Ulrike Schultz and Gisela Shaw, 419–35 (Oxford: Hart Publishing, 2003), 428.

28. De Giorgio, *Le italiane*, 473–76.

29. Olgiati, "Professional Body and Gender Difference," 419.

30. Algardi, *La donna e la toga* (Milan, Giuffrè, 1949), 17. By 1949 she had published, *Il diritto di autore* (with E. Valerio) (Milan: Giuffrè, 1942); *Il processo Caruso* (Darsena, 1944); and *Pagine di storia napoletana* (Bari: L'Ape, 1945).

31. Clara Bounous, *La toga negate: da Lidia Poët all'atttuale realtà torinese: il cammino delle donne nelle professioni giuridiche* (Pinerolo: Alzani, 1997), 95, 101–4.

32. Lombroso, *The Soul of a Woman*, 111–15.

33. Marina Addis Saba, "La donna 'muliebre'," in *La corporazione delle donne: ricerche e studi sui modelli femminili nel ventennio fascista*, ed. Marina Addis Saba, 1–71 (Florence: Vallecchi Editore, 1988), 34.

34. Pieraccini, *La donna*, 471.

35. Horn, *Social Bodies*, 19.

36. Castellani, *Donne italiane*, 13, 42.

37. Meldini, *Sposa e madre esemplare*, 227–28, reprint of Wanda Gorjux, "La festa del popolo che si eterna," *Augustea* 23 (1933): 23, 651–53.

38. On Loffredo, see Re, "Fascist Theories," 85–89, and Rosella Isidori Frasca, "L'educazione fisica e la "preparazione materna'," in *La Corporazione delle donne*, ed. Saba, 273–304, 276–77, 286–87.

39. Frasca, "L'educazione fisica e sportiva," 282–83.

40. On Ondina Valla and other women athletes and the fascist promotion of health through sport, see Gigliola Gori, *Italian Fascism and the Female Body: Sport, Submissive Women, and Strong Mothers* (Oxfordshire: Routledge, 2004).

41. Frasca, "L'educazione fisica," 278.

42. Eugenio Comba, *Donne illustri italiane* (Turin: G. B. Paravia, 1935), v–vii. See Davis, "Women's History," 83, on studies of "worthy women."

43. Comba, *Donne illustri italiane*, 129–31.

44. On the conception of women as "female citizens" in the era of World War I, see Allison Scardino Belzer, *Women and the Great War: Femininity Under Fire in Italy* (New York: Palgrave Macmillan, 2010), 35.

45. Comba, *Donne illustri italiane*, 194–96, and H. Nelson Gay, T.Sillani, and N. Hodnig, ed., *Italy's Great War and Her National Aspirations* (Milan: Alfieri & Lacroix, 1917), 50.

46. Belzer, *Women and the Great War*, 35.

47. TS, AdS, Pref. di Trieste, Gab., b. 139 (1927), "*Il Popolo d'Italia.*"

48. Francesca Lagorio, "Appunti per una storia delle vedove di guerra italiane nei conflitti mondiali," *Rivista di storia contemporanea* 23–24, no. 1–2 (1994–95): 183.

49. TS, AdS, Pref. di Trieste, Gab., b. 33 (1923), "Battisti, Sauro, Rismondo— Assegno pensione alle vedove," and Gay, Sillani, and Hodnig, *Italy's Great War*, 50. Fascists were not alone in reverence for war widows. In 1947 the postwar Italian government voted to augment Bugliovaz's pension. "Disegno di legge," http://legislature.camera.it/_dati/leg01/lavori/stampati/pdf/02220001.pdf.

50. Lagorio, "Italian widows," 191.

51. TS, AdS, Pref. di Trieste, Gab. (1923–1952), b. 134 (1927); and Bruno Coceani, "Salari d'anteguerra e dopoguerra nelle industrie di Trieste," La porta orientale 1, no. 4 (1931): 351.

52. Lagorio, "Italian Widows," 176.

53. De Grand, "Women under Italian Fascism," 954.

54. Lagorio, "Italian Widows," 176.

55. Bonsaver, Censorship and Literature in Fascist Italy, 95–107.

56. On relationships between white women and black men and colonial policy in Eritrea at the turn of the twentieth century, see Giulia Barrera, "Sex, citizenship, and the state: The Construction of the Public and Private Spheres in Colonial Eritrea," in Gender, Family, and Sexuality, ed. Willson, 158.

57. Pieraccini, La donna, 454–56.

58. The categorizations of feminine and masculine are from the original. They do not imply that Canella intended anything related to contemporary definitions that offer nuanced gendered understandings that transcend binary sexual categories of male and female. Meldini, Sposa e madre esemplare, 273–75, reprint of Mario Cannella [sic], Principi di psicologia razziale (Florence: Sansoni, 1941), 71–74.

59. Veronesi, Un viaggio al femminile, 46. On Weininger's reception in Italy and particularly in Trieste, see Alberto Cavaglion, Otto Weininger in Italia (Rome: Carucci, 1982), 195–220.

60. Cited in De Giorgio, Le italiane, 16–17.

61. Meldini, Sposa e madre esemplare, 228, reprint of Wanda Gorjux, "La festa del popolo che si eterna," Augustea 23 (1933): 651–53.

62. Angelantonio Mancini, La donna fascista nell'irrobustimento della razza (Rome: Vittorio Ferri, 1937), 5.

63. Quoted in Dittrich-Johansen, Le "militi dell'idea," 55.

64. Belzer, Women and the Great War, 2–3.

65. Dittrich-Johansen, Le "militi dell'idea," 26, quoting T. Labriola, I problemi sociali della donna.

66. Emilia Sarogni, La donna italiana: il lungo cammino verso i diritti, 1861–1994 (Parma: Nuova Pratiche, 1995), 37, 139.

67. Graziosi, "Gender Struggle," 39, and De Grand, "Women under Italian Fascism," 955. The measure was moot. In 1926 the fascists eliminated the local elections in favor of government appointment.

68. De Grand, "Women under Italian Fascism," 949–50.

69. Graziosi, "Gender Struggle," 37–38.

70. Sara Follacchio, "Conversando di femminismo: 'la donna italiana'" in La corporazione delle donne, ed. Saba, 171–225.

71. Cited in Follacchio, "Conversando il femminismo," 213.

72. Castellani, *Donne italiane*, 42.

73. Mancini, *La donna fascista*, 5.

74. Castellani, *Donne italiane*, 29.

75. Horn, *Social Bodies*, 12.

76. Grilli, "L'opera nazionale per la protezione della maternità e dell'infanzia," 155.

77. "Prefazione," *Almanacco della donna* 8 (1927).

78. Veronesi, *Un viaggio al femminile*, 194–95.

79. Armando Michielj, "La donna nella scuola," *Almanacco della donna* 10 (1929): 100.

80. Astaldi, "La posizione della donna," 96–98. The author cites the conference as having taken place "three years ago" (which would be 1934), but the tenth anniversary of the fascist revolution was celebrated in 1932, and Frida Ceccon Marx, Lina Furlan, and Maria Laetitia Riccio, ed., *La donna e la famiglia nella legislazione fascista* (Naples: "La Toga, 1933) was published in 1933.

81. B. Maineri, "Le nozze e la potenza demografica dell'Italia," *Almanacco della donna* 12 (1931): 314.

82. The numbers are national averages that do not reflect regional specificities, which were marked, particularly between north and south.

83. De Giorgio, *Le italiane*, 353–61. The percentage of childless women did not change significantly from unification to 1931, rising from 8 to 9 percent.

84. "Poi dicono che la quantità va a scapito della qualità!," *Guerin meschino* 47, no. 32 (1928): 3.

85. Postscript to Maineri, "Le nozze e la potenza demografica," 318.

86. Grilli, "L'opera nazionale per la protezione della maternità e dell'infanzia," 156.

87. De Grand, "Women under Italian Fascism," 956.

88. Olgiati, "Professional Body and Gender Difference," 422.

89. Veronesi, *Un viaggio al femminile*, 27, 31.

90. Astaldi, "La posizione della donna nel regime fascista," 96–97.

91. Orestano, *Opera omnia: opere giuridico-politiche*, 137–38.

92. Rome, ACS, CdS-Sez. IV, 1931–1936, *passim*.

93. Mazzarolli, "La protezione del cittadino," 10.

94. Rome, ACS, CdS-Sez. IV, 1932, vol. 4, decisione 166.

95. Rome, ACS, CdS-Sez. IV, 1932, vol. 5, decisione 254.

96. Rome, ACS, CdS-Sez. IV, 1937, vol. 1, decisione 66.

97. TS, AdS, Pref. di Trieste, Gab., b. 189 (1930).

98. TS, AdS, Pref. di Trieste, Gab., b. 223 (1932).

99. Rome, ACS, CdS-Sez. IV, 1932, vol. 1, decisione 17.

100. Rome, ACS, CdS-Sez. IV, 1935, vol. 1, decisione 36.

101. Michielj, "La donna nella scuola," 104. In Venezia Giulia, 34 percent of teachers were males, while in Sardegna and Toscana, at the other end of the spectrum, 23 percent and 14 percent were males.

102. Denise Detragiache, "Il fascismo femminile da San Sepolcro all'affare Matteotti (1919–1925)," *Storia contemporanea* 14, no. 2 (1983): 220–23.

103. Graziosi, "Gender Struggle," 41.

104. Detragiache, "Il fascismo femminile," 222–33.

105. Roberto Curci and Gabrielle Ziani, *Bianco, rosa e verde: scrittici a Trieste fra '800 e '900* (Trieste: Lint, 1993), 154.

106. Saba, "La donna 'muliebre,'" 23, cites Denise Detragiache.

107. Ibid., 29–30.

108. TS, AdS, Pref. di Trieste, Gab., b. 173 (1929), "CNDI - Sezione di Trieste."

109. Ibid.

110. Dittrich-Johansen, *Le "militi dell'idea,"* 253.

111. Cogni, *I valori,* 152.

112. TS, AdS, Pref. di Trieste, Gab., b. 260 (1934).

113. On James Joyce and Amalia Popper, see Vicki Mahaffey, "The Case Against Art: Wunderlich on Joyce," *Critical Inquiry* 17, no. 4 (1991): 672–74.

114. TS, AdS, Pref. di Trieste, Gab. (1923–1952), b. 260 (1934).

115. Elisabetta Mondello, *La nuova italiana: la donna nella stampa e nella cultura del ventennio* (Rome: Editori Riuniti, 1987), 14, 74, 163.

116. Reprinted in "La donna e la caricatura dei giornali italiani," *Almanacco della donna* 8 (1927): 371.

117. "Vademecum per riconoscere la donna moderna," *Guerin meschino* 49, no. 20 (1930): 7.

118. Veronesi, *Un viaggio al femminile,* identifies four major periodicals for women *Rassegna femminile italiana, Vita femminile, La donna italiana,* and *Cordelia.*

119. Mondello, *La nuova italiana,* 58, 163.

120. Rome, ACS, PCM (1928–1930), "1° Mostra Femminile d'Arte Decorativa."

121. Mondello, *La nuova italiana,* 74.

122. Bonsaver, *Censorship and Literature in Fascist Italy,* 132.

123. Alessandra Gissi, "Between tradition and profession: Italian Midwives during the Fascist Period," in *Gender, Family, and Sexuality,* ed. Willson, 122–38.

124. Yves Aubry, "Pour une étude du veuvage feminine a l'époque moderne," *Histoire, Économie et Société* 8, no. 2 (1989): 228.

125. See Anne Wingenter, "Le veterane del dolore: Mothers and Widows of the 'Fallen' in Fascist Italy," (MA thesis Loyala University of Chicago, 2003).

126. Wingenter, "Le veterane del dolore," 63–66.

127. De Grazia, *How Fascism Ruled Women*, 3, discusses this generational dilemma. Kertzer, *Amalia's Tale* demonstrates that the legal system afforded little protection to the general populace in the nineteenth century.

128. Wingenter, "Le veterane del dolore," 161–78.

129. See Fried, *Italian Prefects*, 297.

130. Lagorio, "Appunti per una storia," 172, 182.

131. Gabrielli, *Tempio di virilità*, 16–17.

132. Morpurgo failed to mention, and the court neglected to note here that the contract had been with the Church in the Habsburg monarchy. The Italian state had no role in certifying the legitimacy of the marriage contract.

133. Rome, ACS, CdS-Sez. IV, 1932, vol. 1, decisione 2.

7. A Matter of Law

1. Piero Calamandrei, *Eulogy of Judges* (Princeton: Princeton University Press, 1942), 3.

2. Judson, *Guardians of the Nation*, 5, observes this for Bohemians and Czechs.

3. TS, AdS, PPT/DI-11419.

4. Ibid.

5. Rava, "Italian Administrative Courts," 664.

6. Petrone, *Il nuovo diritto*, 173.

7. Consiglio di stato, *Il consiglio di stato nel quinquennio 1931–1935*, 2:876.

8. Curci and Ziani, *Bianco, rosa e verde*, 290.

9. "Teatro Fenice," *Il Piccolo*, January 19, 1932, 3 (advertisement).

10. "Il prossimo 'Giugno Triestino': una riunione preliminare nell'Ufficio del Podestà," *Il Piccolo*, January 19, 1932, 3.

11. On the prefect's powers and responsibilities with regard to court decisions see Rava, "Italian Administrative Courts," 663.

12. Rava, "Italian Administrative Courts," 658–59.

13. Consiglio di stato, *Il consiglio di stato nel quinquennio 1931–1935*, vol. 2, appendix 2, Tables 7, 8, and 9.

14. Vittorio Emanuele Orlando, *Principii di diritto costituzionale*, 5th ed. (Florence: G Barbèra, 1928).

15. Shifting alliances and associations among government branches in fascist Italy stood in contrast to the situation in Nazi Germany, where Hitler separated political leadership from the administration to create an antagonistic relationship. On Nazi Germany, see Majer, *Non-Germans in the Third Reich*, 2.

16. A cursory review of the case records for Section IV in 1931 and 1932 suggests that the magistrates of the Council of State generally ordered only partial or no reimbursement.

17. Rava, "Italian Administrative Courts," 664.

18. Pappalardo, "L'eccesso di potere," 2:437, 486.

19. Rome, ACS, CdS - Sez. IV, 1932, vol. 1, decisione 2.

20. Rome, ACS, CdS - Sez. IV, 1932, vol. 5, decisione 239. Bertorsi was judged acceptable in Gorizia although it did not appear to conform to the typical or *elegant* Italian standards Pizzagalli sought to enforce in Trieste.

21. Tamaro, *Vénétie Julienne*, 2:277.

22. Nani, *Notizie storiche*, 115.

23. Raicich, "La scuola triestina," 301.

24. Corner, "Everyday Fascism," 201–3.

25. Pasini, "Ufficio della letteratura," 877.

26. TS, BC, Racc. Pat. Attilio Tamaro papers (correspondence received), from Rino Alessi, 21 June 1927.

27. Apollonio, *Venezia Giuilia e fascismo*, 78–80.

28. TS, AdS, Pref. di Trieste, Gab., b. 133, 1927.

29. Apollonio, *Venezia Giuilia e fascismo*, 71–72.

30. In a telegram to Rome, Pettorelli-Finzi, an active duty colonel of a well-known irredentist Jewish family, denied the allegations of Aventine or Masonic tendencies and protested the invasion of his home. Lupetina maintained that he entered the Masonic Lodge with permission and intending to engage in "the work of pacification." TS, AdS, Pref. di Trieste, Gab. (1927).

31. Dario Mattiussi, *Il partito nazionale fascista a Trieste: uomini e organizzazione del potere 1919–1932* (Trieste: Istituto regionale per la storia del movimento di liberazione nel Friuli-Venezia Giulia), 78–80. Apollonio, *Venezia Giuilia e fascismo*, 70–2.

32. TS, AdS, Pref. di Trieste, Gab., b. 133, 1927.

33. Cited in Apollonio, *Venezia Giulia e fascismo*, 181.

34. Marchetti, *Mussolini, i prefetti e i podestà*, 28, 34, 42.

35. Apollonio, *Venezia Giulia e fascismo*, 101.

36. Melis, *Storia dell'amministrazione italiana*, 345–50.

37. Corner, "Everyday Fascism," 203.

38. On the career of Pitacco, see "Giorgio Pitacco," http://tinyurl.com/pitacco -career. The practice of appointing a local candidate as *podestà* continued in Trieste throughout the fascist period. In the years of Nazi occupation from 1943 to 1945 the ties to Rome were severed and a local candidate Bruno Coceani (born Coceanig) was chosen as prefect.

39. On the elite, see Anna Millo, *L'Élite del potere a Trieste: una biografia collettiva, 1891–1938* (Milan: Franco Angeli, 1989).

40. TS, AdS, Pref. di Trieste, Gab., b. 205, 1931. The government's difficult relationship with Giulian elites continued throughout the *ventennio*. The Cosulich family actively participated in fascist economic programs, but after 1943 members of the family were recognized for their resistance against the Nazis.

41. Morgan, Years of Consent," 166, suggests that the police had the power to "dispense their own justice."

42. TS, AdS, Pref. di Trieste, Gab., b. 171, 1929.

43. Morgan, "Years of Consent," 168.

44. Dal Pont et. al., *Aula IV*, 142.

45. Ibid., 159–60. In World War II, Basovizza became famous as the town near the site where victims were thrown into limestone pits (*foibe*).

46. TS, AdS, Pref. di Trieste, Gab., b. 191, 1930.

47. Ibid. OVRA later admitted that the harsh sentences and the executions were meant to intimidate the local population.

48. TS, AdS, Pref. di Trieste, Gab., b. 208, 1931. In fact, some of the suspects in the *Il Popolo* case had fled through the Carso and across the border through Planina.

49. Livio Ragusin Righi, "Guardia al confine," *La porta orientale* 1, no. 1 (1931): 111–12.

50. While citizenship granted to "Slavs" was revoked only in conjunction with other charges regarding acts of disloyalty, with the passage of the racial laws in 1938, the fascist government revoked the citizenship of those Jews who, under the treaties, had gained it through option or election rather than automatically with full rights.

51. TS, AdS, PPT/DI-11419.

52. Apollonio, *Venezia Giulia e fascismo*, 180.

53. Judson, *Guardians of the Nation*, 53.

54. Federico Pagnacco, "L'italianità giuliana (postilla ad un processo)," *La porta orientale* 2, no. 3–4 (1932): 300–1.

55. Pizzagalli, *Per l'italianità dei cognomi*, 84, 110.

56. Ibid., 99–100.

57. Dietz Bering, *The Stigma of Names: Antisemitism in German Daily Life, 1812–1933* (Cambridge: Polity Press, 1992) discusses the alteration of Jewish surnames in relation to anti-Semitism and assimilation in Germany.

58. Pizzagalli, *Per l'italianità dei cognomi*, 64–65.

59. TS, AdS, PPT/DI-11419.

60. Pizzagalli, *Per l'italianità dei cognomi*, 105.

61. TS, AdS, PPT/DI-11419.

62. Pizzagalli, *Per l'italianità dei cognomi*, 33–34.

63. Posthumia in now known as Postojna, Slovenia.

64. TS, AdS, PPT/DI-11419.

65. Ibid.

66. Ibid.

67. Ibid.

68. Rava, "Italian Administrative Courts," 663.

69. Fried, *Italian Prefects*, viii.

70. Orestano, *Opera Omnia: Opere giuridico-politiche*, 37.

71. Pizzagalli, *Per l'italianità dei cognomi*, 72–73.

72. TS, AdS, PPT/DI-11419.

73. Ibid.

Conclusion

1. Mauro Covacich, "Il cimitero di Sant'Anna: la verità dei nomi," in *Trieste sottosopra: quindici passeggiate nella città del vento*, ed. Mauro Covacich, 113–21 (Rome: Laterza, 2006), 113.

2. Covacich, "Il cimitero," 114–17. Monuments and markers designed by renowned Triestine and European artists dot the cemetery established in 1825. The monumental iron gate that graces the entrance dates from 1932, the year the Paulovich case was settled. "A Trieste: il cimitero cattolico di Sant'Anna," *Oltre Magazine: Periodico di informazione dell'imprenditoria funeraria e cimiteriale* 11 (November 2004), http://tinyurl.com/catholic-cemetery.

3. Svevo's remains are in the Veneziani tomb of his wife's family.

4. Quoted in Renzo S. Crivelli and Elvio Guagnini, eds. *Umberto Saba: itinerary triestini/Trieste Itineraries* (Trieste: Lint, 1993), 16, 22.

5. Čermelj, *Life-and-Death Struggle*, 114–15.

6. Pupo, "Guerra civile e conflitto etnico," 504.

7. David Roberts, "How not to think about Fascism and Ideology, Intellectual Antecedents and Historical Meaning," *Journal of Contemporary History* 35, no. 2 (2000): 193.

8. Collotti, "Sul razzismo antislavo," 54–55.

9. Cattaruzza, *L'Italia e il confine orientale*, 377–79.

10. Quoted by Mikulas Teich and Roy Porter, eds., *The National Question in Europe in Historical Context* (Cambridge: Cambridge University Press, 1993), xx.

11. Furlan, *Fighting Jugoslavia*, 7.

12. Parovel, *L'identità cancellata*, 30.

13. Cattaruzza, *L'Italia e il confine orientale*, 327.

14. For a recent scholarly assessment of the *foibe*, see Jože Pirjevec, *Foibe: Una storia d'Italia* (Turin: Einaudi, 2009). Its publication ignited a firestorm once again over the question of what happened in the *foibes*.

15. See Pamela Ballinger, *History in Exile: Memory and Identity at the Borders of the Balkans* (Princeton: Princeton University Press, 2003).

16. Grbelja, Josip. "Molat-Najstraštrašniji fašisticki konclogor na svijetu," *Slobodna Dalmacija*, January 10, 2002, http://tinyurl.com/molat-najstra.

17. For information on the Molat camp in Jaza Bay, see "Italian concentration camp in Jaza bay on the island Molat," http://tinyurl.com/molat-jb.

18. Davide Rodogno, *Fascism's European Empire: Italian Occupation During the Second World War* (Cambridge: Cambridge University Press), 355–56.

19. Rodogno, *Fascism's European Empire*, 304–8.

20. Harnett T. Kane, "Trieste—Side Door to Europe," *National Geographic Magazine* 109 (1956): 840–49.

21. For a text of the 1991 law, see Maura E. Hametz, "Surnames and Nationality," case study at "Making the History of 1989," http://tinyurl.com/hametz -study. On individuals' attempts to reclaim prefascist forms, see Maura E. Hametz, "To have what was mine: Reclaiming surnames in Trieste," *Names* 50, no. 1 (2002): 3–22.

22. Cattaruzza, *L'Italia e il confine orientale*, 12, proposes the eastern borderland as the site from which to view the "parabola of Italian patriotism."

23. Cited in Crivelli and Guagnini, *Umberto Saba*, 30.

24. Ballinger, "Authentic Hybrids," 38–49, and "Comments," 49–57, in response to her analysis demonstrate the contours of this lively debate.

25. On administrative reformulation under Nazism, see Majer, *Non-Germans in the Third Reich*, 531–32.

26. See Corner, "Everyday Fascism," 211.

27. Corner, "Everyday Fascism," 220.

28. Ibid., 221.

29. Judson, *Guardians of the Nation*, 18.

30. Bonsaver, *Censorship and Literature in Fascist Italy*, 261, 266.

31. De Grand, "Women under Italian Fascism," 947.

32. De Grazia, *How Fascism Ruled Women*, 2.

33. Ibid., 6.

34. The idea of occupying a specific place on the fascist social scale was quoted in Ben-Ghiat, *Fascist Modernities*, 3, and taken from Umberto Bernasconi, "Vita di masse," *Gioventù fascista* (May 1, 1935).

35. Orestano, *Opera Omnia: Opere giuridico-politiche*, 46.

36. Olgiati, "Organizational Totalitarianism," 134.

37. Fried, *Italian Prefects*, 300.

38. Orestano, *Opera Omnia: Opere giuridico-politiche*, 38.

39. Nicolas Sarkozy, "Discours de Nicolas Sarkozy sur l'identité française," November 12, 2009, at La Chapelle en Vercors, http://tinyurl.com/sarkozy -french-id.

40. On the statutes of December 14, 2000, and Law 124 of 2006, see Giovanna Zincone, "The Making of Italian Nationality Law," *Italian Politics and Society* 69 (2010): 23–53.

41. Guido Posar, "Sono proprio slavi i nomi terminanti in ich?," *Pagine Istriane* 2, series 3, no. 5 (1951): 34–36.

42. W. F. H. Nicolaisen, "Placenames and Politics," *Names* 38, no. 3 (1990): 199–200. The author wishes to thank Prof. Nicolaisen for information related to the conference.

43. Scott, Tehranian, and Mathias, "The Production of Legal Identities," 31.

44. Pupo, "Guerra civile e conflitto etnico," 497.

45. Marino Bonifacio, *Cognomi triestini: Origini, Storia, Etimologiche* (Trieste: Lint, 2004), 198.

46. Pagine Bianchi, http://www.paginebianche.it/.

47. Scott, Tehranian, and Mathias, "The Production of Legal Identities," 5.

Bibliography

Adamson, Walter L. "Gramsci's Interpretation of Fascism." *Journal of the History of Ideas* 41, no. 4 (1980): 615–33.

Albrecht-Carrié, René. *Italy at the Paris Peace Conference*. Hamden, CT: Archon Books, 1996.

Algardi, Zara. *La donna e la toga*. Milan: Giuffrè, 1949.

———. *Processi ai fascisti*. Florence: Vallecchi, 1992.

Anderson, Benedict. *Imagined Communities: Reflections on the Origin and Spread of Nationalism*. London: Verso, 1991.

Andri, Adriano. "I cambiamenti di cognome nel 1928 e la scuola triestina." *Qualestoria* (new series a) 11, no. 1 (1983): 9–16.

———. "La scuola e il regime fascista." *Friuli e Venezia Giulia: storia del '900*. Istituto regionale per la storia del movimento di liberazione nel Friuli-Venezia Giulia, 325–43. Gorizia: Libreria Editrice Goriziana, 1997.

Annoni, Antonio Marcello. "Le lingue straniere e gli stranieri in Italia." *Vita Internazionale* 25 (1922): 310–14, 329–32.

Anzilotti, Giulia Mastrelli. "Restituire, sostituire, creare: il metodo toponomastico di Ettore Tolomei nel *Prontuario dei nomi locali dell'Alto Adige*." In *Ettore Tolomei (1865–1952): Un nazionalista di Confine. Die Grenzen Des Nationalismus*, edited by Sergio Benvenuti and Christoph H. von Hartungen, 319–23. Trent: Museo Storico Trento, 1998.

Apollonio, Almerigo. *Venezia Giulia e il fascismo 1922–1935*. Gorizia: Libreria Editrice Goriziana, 2004.

Aquarone, Alberto. *L'organizzazione dello stato totalitario*. Turin: Einaudi, 1965.

Astaldi, Maria Luisa. "La posizione della donna nel regime fascista," *Almanacco della donna* 18 (1937): 95–8.

"A Trieste: il cimitero cattolico di Sant'Anna," *Oltre magazine: periodico di informazione dell'imprenditoria funeraria e cimiteriale* 11 (November 2004).

Aubry, Yves. "Pour une étude du veuvage féminin à l'époque moderne." *Histoire, Économie et Société* 8, no. 2 (1989): 223–36.

Ballinger, Pamela. "'Authentic Hybrids' in the Balkan Borderlands." *Current Anthropology* 45, no. 1 (2004): 31–49.

———. *History in Exile: Memory and Identity at the Borders of the Balkans*. Princeton: Princeton University Press, 2003.

Barrera, Giulia. "Sex, Citizenship and the State: The Construction of the Public and Private Spheres in Colonial Eritrea." In *Gender, Family, and Sexuality: The Private Sphere in Italy, 1860–1945*, editor Perry Willson, 157–72. Houndsmills: Palgrave Macmillan, 2004.

Battaglini, Giulio. "The Fascist Reform of the Penal Law." *Journal of Criminal Law and Criminology* 24, no. 1 (1933): 278–89.

Battente, Saverio. *Alfredo Rocco: dal nazionalismo al fascismo, 1907–1935*. Milan: Franco Angeli, 2005.

Baxa, Paul. *Roads and Ruins: The Symbolic Landscape of Fascist Rome*. Toronto: University of Toronto Press, 2010.

Behan, Tom. *The Italian Resistance: Fascists, Guerillas, and the Allies*. New York: Pluto, 2009.

Belci, Corrado. *Il libro della bora*. Trieste: Lint, 2002.

Belzer, Allison Scardino. *Women and the Great War: Femininity under Fire in Italy*. New York: Palgrave Macmillan, 2010.

Ben-Ghiat, Ruth. *Fascist Modernities, Italy 1922–1945*. Berkeley: University of California Press, 2001.

Benedetti, Andrea. "Postumia." *La porta orientale* 1, no. 2 (1931): 114–17.

Benvenisti, Meron. *Sacred Landscape: The Buried History of the Holy Land Since 1948*. Berkeley: University of California Press, 2002.

Berenson, Edward. *The Trial of Madame Caillaux*. Berkeley: University of California Press, 1992.

Bering, Dietz. *The Stigma of Names: Antisemitism in German Daily Life, 1812–1933*. Cambridge: Polity Press, 1992.

Bloch, Marc. "Noms de personne et histoire sociale." *Annales d'histoire économique et sociale* 4, no. 13 (1932): 67–69.

Bongioanni, Angelo. *Nomi e cognomi: saggio di ricerche etimologiche e storiche*. Turin: Fratelli Bocca, 1928.

Bonifacio, Marino. *Cognomi triestini: origini, storia, etimologia*. Trieste: Lint, 2004.

Bonsaver, Guido. *Censorship and Literature in Fascist Italy*. Toronto: University of Toronto Press, 2007.

Bosworth, R. J. B. *Mussolini's Italy: Life under the Fascist Dictatorship, 1915–1945*. New York: The Penguin Press, 2006.

Bounous, Clara. *La toga negata: da Lidia Poët all'attuale realtà Torinese: il cammino delle donne nelle professioni giuridiche*. Pinerolo: Alzani, 1997.

Brienza, Giuseppe. "1908–2008: riflessioni nel centenario della nascita di Ferdinando Loffredo: 'in memorium' di un intellettuale italiano controcorrente." http://orientamentistorici.blogspot.com/2008/08/1908-2008-cento-anni-dalla-nascita-di.html.

Brunet, Guy, and Alain Bideau. "Surnames: History of the Family and History of Populations." *The History of the Family* 5, no. 2 (2000): 153–60.

Burgwyn, James. *The Legend of the Mutilated Victory: Italy, The Great War, and the Paris Peace Conference, 1915–1919*. Westport, CT: Greenwood Press, 1993.

Burić, Olivera. "The Zadruga and the Contemporary Family in Yugoslavia." In *Communal Families in the Balkans: The Zadruga: Essays by Philip E. Mosely and Essays in His Honor*, edited by Robert F. Byrnes, 117–38. Notre Dame: University of Notre Dame Press, 1976.

Calamandrei, Piero. *Eulogy of Judges*. Princeton: Princeton University Press, 1942.

Candeloro, Giorgio. *Storia dell'Italia moderna: il fascismo e le sue guerre (1922–1939)*, vol. 9. Milan: Feltrinelli, 1981.

Cannistraro, Philip V., ed. *Historical Dictionary of Fascist Italy*. Westport, CT: Greenwood Press, 1982.

Cassese, Sabino. *Cultura e politica del diritto amministrativo*. Bologna: Il Mulino, 1971.

Castaldi, Luigi. "Prefazione." In *La donna nella conservazione e nel perfezionamento della specie*, Gaetano Pieraccini, v–vi. Siena: S. Bernardino, 1931.

Castellani, Maria. *Donne italiane di ieri e di oggi*. Florence: Bemporad, 1937.

"Casti Connubii Encyclical of Pope Pius XI on Christian Marriage to the Venerable Brethren, Patriarchs, Primates, Archbishops, Bishops, and Other Local Ordinaries Enjoying Peace and Communion With the Apostolic See," December 31, 1930. http://www.vatican.va/holy_father/pius_xi/encyclicals/documents/hf_p-xi_enc_31121930_casti-connubii_en.html.

Cattaruzza, Marina. *L'Italia e il confine orientale*. Bologna: Il Mulino, 2007.

———. "Slovenes and Italians in Trieste, 1850–1914." In *Ethnic Identity in Urban Europe*, edited by Max Engman, 189–219. New York: New York University Press, 1992.

Cavaglion, Alberto. *Otto Weininger in Italia*. Rome: Carucci, 1982.

Čermelj, Lavo. *Life-and-Death Struggle of a National Minority (The Jugoslavs in Italy)*. Ljubljana: Jugoslav Union of League of Nations Societies, 1936.

Cerutti, Simona. "Microhistory: Social Relations versus Cultural Models?" In *Between Sociology and History: Essays on Microhistory, Collective Action, and Nation-Building*, edited by Anna-Maija Castrén, Markku Lonkila, and Matti Peltonen, 17–40. Helsinki: SKS Finnish Literature Society, 2004.

Chi è?: dizionario degli italiani d'oggi. Rome: A. F. Formiggini Editore, 1936.

Choate, Mark. *Emigrant Nation: The Making of Italy Abroad*. Cambridge: Harvard University Press, 2009.

Cicu, Antonio. *Scritti minori: volume primo: scritti di teoria generale del diritto, diritto di famiglia*. Milan: Giuffrè, 1965.

Cobolli, Nicolò. "Le alterazioni dei toponomi nella Venezia Giulia," *La porta orientale* 2, no. 5 (1932): 462–71, 575–83, 921–38.

Coceani, Bruno. "Salari d'anteguerra e dopoguerra nelle industrie di Trieste." *La porta orientale* 1, no. 4 (1931): 339–76.

Cogni, Giulio. *I valori della stirpe italiana*. Milan: Fratelli Bocca, 1937.

Collotti, Enzo. "Sul razzismo antislavo." In *Nel nome della razza: il razzismo nella storia d'Italia, 1870–1945*, edited by Alberto Burgio, 33–62. Bologna: Il Mulino, 1999.

Comba, Eugenio. *Donne illustri italiane*. Turin: G. B. Paravia, 1935.

"Conciliation Treaty, Lateran Pacts of 1929." http://uniset.ca/nold/lateran.htm.

Confino, Alon. *The Nation as a Local Metaphor: Württemberg, Imperial Germany, and National Memory, 1871–1918*. University of North Carolina Press: Chapel Hill, 1997.

Consiglio di stato. *Il consiglio di stato nel quinquennio 1931–1935: relazione del presidente a s.e. il capo del governo*. Rome: Istituto poligrafico dello stato, 1937.

Corner, Paul. "Everyday Fascism in the 1930s: Centre and Periphery in the Decline of Mussolini's Dictatorship." *Contemporary European History* 15, no. 2 (2006): 195–222.

———. "Italian Fascism: Whatever Happened to Dictatorship?" *Journal of Modern History* 74, no. 2 (2002): 325–51.

Covacich, Mauro. "Il cimitero di Sant'Anna: la verità dei nomi." *Trieste sottosopra: quindici passeggiate nella città del vento*, edited by Mauro Covacich, 113–21. Rome: Laterza, 2006.

Crivelli, Renzo S., and Elvio Guagnini, eds. *Umberto Saba: itinerari triestini / Triestine Itineraries*. Trieste: MSG Press, 2007.

Curci, Roberto, and Gabriella Ziani. *Bianca, rosa, e verde: scrittici a Trieste fra '800 e '900*. Trieste: Lint, 1993.

Dainelli, Giotto. *La Dalmazia: cenni geografici e statistici*. Novara: Istituto geografico de Agostini, 1918.

Dal Pont, Adriano, and Simonetta Carolini. *L'Italia dissidente e antifascista: le ordinanze, le sentenze istruttorie e le sentenze in camera di consiglio emesse dal tribunale speciale fascista contro gli imputati di antifascismo dall'anno 1927 al 1943*. Milan: La Pietra, 1980.

Dal Pont, Adriano, Alfonso Leonetti, Pasquale Maiello, and Lino Zocchi, eds. *Aula IV: tutti i processi del tribunale speciale fascista*. Milan: La Pietra, 1976.

Davis, Natalie Zemon. "'Women's History' in Transition: The European Case." *Feminist Studies* 3, no. 3/4 (1976): 83–103.

De Felice, Renzo, ed. *Mussolini il duce: gli anni del consenso, 1929–1936*. Turin: Einaudi, 1974.

De Giorgio, Michela. *Le italiane dall'Unità a oggi: modelli culturali e comportamenti sociali*. Bari: Laterza, 1993.

De Grand, Alexander J. "Women under Italian Fascism." *The Historical Journal* 19, no. 4 (1976): 947–68.

———. *The Italian Nationalist Association and the Rise of Fascism in Italy*. Lincoln: University of Nebraska Press, 1978.

De Grazia, Victoria. *How Fascism Ruled Women, 1922–1945*. Berkeley: University of California Press, 1992.

De Luna, Giovanni. *Donne in oggetto: l'antifascismo nella società italiana, 1922–1939*. Turin: Bollati Boringhieri, 1995.

De Marco, Roland R. *The Italianization of African Natives: Government Native Education in the Italian Colonies 1890–1937*. New York: Teachers College, Columbia University, 1943.

Detragiache, Denise. "Il fascismo femminile da San Sepolcro all'affare Matteotti (1919–1925)." *Storia contemporanea* 14, no. 2 (1983): 211–51.

Dittrich-Johansen, Helga. *Le "militi dell'idea": storia delle organizzazioni femminili del partito nazionale fascista*. Città di Castello: Leo S. Olschki, 2002.

"La donna e la caricatura dei giornali italiani," *Almanacco della donna* 8 (1927): 371.

Fascist War on Women: Facts From Italian Gaols. London: Martin Lawrence, n.d.

Febbrajo, Alberto. "Higher Legal Education and Models of Legal Culture in Italy." In *Higher Legal Culture and Postgraduate Legal Education in Europe*, edited by Vittorio Olgiati, 93–110. Naples: Edizioni Scientifiche Italiane, 2007.

Fiume, Giovanna. "Women's History and Gender History: The Italian Experience." *Modern Italy* 10, no. 2 (2005): 207–31.

Fogar, Galliano. *Trieste in guerra 1940–1945: società e resistenza*. Trieste: Istituto regionale per la storia del movimento di liberazione nel Friuli-Venezia Giulia, 1999.

Follacchio, Sara. "Conversando di femminismo: 'la donna italiana.'" In *La corporazione delle donne: ricerche e studi sui modelli femminili nel ventennio fascista*, edited by Marina Addis Saba, 171–225. Florence: Vallecchi Editore, 1988.

Fontanot, Walter, and Fabiana Romanutti. *Tramway: Trieste-Opicina*. Trieste: Danubio, 1992.

Franzinelli, Mimmo. *I tentacoli dell' Ovra: agenti, collaboratori, e vittime della polizia politica fascista*. Turin: Bollati Boringhieri, 1999.

———. *Squadristi: protagonisti e techniche della violenza fascista 1919–1922*. Milan: Mondadori, 2003.

Frasca, Rosella Isidori. "L'educazione fisica e sportiva e la 'preparazione materna.'" In *La corporazione delle donne: ricerche e studi sui modelli femminili nel ventennio fascista*, edited by Marina Addis Saba, 273–304. Florence: Vallecchi Editore, 1988.

Fried, Robert C. *The Italian Prefects: A Study in Administrative Politics*. New Haven: Yale University Press, 1963.

Friends of Italian Freedom. "The Provisions of the Special Tribunal." *Italy To-Day* (1931): 1–5.

Furlan, Boris. *Fighting Yugoslavia: The Struggle of the Slovenes*. New York: Yugoslav Information Center, 1942.

Gabaccia, Donna. *Italy's Many Diasporas.* Seattle: University of Washington Press, 2000.

Gabrielli, Patrizia. *Tempio di virilità: l'antifascismo, il genere, la storia.* Milan: Franco Angeli, 2008.

Gasparini, Lina, ed. *Impressioni Su Trieste, 1793–1887.* Trieste: Zibaldone, 1951.

Gay, Nelson H., T. Sillani, and N. Hodnig, eds. *Italy's Great War and Her National Aspirations.* Milan: Alfieri & Lacroix, 1917.

Gayda, Virgilio. *Gli slavi della Venezia Giulia.* Milan: Ravà & Co., 1915.

Gayda, Virginio. *L'Italia d'oltre confine.* Turin: Fratelli Bocca, 1914.

Gentile, Emilio. *Fascismo di pietra.* Bari: Laterza, 2007.

———. "The Fascist Anthropological Revolution." In *Culture, Censorship and the State in Twentieth-Century Italy,* edited by Guido Bonsaver and Robert S. C. Gordon, 22–33. London: Legenda, 2005.

———. *The Sacralization of Politics.* Cambridge: Harvard University Press, 1996.

Gentile, Giovanni. "The Philosophic Basis of Fascism." *Foreign Affairs* 6, no. 2 (1928): 290–304.

———. *The Reform of Education.* New York: Harcourt, Brace, and Company, 1922.

Gianturco, Luigi E. *Gli avvocati colonne del regime.* Naples: Edizioni del giornale "La Toga," 1937.

Gibson, Mary. *Born to Crime: Cesare Lombroso and the Origins of Biological Criminology.* Westport, CT: Praeger, 2002.

Giddens, Anthony. *The Nation-State and Violence: Volume 2 of a Contemporary Critique of Historical Materialism.* Berkeley: University of California Press, 1987.

Gini, Corrado. "Enrico Haskel Sonnabend." *Revue de l'Institut international de statistique/Review of the International Statistical Institute* 24, no. 1/3 (1956): 162–64.

Ginzburg, Carlo. *The Cheese and the Worms: The Cosmos of a Sixteenth-Century Miller.* Baltimore: Johns Hopkins University Press, 1980.

Gissi, Alessandra. "Between Tradition and Profession: Italian Midwives During the Fascist Period." In *Gender, Family, and Sexuality: The Private Sphere in Italy, 1860–1945,* edited by Perry Willson, 122–38. Houndsmills: Palgrave Macmillan, 2004.

Giuriati, Giovanni. *Con D'Annunzio e Millo in difesa dell'adriatico.* Florence: G. C. Sansoni, 1954.

Goldring, Douglas. *Dream Cities: Notes of an Autumn Tour in Italy and Dalmatia.* London: T. Fisher Unwin, 1913.

Gori, Gigliola. *Italian Fascism and the Female Body: Sport, Submissive Women, and Strong Mothers.* Oxfordshire: Routledge, 2004.

Graziosi, Mariolina. *La donna e la storia: identità di genere e identità collettiva nell'Italia liberale e fascista.* Naples: Liguori, 2000.

———. "Gender Struggle and the Social Manipulation and Ideological Use of Gender Identity in the Interwar Years." In *Mothers of Invention: Women, Italian Fascism, and Culture*, edited by Robin Pickering-Iazzi, 26–51. Minneapolis: University of Minnesota Press, 1995.

Grbelja, Josip. "Molat-Najstraštrašniji fašisticki konclogor na svijetu," *Slobodna Dalmacija*, January 10, 2002. http://arhiv.slobodnadalmacija.hr/20020110 /feljton.htm.

Gregor, A. James. *Giovanni Gentile: Philosopher of Fascism*. New Brunswick: Transaction Publishers, 2001.

Griffin, Roger. *Modernism and Fascism: The Sense of a Beginning under Mussolini and Hitler*. New York: Palgrave Macmillan, 2007.

———. *The Nature of Fascism*. New York: St. Martin's Press, 1991.

Grilli, Carlotta. "L'opera nazionale per la protezione della maternità e dell'infanzia." *Almanacco della donna* 12 (1931): 152–63.

Grossi, Paolo. *Scienza giuridica italiana: un profilo storico 1860–1950*. Milan: Giuffrè Editore, 2000.

Hametz, Maura. "The Carabinieri Stood by: The Italian State and the 'Slavic Threat' in Trieste, 1919–1922." *Nationalities Papers* 29, no. 4 (2001): 559–74.

———. "Naming Italians in the Borderland, 1926–1943." *Journal of Modern Italian Studies* 15, no. 3 (2010): 410–30.

———. "Surnames and Nationality," case study at "Making the History of 1989." http://chnm.gmu.edu/1989/exhibits/restructuring/essay.

———. "The Nefarious Former Authorities: Name Change in Trieste, 1918–1922." *Austrian History Yearbook* 35 (2004): 233–52.

———. "To Have What Was Mine: Reclaiming Surnames in Trieste." *Names* 50, no. 1 (2002): 3–22.

Horn, David G. *Social Bodies: Science, Reproduction, and Italian Modernity*. Princeton, New Jersey: Princeton University Press, 1994.

"I leoncini:—Passa via! Non stancare papà!" *Guerin meschino* 47, no. 48 (1928): 5.

Inghilleri, Domenico Caruso. "Politica, amministrazione, e giurisdizione amministrativa." In *Il consiglio di stato nel quinquennio 1931–1935: relazione del presidente a s.e. il capo del governo*, edited by Consiglio di stato, 323–59. Rome: Istituto poligrafico dello stato, 1937.

Ipsen, Carl. *Dictating Demography: The Problem of Population in Fascist Italy*. Cambridge: Cambridge University Press, 1996.

Isolera, Italo. *Roma fascista nelle fotografie dell'Istituto Luce*. Rome: Editori Riuniti, 2001.

Jackson, Thomas Graham. *Dalmatia, The Quarnero, and Istria With Cettigne in Montenegro and the Island of Grado*. Oxford: Clarendon Press, 1887.

Jackson Lears, T. J. "The Concept of Cultural Hegemony: Problems and Possibilities." *American Historical Review* 90, no. 3 (June 1985): 567–93.

Judson, Pieter M. *Guardians of the Nation: Activists on the Language Frontiers of Imperial Austria*. Cambridge, MA: Harvard University Press, 2006.

Kadić, Ante. "'Democratic Spirit' of the Poljica Commune." In *Communal Families in the Balkans: The Zadruga: Essays by Philip E. Mosely and Essays in His Honor*, edited by Robert F. Byrnes, 201–14. Notre Dame: University of Notre Dame Press, 1976.

Kane, Harnett T. "Trieste—Side Door to Europe." *National Geographic Magazine* 109 (1956): 824–57.

Kershaw, Angela, and Angela Kimyongür. "Women in Europe Between the Wars: a Culture of Contradictions." In *Women in Europe Between the Wars: Politics, Culture, and Society*, edited by Angela Kershaw and Angela Kimyongür, 1–22. Aldershot: Ashgate, 2007.

Kertzer, David. *Amalia's Tale: An Impoverished Peasant Woman, an Ambitious Attorney, and a Fight for Justice*. Boston: Houghton Mifflin Company, 2008.

———. *The Kidnapping of Edgardo Mortara*. New York: Knopf, 1997.

Kirk, Tom, and Anthony McElligott. "Introduction: Community, Authority and Resistance to Fascism." In *Opposing Fascism: Community, Authority and Resistance in Europe*, edited by Tom Kirk and Anthony McElligott, 1–11. Cambridge: Cambridge University Press, 1999.

Klein, Gabriella. *La politica linguistica del fascismo*. Bologna: Il Mulino, 1986.

Koon, Tracy. *Believe, Obey, Fight: Political Socialization of Youth in Fascist Italy, 1922–1943*. Chapel Hill: University of North Carolina Press, 1985.

Koonz, Claudia. *Mothers in the Fatherland: Women, the Family and Nazi Politics*. New York: St. Martin's Press, 1987.

Kramer, Johannes. "Ettore Tolomeis Italianisierung Der Südtiroler Ortsnamen Im Europäischen Kontext." In *Ettore Tolomei (1865–1952): un nazionalista di confine. Die Grenzen Des Nationalismus*, edited by Sergio Benvenuti and Christoph H. von Hartungen, 295–313. Trent: Museo Storico Trento, 1998.

Kuehn, Thomas. "Review: Reading Microhistory: The Example of Giovanni and Lusanna." *Journal of Modern History* 61, no. 3 (1989): 512–34.

Lagorio, Francesca. "Appunti per una storia delle vedove di guerra italiane nei conflitti mondiali." *Rivista di storia contemporanea* 23–24, no. 1–2 (1994–1995): 170–93.

———. "Italian Widows of the First World War." In *Authority, Identity and the Social History of the Great War*, edited by F. Shevin-Coetzee and Marilyn Coetzee, 175–98. Providence: Berghahn Books, 1995.

Lanchester, Fulco. *Pensare lo stato: i giuspubblicisti nell'Italia unitaria*. Rome: Laterza, 2004.

Lapierre, Nicole. *Changer de nom*. Paris: Gallimard, 2006.

Ledeen, Michael. *The First Duce: D'Annunzio at Fiume*. Baltimore: Johns Hopkins University Press, 1977.

Liberson, Stanley. *A Matter of Taste: How Names, Fashions and Culture Change*. New Haven: Yale University Press, 2000.

Loffredo, Ferdinando. *Politica della famiglia*. Verona: Bompiani, 1938.

Lombroso, Cesare and Guglielmo Ferrero. *Criminal Woman, the Prostitute, and the Normal Woman*, edited by Nicole Hahn Rafter and Mary Gibson. Durham: Duke University Press, 2004.

Lombroso, Gina. *The Soul of a Woman*. New York: E. P. Dutton & Company, 1923.

Lombroso Ferrero, Gina. *Nuove vite di donna*. Bologna: Zanichelli, 1929.

Lyttelton, Adrian. *The Seizure of Power: Fascism in Italy 1919–1929*. Princeton: Princeton University Press, 1988.

Lüdtke, Alf. "Introduction: What Is the History of Everyday Life and Who Are Its Practitioners?" In *The History of Everyday Life: Reconstructing Historical Experiences and Ways of Life*, edited by Alf Lüdtke, 3–40. Princeton: Princeton University Press, 1995.

"M. Raffaele Paolucci," http://www.orsogna.net/personaggi.asp?titolo =Raffaele+Paolucci%3A+la+vita.

Mahaffey, Vicki. "The Case Against Art: Wunderlich on Joyce." *Critical Inquiry* 17, no. 4 (1991): 667–92.

Maineri, B. "Le nozze e la potenza demografica dell'Italia," *Almanacco della donna* 12 (1931): 313–8.

Majer, Diemut. *"Non-Germans" Under the Third Reich: the Nazi Judicial and Administrative System in Germany and Occupied Eastern Europe With Special Regard to Occupied Poland, 1939–1945*. Baltimore: Johns Hopkins University Press, 2003.

Mancini, Angelantonio. *La donna fascista nell'irrobustimento della razza*. Rome: Vittorio Ferri, 1937.

Maranelli, Carlo, ed. *Dizionario geografico: Alto Adige-Trentino-Venezia Giulia-Dalmazia*. Bari: Giuseppe Laterza & Figli, 1915.

Marchetti, Ugo. *Mussolini, i prefetti e i podestà: lo stile e l'opera di un prefetto fascista*. Mantova: "Mussolinia" Edizione Paladino, 1927.

Mattiussi, Dario. *Il partito nazionale fascista a Trieste: uomini e organizzazione del potere 1919–1932*. Trieste: Istituto regionale per la storia del movimento di liberazione nel Friuli-Venezia Giulia, 2002.

Mazzacane, Aldo. "A Jurist for United Italy: the Training and Culture of Neapolitan Lawyers in the Nineteenth Century." In *Society and the Professions in Italy, 1860–1914*, edited by Maria Malatesta, 80–110. Cambridge: Cambridge University Press, 1995.

Mazzarolli, Leopoldo. "La protezione del cittadino—il consiglio di stato durante la presidenza di Santi Romano." http://www.giustizia-amministrativa.it /documentazione/studi_contributi/mazzarolli_santiromano.htm.

Mazzini, Giuseppe. "To the Young Men of Italy," *The World's Famous Orations, Vol. II: Continental Europe (1906)*, reprint, edited and translated by William Jennings Bryan. http://www.bartleby.com/268/7/43.html.

Mc Elligott, Anthony. "Dangerous Communities and Conservative Authority: the Judiciary, Nazis and Rough People, 1932–1933." In *Opposing Fascism: Community, Authority and Resistance in Europe*, edited by Tom Kirk and Anthony Mc Elligott, 33–47. Cambridge: Cambridge University Press, 1999.

Meldini, Piero. *Sposa e madre esemplare*. Rimini: Guaraldi, 1975.

Melis, Guido. *Due modelli di amministrazione tra liberalismo e fascismo*. Rome: Ministero per i beni culturali e ambientali, 1988.

———. *Storia dell'amministrazione italiana, 1861–1993*. Bologna: Il Mulino, 1996.

Michielj, Armando. "La donna nella scuola." *Almanacco della donna* 10 (1929): 99–110.

Millo, Anna. *L'élite del potere a Trieste: una biografia collettiva, 1891–1938*. Milan: Franco Angeli, 1989.

———. "La società triestina agli inizi del novecento." In *Friuli e Venezia Giulia: storia del '900*, edited by Istituto Regionale per la storia del movimento di liberazione nel Friuli-Venezia Giulia, 43–52. Gorizia: Libreria Editrice Goriziana, 1997.

Missiroli, Mario, and Olivia Rossetti Agresti. *The Organisation of the Arts and Professions in the Fascist Guild State*. Rome: Laboremus, 1938.

Mondello, Elisabetta. *La nuova italiana: la donna nella stampa e nella cultura del ventennio*. Rome: Editori Riuniti, 1987.

Monzali, Luciano. *The Italians of Dalmatia: From Italian Unification to World War I*. Toronto: University of Toronto Press, 2009.

Morgan, Philip. "'The Years of Consent'? Popular Attitudes and Forms of Resistance to Fascism in Italy, 1925–1940." In *Opposing Fascism: Community, Authority and Resistance in Europe*, edited by Tom Kirk and Anthony McElligott, 163–79. Cambridge: Cambridge University Press, 1999.

Mosely, Philip E. "The Peasant Family: The Zadruga, or Communal Joint-Family in the Balkans, and Its Recent Evolution." In *Communal Families in the Balkans: The Zadruga: Essays by Philip E. Mosely and Essays in His Honor*, edited by Robert F. Byrnes, 19–30. Notre Dame: University of Notre Dame Press, 1976.

Moss, M. E. *Mussolini's Fascist Philosopher*. Peter Lang: New York, 2004.

Murru-Corriga, Gianetta. "The Patronymic and the Matronymic in Sardinia: A Long-Standing Competition." *The History of the Family* 5, no. 2 (2000): 161–80.

Nani, Angelo. *Notizie storiche della città di Zara*. Zara: G. Woditzka, 1883.

Nasalli Rocca, Amedeo. *Memorie di un prefetto*. Rome: Casa Editrice Mediterranea, 1946.

Negrelli, Giorgio. "In tema di irredentismo e di nazionalismo." In *Intellettuali di frontiera: triestini a Firenze (1900–1950)*, edited by Roberto Pertici, 251–92. Florence: Olschki, 1985.

Nepitello, Santi. *The History of Trieste*. Trieste: Zigiotti, 1951.

Nerenberg, Ellen. *Prison Terms: Representing Confinement During and After Italian Fascism*. Toronto: University of Toronto Press, 2001.

Olgiati, Vittorio. "Law as an Instrument of 'Organizational Totalitarianism': Fascist Rule over Italian Lawyers." In *Totalitarian and Post-Totalitarian Law*, edited by Adam Podgorecki and Vittorio Olgiati, 123–67. Aldershot: Oñati International Institute for the Sociology of Law (Dartmouth), 1996.

———. "Professional Body and Gender Difference in Court: the Case of the First (Failed) Woman Lawyer in Modern Italy." In *Women in the World's Legal Professions*, edited by Ulrike Schultz and Gisela Shaw, 419–35. Oxford: Hart Publishing, 2003.

Orestano, Francesco. *Opera omnia, volume terzo: Opere giuridico-politiche*. Padua: Cedam, 1961.

Orlando, Vittorio Emanuele. *Principii di diritto costituzionale*, fifth edition. Florence: G. Barbèra, 1928.

Owings, Alison. *Frauen: German Women Recall the Third Reich*. New Brunswick: Rutgers University Press, 1993.

Pagnacco, Federico. "Italiani di Dalmazia." *La porta orientale* 1, no. 2 (1931): 164–80.

———. "L'italianità giuliana (postilla ad un processo)." *La porta orientale* 2, no. 3–4 (1932): 300–1.

Painter, Borden. *Mussolini's Rome: Rebuilding the Eternal City*. London: Palgrave Macmillan, 2005.

Pappalardo, Nino. "L'eccesso di potere 'amministrativo' secondo la giurisprudenza del consiglio di stato." In *Il consiglio di stato nel quinquennio 1931–1935: relazione del presidente a s.e. il capo del governo*, edited by Consiglio di stato, 429–95. Rome: Istituto poligrafico dello stato, 1937.

Parovel, Paolo. *L'identità cancellata: l'italianizzazione forzata dei cognomi, nomi e toponimi nella "Venezia Giulia" dal 1919 al 1945, con gli elenchi delle province di Trieste, Gorizia, Istria ed i dati dei primi 5300 decreti*. Trieste: Eugenio Parovel, 1985.

Pasini, Ferdinando. "Ufficio della letteratura in terra di confine." *La porta orientale* 2, no. 12 (1932): 874–908.

Passerini, Luisa. *Torino operaia e fascismo: una storia orale*. Rome: Laterza, 1984.

Patriarca, Silvana. *Italian Vices: Nation and Character from the Risorgimento to the Republic*. Cambridge: Cambridge University Press, 2010.

Peixotto, Ernest. *By Italian Seas*. New York: Charles Scribner's Sons, 1907.

Pertici, Roberto. "Irredentismo e questione adriatica a Firenze." In *Intellettuali di frontiera: triestini a Firenze (1900–1950)*, edited by Roberto Pertici, 635–59. Florence: Olschki, 1985.

Petrone, Corrado. *Il nuovo diritto costituzionale e amministrativo*. Rome: Attilio Sampaolesi, 1927.

Pickering-Iazzi, Robin. "Introduction." In *Mothers of Invention: Women, Italian Fascism, and Culture*, edited by Robin Pickering-Iazzi, ix–xxxii. Minneapolis: University of Minnesota Press, 1995.

———. "Unseduced Mothers: The Resisting Female Subject in Italian Culture of the Twenties and Thirties." University of Wisconsin-Milwaukee, Center for Twentieth Century Studies, Working Paper No. 1 (1990): 1–31.

Pieraccini, Gaetano. *La donna nella conservazione e nel perfezionamento della specie*. Siena: S. Bernardino, 1931.

Pirjevec, Jože. *Foibe: una storia d'Italia*. Turin: Einaudi, 2009.

Pivato, Stefano. *Il nome e la storia: onomastica e religioni politiche nell'Italia contemporanea*. Bologna: Il Mulino, 1999.

Pizzagalli, Aldo. *Per l'italianità dei cognomi nella provincia di Trieste*. Trieste: Treves-Zanichelli, 1929.

Ploscowe, Morris. "Jury Reform in Italy." *Journal of Criminal Law and Criminology* 25, no. 4 (1934), 576–85.

"Poi dicono che la quantità va a scapito della qualità!" *Guerin meschino* 47, no. 32 (1928): 3.

Posar, Guido. "Sono proprio slavi i nomi terminanti in ich?" *Pagine istriane* 2, no. 5 (1951): 34–6.

"Il prossimo 'Giugno Triestino': una riunione preliminare nell'ufficio del podestà," *Il Piccolo*, 19 January 1932, 3.

Pugliese, Stanislao. *Fascism, Anti-Fascism, and the Resistance in Italy, 1919 to the Present*. Lanham: Rowman and Littlefield, 2004.

Pupo, Raoul. "Guerra civile e conflitto etnico; italiani, sloveni e croati." *Clio: Rivista trimestrale di studi storici* 36, no. 3 (2000): 497–530.

"Raffaele Paolucci di Valmaggiore." *Annali italiani di chirurgia* 63, no. 6 (1992): 835–9. http://www.annaliitalianidichirurgia.it/index.php?option=com _content&view=article&id=36&Itemid=3&lang=it.

Raicich, Marino. "La scuola triestina tra 'La Voce' e Gentile 1910–1925." In *Intellettuali di frontiera: triestini a Firenze (1900–1950)*, edited by Roberto Pertici, 320–44. Florence: Olschki, 1985.

Ranelletti, Oreste. *Istituzioni di diritto pubblico: il nuovo diritto pubblico italiano*. Padua: CEDAM, 1935.

Rava, Paul B. "Italian Administrative Courts under Fascism." *Michigan Law Review* 40, no. 5 (1942): 654–78.

Ravasini, Oscarre. *Toponomastica stradale: compendio di notizie sulla nomencla-tura di località e strade di Trieste*. Trieste: La Editoriale Libraria, 1929.

Re, Lucia. "Fascist Theories of 'Woman' and the Construction of Gender." In *Mothers of Invention: Women, Italian Fascism, and Culture*, edited by Robin Pickering-Iazzi, 76–99. Minneapolis: University of Minnesota Press, 1995.

Reale Società Geografica Italiana. *Prontuario dei nomi locali della Venezia Giulia*. Rome: La Reale Società Geografica Italiana, 1917.

Reale Società Geografica Italiana. *Prontuario dei nomi locali dell'Alto Adige*. Rome: La Reale Società Geografica Italiana, 1916.

Reill, Dominique. "From Bond to Border: The Position of the Adriatic in the Mid-Nineteenth Century." PhD dissertation, Columbia University, 2007.

Renan, Ernest. "What Is a Nation?" In *Becoming National: A Reader*, edited by Geoff Eley and Ronald Grigor Suny, 42–55. New York: Oxford University Press, 1996.

Reut-Nicolussi, Eduard. *Tyrol Under the Axe of Italian Fascism*. London: George Allen & Unwin, 1930.

Righi, Livio Ragusin. "Guardia al confine." *La porta orientale* 1, no. 1 (1931): 111–13.

Rizzo, Domenico. "Marriage on Trial: Adultery in Nineteenth Century Rome." In *Gender, Family, and Sexuality: The Private Sphere in Italy, 1860–1945*, edited by Perry Willson, 20–36. Houndsmills: Palgrave Macmillan, 2004.

Roberts, David. "How Not to Think About Fascism and Ideology, Intellectual Antecedents and Historical Meaning." *Journal of Contemporary History* 35, no. 2 (2000): 185–211.

Rocco, Alfredo. "The Transformation of the State." In *What Is Fascism and Why?*, edited by Tomaso Sillani, 15–29. London: Ernest Benn Limited, 1931.

Rodogno, Davide. *Fascism's European Empire: Italian Occupation During the Second World War*. Cambridge: Cambridge University Press, 2006.

Romano, Santi. *Corso di diritto amministrativo: principii generali*. Padua: CEDAM, 1937.

———. "La funzione e i caratteri del consiglio di stato." In *Il consiglio di stato, studi in occasione del centenario*, edited by Consiglio di stato, 1–28. Rome: Istituto poligrafico dello stato, 1932.

Rosenthal, Joel T. "Onomastics and Its Uses." *Journal of Interdisciplinary History* 36, no. 1 (2005): 57–62.

Rusinow, Dennison. *Italy's Austrian Heritage, 1919–46*. Oxford: Oxford University Press, 1969.

Saba, Marina Addis. "La donna 'muliebre.'" In *La corporazione delle donne: ricerche e studi sui modelli femminili nel ventennio fascista*, edited by Marina Addis Saba, 1–71. Florence: Vallecchi Editore, 1988.

Sadkovich, James. *Italian Support for Croatian Separatism 1927–1937*. New York: Garland, 1987.

Salvemini, Gaetano. *Racial Minorities under Fascism in Italy*. Chicago: Women's International League for Peace and Freedom, 1934.

Sarogni, Emilia. *La donna italiana: il lungo cammino verso i diritti, 1861–1994*. Parma: Nuova Pratiche, 1995.

Sator (pseud. Battara, Pietro). *La popolazione della Venezia Giulia*. Rome: Darsena, 1945.

Saunders, Frances Stonor. *The Woman Who Shot Mussolini*. London: Faber and Faber, 2010.

Savini, Pietro. *Le origini e le evoluzioni storiche della civiltà latina e della nomenclatura locale nella Venezia Giulia*. Venice: R. Deputazione veneta di storia patria, 1918.

Savino, Edoardo. *La nazione operante: albo d'oro del fascismo: profili e figure*. Novara: Istituto Geografico de Agostini, 1937.

Schiffrer, Carlo. *Venezia Giulia: Study of a Map of the Italo-Yugoslav National Borders*. Rome: C. Colombo, 1946.

Schneider, Herbert Wallace. "Italy's New Syndicalist Constitution." *Political Science Quarterly* 42, no. 2 (1927): 161–202.

Scocchi, Angelo. "I nomi pagani slavi e l'onomastica italiana." *La porta orientale* 2, no. 3–4 (1932): 275–83.

———. "Onomastica romana e onomastica slava meridionale." *La porta orientale* 2, no. 5 (1932): 390–401.

———. "Toponomistica italiana." *La porta orientale* 1, no. 3 (1931): 306–11.

Scott, James C., John Tehranian, and Jeremy Mathias. "The Production of Legal Identities Proper to States: The Case of the Permanent Family Surname." *Comparative Studies in Society and History* 44, no. 1 (2002): 4–44.

Semelin, Jacques. *Unarmed Against Hitler: Civilian Resistance in Europe, 1939–1943*. Westport, Connecticut: Praeger, 1993.

Semi, Francesco and Vanni Tacconi. "Italiani e slavi in Dalmazia: aspetti e problemi di una convivenza secolare." In *Istria e Dalmazia: uomini e tempi, Dalmazia, le figure più rappresentative della civiltà dalmata nei diversi momenti della storia*, vol. 2, edited by Francesco Semi and Vanni Tacconi, 603–22. Udine: Del Bianco, 1991.

Serao, Matilde. *Parla una donna: diario femminile di guerra, maggio 1915–marzo 1916*. Milan: Treves, 1916.

Seton-Watson, Robert William. *The Southern Slav Question and the Habsburg Monarchy*. New York: Howard Fertig, 1969.

Sigmund, Anna Maria. *Women of the Third Reich*. Richmond Hill: NDE, 2000.

Smith, Helmut Walser. *The Butcher's Tale: Murder and Anti-Semitism in a German Town*. New York: W. W. Norton, 2002.

Sonnabend, Haskel. *L'espansione degli slavi*. Rome: Tipografia Failli, 1930.

Soppelsa, Giancarlo. "Luigi Ziliotto." In *Istria e Dalmazia: uomini e tempi, Dalmazia, le figure più rappresentative della civiltà dalmata nei diversi momenti della storia*, vol. 2, edited by Francesco Semi, and Vanni Tacconi, 479–81. Udine: Del Bianco, 1991.

Staderini, Tito. *Legislazione per la difesa della razza*. Rome: Carlo Colombo, 1940.

Stephenson, Jill. *Women in Nazi Germany*. New York: Longman, 2001.

Stibbe, Matthew. *Women in the Third Reich*. London: Arnold, 2003.

Stolleis, Michael. *The Law under the Swastika: Studies on Legal History in Nazi Germany*. Chicago: University of Chicago Press, 1998.

Stone, Julius. "Theories of Law and Justice of Fascist Italy." *The Modern Law Review* 1, no. 3 (1937): 177–202.

Stone, Marla. *The Patron State: Culture and Politics in Fascist Italy*. Princeton: Princeton University Press, 1998.

Stravisi, Franco. *Considerazioni statistiche sui valori medi mensili di cinque elementi meteorologici — Trieste 1841–1975*. Trieste: Istituto Sperimentale Talassografico: "Francesci Vercelli," 1976.

Sucur, Ante. "The Sinking of Viribus Unitis in Austro-Hungarian Tegetthoff Class Dreadnoughts." http://croatian-treasure.com/viribus.html.

T. D. M. *Italy and the Jugo-Slavs in Istria and Dalmatia*. Philadelphia: Joseph Bruno, 1919.

Tacchi, Francesca. "Un professionista della classe dirigente: l'avvocato negli anni '20." In *Libere professioni e fascismo*, edited by Gabriele Turi, 49–86. Milan: Franco Angeli, 1994.

Taddei, Berardo. *Donne processate dal Tribunale Speciale 1927–1943*. Verona: G. Grazia, 1969.

Tamaro, Attilio. *L'Adriatico—golfo d'Italia: l'italianità di Trieste*. Milan: Fratelli Treves, 1915.

———. *Italiani e slavi nell'Adriatico*. Rome: Athenaeum, 1915.

———. *Trieste*. Rome: S. A. Edizioni Tiber, 1930.

———. *La Vénétie Julienne et la Dalmatie: histoire de la nation italienne sur ses frontières orientales*. Rome: Imprimerie du sénat, 1918.

Tasso, Miro. *Un onomasticidio di stato*. Trieste: Mladika, 2010.

Teich, Mikulas and Roy Porter, ed., *The National Question in Europe in Historical Context* (Cambridge: Cambridge University Press, 1993), xx.

Todeschini, Mario. "La scuola primaria della Venezia Giulia." *La porta orientale* 3, no. 5 (1933): 327–47.

Tolomei, Ettore. "Elenco dei cognomi dell'Alto Adige: la restituzione del cognome atesino." In *Die Gewaltsame Italianisierung Der Familiennamen in Südtirol: Wie Wären Heute Mein Familienname?* Meran: Südtiroler Heimatbund, 2003.

———. "Il discorso di Bolzano," Teatro di Bolzano, 15 luglio 1923. Trent: Tipografia Cooperative Trentina, 1923.

———. *Memorie Di Vita*. Rome: Garzanti, 1948.

Tosatti, Giovanna. "Il prefetto e l'esercizio del potere durante il periodo fascista." *Studi storici* 42, no. 4 (2001): 1021–39.

Trampus, Antonio. *Vie e piazze di Trieste moderna: toponomastica stradale e topografia storica*. Trieste: Edizioni "Italo Svevo," 1989.

Türköz, Meltem. "Surname Narratives and the State-Society Boundary: Memories of Turkey's Family Name Law of 1934." *Middle Eastern Studies* 43, no. 6 (2007): 893–908.

Ungari, Paolo. *Il diritto di famiglia in Italia dalla costituzioni "giacobine" al codice civile del 1942*. Bologna: Il Mulino, 1970.

Valdevit, Giampaolo. *Chiesa e lotte nazionali: il caso di Trieste (1850–1919)*. Udine: Aries Edizioni, 1979.

Valiani, Leo. *The End of Austria-Hungary*. New York: Knopf, 1973.

"Vademecum per riconoscere la donna moderna," *Guerin meschino* 49, no. 20 (1930): 7.

Veronesi, Enrico. *Un viaggio al femminile lungo quarant'anni: dai congressi femministi italiani del 1908 alla caduta del fascismo*. Milan: M&B Publishing, 2004.

Vivante, Angelo. *Irredentismo adriatico*. Trieste: Edizioni "Italo Svevo," 1984 (reprint 1912).

Vodopivec, Peter. "Slovene Intellectuals' Response to Political and Social Modernization in the Nineteenth and at the Beginning of the Twentieth Centuries." *Slovene Studies* 23, no. 1–2 (2001): 3–13.

Voinovitch, Louis. *Dalmatia and the Jugoslav Movement*. London: George Allen & Unwin, 1920.

Volk, Alessandro. "Sloveni e Croati in Italia tra le due guerre." In *Friuli e Venezia Giulia: storia del '900*, edited by Istituto Regionale per la storia del movimento di liberazione nel Friuli-Venezia Giulia, 297–308. Gorizia: Libreria Editrice Goriziana, 1997.

Vucinich, Wayne. "A Zadruga in Bileća Rudine." In *Communal Families in the Balkans: The Zadruga: Essays by Philip E. Mosely and Essays in His Honor*, edited by Robert F. Byrnes, 162–86. Notre Dame: University of Notre Dame Press, 1976.

Welk, William G. *Fascist Economic Policy: An Analysis of Italy's Economic Experiment*. Cambridge, MA: Harvard University Press, 1938.

Willson, Perry. *The Clockwork Factory: Women and Work in Fascist Italy*. Oxford: Clarendon Press, 1993.

———, ed. *Gender, Family, and Sexuality: The Private Sphere in Italy, 1860–1945*. Houndsmills: Palgrave Macmillan, 2004.

———. *Peasant Women and Politics in Fascist Italy: The Massaie Rurali*. London: Routledge, 2002.

Wingenter, Anne. "Le veterane del dolore: Mothers and Widows of the 'Fallen' in Fascist Italy." MA thesis, Loyola University of Chicago, 2003.

Wingfield, Nancy M. *Flag Wars and Stone Saints: How the Bohemian Lands Became Czech*. Cambridge, MA: Harvard University Press, 2007.

Winner, Irene Portis. "The Question of the Zadruga in Slovenia: Myth and Reality in Žerovnica." *Anthropological Quarterly* 50, no. 3 (1977): 125–34.

Wolff, Larry. *Inventing Eastern Europe: The Map of Civilization on the Mind of the Enlightenment*. Stanford: Stanford University Press, 1994.

Zanetti, Sperato. "Il movimento turistico nelle stazioni balneari della Venezia Giulia." *La porta orientale* 3, no. 1 (1933): 62–75.

Ziliotto, Luigi. *Lettera ad Enzo Bettiza: la risposta di un dalmata di Zara all'esilio*. Rome: La Società Dalmata di Storia Patria, 2004.

Zincone, Giovanna. "The Making of Italian Nationality Law." *Italian Politics and Society* 69 (2010): 23–53.

Zubini, Fabio. *Scorcola e Cologna: amene colline di periferia, sin dal secolo scorso residenza di cittadini laboriosi e benestanti di differenti provenienze e religioni, che nascondono ancora angoli tranquilli in mezzo al verde*. Trieste: Edizioni Italo Svevo, 1997.

Index